Fallenness in Victorian Women's Writing

Fallenness in Victorian Women's Writing

Marry, Stitch, Die, or Do Worse

Deborah Anna Logan

University of Missouri Press • Columbia and London

Copyright ©1998 by
The Curators of the University of Missouri
University of Missouri Press, Columbia, Missouri 65201
Printed and bound in the United States of America
All rights reserved
5   4   3   2   1   02   01   00   99   98

Library of Congress Cataloging-in-Publication Data

Logan Deborah Anna, 1951–
    Fallenness in Victorian women's writing : marry, stitch, die, or
do worse / Deborah Anna Logan.
        p.   cm.
    Includes bibliographical references and index.
    ISBN 0-8262-1175-5 (alk. paper)
    1. English literature—Women authors—History and criticism.
    2. Women and literature—Great Britain—History—19th century.
    3. English literature—19th century—History and criticism.
    4. Unmarried mothers in literature.   5. Moral conditions in
literature.   6. Social problems in literature.   7. Prostitution in
literature.   8. Prostitutes in literature.   9. Women in literature.
    I. Title.
    PR115.L64   1998
    820.8'09287'09034—dc21   98-6618
                                                              CIP

⊗™ This paper meets the requirements of the
American National Standard for Permanence of Paper
for Printed Library Materials, Z39.48, 1984.

Designer: Mindy Shouse
Typesetter: BookComp, Inc.
Printer and Binder: Thomson-Shore, Inc.
Typefaces: Minion and Medici Script

For Jacob, Lauren, and Zachary, with all my love

Contents

PREFACE

T HE TOPIC of women's fallenness, with its long and varied history of cultural silences, thwarted ambitions, and misrepresentations, has interested me since my first girlhood reading of Alcott's *Little Women*. The image of Jo March in her ink-stained pinafore, furiously scribbling away in her garret studio, fascinates me still, and resonates with the unconvention-alities of the women writers and characters that are the focus of this book. The intersections of silencing and fallenness resulting from the Victorian period's sexual ideology provide a rich field of study, not only for our understanding of the period's literary and social history but also for the understanding of our own.

My greatest creative debt in this project is to Beverly Taylor of the University of North Carolina at Chapel Hill. I am indeed fortunate to have acquired a teacher, mentor, adviser, critic, and friend all in one person. That which is most effective and inspired in this book is due to her patient cultivation, to her unflagging encouragement, and to her commitment to excellence.

I thank also John McGowan, Pam Cooper, and Joy Kasson of UNC at Chapel Hill, and Jan Radway of Duke University for their thoughtful comments and especially for the broad perspectives they were able to offer on the work as a whole.

At Western Kentucky University I thank Mary Ellen Pitts for her en-couragement and support of my work during the editing and revising process.

At the University of Missouri Press, I thank Beverly Jarrett for her initial enthusiasm for and continued support of this project. I also thank Managing Editor Jane Lago for her advice and guidance during the book's final stages and Annette Wenda for her excellent editing suggestions.

For their gracious permission to reprint earlier versions of parts of my analysis I thank the following: Pierre Steiner of *Women's Studies* for both "Harem Life, West and East" and "The Economics of Sexuality: Elizabeth Barrett Browning and the Victorian 'bad conscience' "; Alan Shelston of the *Gaskell Society Journal* for " 'An unfit subject for fiction': Elizabeth Gaskell and the Duty of Silence"; and Ward Hellstrom of *The Victorian Newsletter* for "Am I My Sister's Keeper? Sexual Deviance and the Social Community."

For moral support in a variety of manifestations I am grateful to Bonnie Wehrle, Joy Johnson, Bob Ramirez, Mickey Adams, Gil Adams, and Jeff Logan. Edna Logan deserves special mention for contributing to this project in a most unexpected and timely way.

Finally, families generally have little choice but to accept the preoccupation a project such as this one requires of a writer. The last word, therefore, is reserved for Jacob, Lauren, and Zachary, who make possible all that is worthwhile.

Fallenness in Victorian Women's Writing

1

Victorian Silences

AN IDEOLOGY OF FALLEN SEXUALITY

There is a silence where hath been no sound,
There is a silence where no sound may be,
In the Cold grave—under the deep, deep, sea . . .
There the true Silence is, self-conscious
and alone.

—Thomas Hood, "Silence"

Has paterfamilias, with his Oriental traditions and veiled female
faces, very successfully dealt with a certain class of evil? What
if materfamilias . . . do more towards their expulsion by simply
looking at them & calling them by their names[?]
    —Elizabeth Barrett Browning, letter to William Thackeray

O NE OF the most remarkable features of Jane Campion's 1993 film
The Piano is its narrative perspective. Campion's Victorian heroine,
Ada McGrath, begins with this astonishing statement: "The voice you
hear is not my speaking voice, but my mind's voice. I have not spoken
since I was six years old. No one knows why, not even me."[1] The device
draws us into a curiously intimate relationship with Ada's mind, just as
Charlotte Brontë's companionable "dear reader" invites us to share the
narrator's privileged perspective. Ada speaks through her "mind's voice"
only twice during the film, at the beginning and at its conclusion, in a sort

---

1. This and subsequent quotations transcribed from the film *The Piano,* directed by
Jane Campion.

of Brontë-esque "winding up." In between there are only two exceptions to Ada's vocal silence: her sharp intake of breath when her lover, Baines, first touches her and her frantic gasping when her husband attempts to rape her. The film concludes with Ada practicing, not her piano, but verbal speech, though she does so only when concealed behind an opaque veil. That her silence is not physiological but, apparently, psychologically self-imposed demonstrates both Ada's prodigious self-control and her internalization of oppressive cultural constructs. Not surprisingly, as Ada's story unfolds, the enigma of her character proves impervious to those who would penetrate it uninvited—in effect, her silence is also her empowerment.

What is notable about Ada's muteness from a narrative standpoint is the fact that viewers are held in her mind through the entire film, sustained by her opening statements and prompted by the energy conveyed through her signing. Like Harriet Martineau's ungainly ear trumpet, Ada's highly visible silence presents a compelling metaphor for a historical tradition of silenced women.[2] The synesthetic qualities of such "visible silence" support the idea that what seems most culturally marginalized—for my purposes, the fallen woman—is in fact the object of most intense scrutiny. The highly suggestive observation that "What is socially peripheral is often symbolically central" is proved by the Victorian period's fascination with deviancy, a fascination evidenced by its trademark sexual euphemisms.[3] The absence of the spoken word in the character Ada creates a narrative distance similar to that which separates modern readers from Victorian literature's fallen heroines, who are typically shrouded in obscure rhetoric.

Ada McGrath not only symbolizes the silent woman archetype but also is that peculiarly Victorian phenomenon, a fallen woman, a woman whose transgression is marked by the presence of an illegitimate child, whose fallenness justifies her social ostracism, and whose outraged father forces her into a mail-order marriage and transports her to New Zealand (at the time, associated with penal colonies and savage natives) like the ideological criminal she is. While acknowledging the multiple meanings currently attached to the term *ideology,* for the sake of simplicity I employ one of Terry Eagleton's general definitions: "a body of ideas . . . characteristic of

2. Tillie Olsen's groundbreaking *Silences,* published in 1965, speculates on the psychic as well as cultural damage that results from imposing silence on creative energies, a damage intensified by women's subordinate social status. Olsen's work paved the way for such studies as Sandra M. Gilbert and Susan Gubar's *The Madwoman in the Attic,* a monumental reconstruction of women's lives, writing, and issues.

3. Peter Stallybrass and Allon White, *The Politics and Poetics of Transgression,* 20.

a particular social group or class . . . which help to legitimate a dominant political power"—here, the Victorian middle class. Perpetuating an ideology involves "*promoting* beliefs and values congenial to it; *naturalizing* and *universalizing* such beliefs so as to render them self-evident and apparently inevitable; *denigrating* ideas which might challenge it; *excluding* rival forms of thought . . . ; and *obscuring* social reality in ways convenient to itself."[4] My discussion aims to clarify fallenness in relation to the period's dominant ideology by analyzing how the points Eagleton outlines manifest in the literature. This book, then, is a study about Victorian fallen women both real and literary, about the surrounding texts and contexts that branded them criminals and outcasts, and about the cultural dynamics that sought to banish such anomalies by transporting them to real and metaphorical penal colonies.

Ada's refusal to speak attests to the strength of her will: "My father says it is a dark talent, and the day I take it into my head to stop breathing will be my last." But he underestimates Ada's will, which is powerful enough both to invite and to resist the "cold grave under the deep, deep, sea" and to transform impending death into a rebirth. From modern perspectives on suppressed psychosexual trauma and the self-negating ways such trauma can erupt, it is tempting to speculate on Ada's decision to silence herself (was she a victim of incest or other sexual abuse?) and on her subsequent sexual falls (does incest or rape predispose one to sexual promiscuity?). But Campion provides little history by which to interpret Ada's silence, which is why watching this film is like reading Victorian fallen-woman literature: we must read between the lines or, in this case, "hear" between the silences.[5]

Ada does speak, however, most eloquently—through her music: "The strange thing is, I don't think myself silent. That is because of my piano." Ada's vocal silence and its link with her sexuality converge in her emblematic piano, and her music conveys different messages to different people. When Ada plays, her mother stares at her with hostility; the town's ladies are disturbed by her sensuality ("She doesn't play the piano like we do"); Ada's

4. Terry Eagleton, *Ideology: An Introduction*, 1, 5–6. See also Stallybrass and White, *Politics and Poetics*, 195.

5. For this, I am indebted to an important—and easily underestimated—insight I heard long ago, the source of which eludes me. This idea was attributed to Mozart, who observed that the silences (rests, pauses) between musical notes are as integral to experiencing music as are the "heard" notes. The idea applies also to fine arts (empty spaces), dance (stillness), and literature (what is left unsaid). By association, fallen women are as necessary to Victorian cultural representation as angels in the house.

husband urges, "Play us a jig," and clumsily beats time on the piano lid; and the tattooed Maori Baines falls in love with her. Because it is her "voice" and, as such, a mode of expression far subtler than words, Ada's piano is inseparable from Ada; accordingly, the gendered drama of husband, lover, and adulteress (this makes her twice fallen) unfolds around the possession of the instrument. Ultimately, however, neither Ada nor her piano is available for the taking.

Demonstrating his authority over his wife, Ada's husband deprives her of her piano and waits with increasing exasperation to consummate their marriage (twice he attempts to rape her), failing to see the connection between the two. In contrast, Baines, who is deeply affected by her playing, restores Ada's piano to her, and the two become lovers. Her husband's response is to violate her at the most profound level: he chops off her finger, vowing to remove each one in turn until she submits her extraordinary will to his. Enriching Campion's version of fallenness are several archetypal myths. A Bluebeard of the Outback, Ada's husband takes an ax to his wife, cutting off her "ideas, feelings, and actions" as well as her mode of articulation. Typically, Bluebeard's wives are conveniently supplied by parents who are content to overlook his dangerous qualities ("Hmmm, his beard isn't really *that* blue") or, in Ada's case, to relieve themselves of an undesirable social burden.[6] Although parents and husbands ostensibly protect women like Ada from savages like Baines, such roles are here dramatically reversed.

Countering Bluebeard is the "Silver Hands" myth, wherein Baines proves he is the worthy lover by fashioning a silver prosthetic finger specially shaped to play the piano. Clarissa Estes notes that the "idea of replacing lost parts with limbs of silver" is associated with compassion for and restoration of those who are crippled in body as well as "those whose hearts or dreams are broken."[7] Baines, whose status as a half-savage native aligns him (in terms of imperialist ideology) with the outcast Ada, serves as the unlikely restorer who assists, but never interferes with, the processes of her will. These influences elevate women's silencing and fallenness to archetypal status, in Campion's treatment enhanced by the husband's murderous Bluebeardian character and the lover's association with the restorative "Silver Hands" myth. The fallen woman's dismembered finger, suggestively prefigured by the piano key she sends to Baines as a token of her passion, serves as the

6. Clarissa P. Estes, *Women Who Run with the Wolves*, 49.
7. Ibid., 427, 434.

symbolic key that will not cease bleeding until she removes herself from the life-threatening, spirit-killing chamber of horrors her marriage represents.

In *The Piano* neither father nor husband succeeds in containing Ada McGrath. Relegated to the wilds of New Zealand by the ethics of civilized society, Ada fashions her own code of conduct in which she destroys her piano, attempts, then aborts, suicide, and selects her own sexual partner rather than accepting the one society has chosen for her. Ada's character resists the victim category, although she cannot fully escape from male authority or social ostracism. That she finally breaks her self-imposed silence with a half-savage man in a half-savage country bears eloquent testimony to the stultifying effects of the sort of protection offered her in middle-class drawing rooms.

Ada's failure to realize the angelic ideal, regarded as a certain sign of a woman's propensity to fall, reveals Victorian social attitudes toward woman's sphere; she is neither domestic, idle, nor emblematic of conspicuous consumption, all middle-class standards of measuring female respectability. Ada is a serious pianist—clearly not a drawing-room dabbler; and when her husband trades her piano for a piece of land, she rejects the domestic role altogether: she stamps her foot, rips down the laundry, and smashes the crockery on the floor. "The piano is mine," she shouts in writing, "it's *mine!*" at once an assertion of ownership and of control over her sexuality, a concept her involuntarily celibate husband only vaguely perceives. Ada's character resonates with what Nina Auerbach calls the "titanic outcast" power of female sexuality that, left uncontrolled by legitimate marriage and motherhood, is by definition imbued with fallenness.[8]

The primary relevance of Ada's character to my study of fallen women inheres in its powerful metaphors of silencing and articulation, metaphors that represent what Harriet Martineau termed the "political invisibility" of women of all classes, races, and ethnicities who are defined solely by sexual functions.[9] By using Coventry Patmore's idea of acceptable and respectable womanhood—the angel in the house—as my point of departure, I will explore both modern and Victorian ideas concerning nineteenth-century

8. Auerbach, *Woman and the Demon: The Life of a Victorian Myth*, 155.

9. Martineau's "The Political Invisibility of Women," in her *Society in America*, challenges the notions of freedom and equality in a nation wherein more than half the population (women, blacks, and all other ethnic minorities) are systematically excluded from the law. Metaphorically, as Olsen and others demonstrate, silence equates with invisibility, articulation with representation.

sexual mores in an attempt to reconcile them with Victorian fallen-woman discourse.[10] As Gilbert and Gubar and other scholars note, most literary angels die before their stories can be written, a convention that seems to belie the domestic bliss promised by the ideology Patmore and others promote, and one that disturbingly suggests that necrophilism is somehow essential to the angelic construct. What readers are left with is a range of nonconforming deviant characters, each of whom challenges the idea that either a woman is respectable or she is not. Since "respectability" in this sense was primarily a middle-class concept, many women found themselves measured by standards foreign to their class and especially to their socioeconomic milieu. Interestingly, the resulting "wayward or un-productive sexualities" are so prominent and visible throughout Victorian literature as to suggest that angelic sexuality is the anomaly rather than the norm.[11]

My methodology, which employs nonliterary as well as literary Victorian texts, is modeled less on a theoretical framework than on a social construc-tion that functions as a "deviance hierarchy." Angels in the house, elevated by their chaste morality, of course occupy the topmost position in such a construction, though not, as we have seen, without complications. This may be accounted for by Mary Poovey's observation that the historical tradition associating all women with the first fallen woman, Eve, the "Mother of our Miseries," was reinvigorated as the Victorian period's madonna-harlot dichotomy. "The place women occupied in liberal, bourgeois ideology," says Poovey, "helps account for the persistence in the domestic ideal of the earlier image of woman as sexualized, susceptible, and fallen. . . . The contradiction between a sexless, moralized angel and an aggressive, car-nal magdalen was therefore written into the domestic ideal as one of its constitutive characteristics."[12] Poovey's observations also account for the curious collapsing of class boundaries between women where appropriate and inappropriate sexualities, or any other behaviors, were concerned.

According to Wendell Johnson, the phrase *madonna-harlot syndrome* is a psychiatric term (despite its inescapably biblical terminology) denoting

10. Together, conduct books (such as Sarah Ellis's *The Women of England* [New York: J. and H. G. Langley, 1844] and Sarah Lewis's *Women's Mission* [Boston: W. Crosby, 1840]) and Victorian prostitution discourse (see my discussion of the latter in Chapter 3) provide a comprehensive picture of the period's sexual ideology, particularly concerning female respectability.
11. Michel Foucault, *The History of Sexuality, Volume One,* 45.
12. Poovey, *Uneven Developments: The Ideological Work of Gender in Mid-Victorian England,* 9, 11.

extremes of female sexual behavior. Elsewhere, Johnson observes that the Victorians' obsessive idealization of angelic women of necessity implies that nonconforming women are "beasts": "there is no in-between," meaning that most Victorians rejected such notions as degrees of fallenness or a hierarchy of fallen behaviors, and, by association, the possibility for redemption and social integration.[13] I have employed the term *madonna-harlot dichotomy* or *polarity* throughout this study because it so aptly invokes the rigidity of acceptable sexual standards, a polarization Victorian writers repeatedly prove is an unrealistic fiction. The literary examples I discuss only begin to suggest the wide range of experiences that fall "in-between."

Perhaps the primary complication offered by in-between deviancies concerns the first part of this ideology's equation: maternity. As my readings will show, that maternity was the most highly valued of women's abilities presents continual challenges to the political and economic agendas motivating the madonna-harlot polarity. In a period threatened by unprecedented shifts in previously "stable" cultural paradigms, maternal ideology also proved to be subject to "the mutability of natural propensities," "mutability" and "natural" being to many Victorians incompatible concepts.[14] What happens when unmarried women bear illegitimate children (an "unnatural" act) toward whom they exhibit "maternal instinct" (promoted as "natural," but only in "good" women)? Is this sufficient to redeem them? Is their redemption to be configured as spiritual? social? or moral? Or is the rhetoric of redemption but a smoke screen for a social economy seeking only to justify, solidify, and perpetuate its own existence? Of the fallen-woman literary convention Tess Cosslett observes, "it is the fallen woman, the 'Magdalen,' who is the mother—her fall being marked by the child she bears. The 'pure' woman is childless and single. Her status as 'Madonna' comes not from maternity, but from her roles as rescuer and as sufferer."[15] But although this is true (at least initially) of Aurora and Marian in *Aurora Leigh*, Dinah and Hetty in *Adam Bede*, and others who represent a seamless madonna-harlot construct, it is complicated by Ruth Hilton, Mrs. Kay, and Janet Dempster, characters who manifest both extremes and therefore require different standards of measurement.

The centrality of the maternal paradigm is further illustrated by the assumption that motherless girls are destined to fall. Consistent with this

13. Johnson, *Sex and Marriage in Victorian Poetry*, 34–35; Johnson, *Living in Sin: The Victorian Sexual Revolution*, 23.
14. Jill Matus, *Unstable Bodies: Victorian Representations of Sexuality and Maternity*, 6.
15. Cosslett, *Woman to Woman: Female Friendship in Victorian Fiction*, 50.

convention, the literature discussed in this study refers obliquely to angelic mothers by presenting them as dead or otherwise unavailable. A farmer's wife, Ruth's mother died young as a result of a "delicacy" that unsuited her to the rigors of farm life. The other Gaskell heroines I consider (the beekeeper, Mary Barton, and Esther) are also motherless, as are Hetty Sorrel and most of Charlotte Brontë's women characters. Some mothers are still alive, but unavailable in various ways: Lizzie Leigh's father forbids any relationship between mother and daughter, which is true also of Sarah Grand's Evadne Frayling. The legacy of Bertha Mason Rochester's mother is hereditary insanity, while Janet Dempster's mother responds to Dempster's abuse of her daughter by praying, as does Edith Beale's mother in *The Heavenly Twins;* the most unavailable of all is Marian Erle's mother, who seeks to dull her own pain by exploiting her daughter's sexuality. Finally, Martineau's various depictions of slavery demonstrate the absence of familial integrity (especially maternal influence) that characterizes this milieu. To the Victorian reading public, the primary significance of the absent mother concerns her inability to foster proper moral growth during her daughter's sexual rites of passage, a device employed by many writers to exonerate their fallen heroines.[16]

Similarly, the "harlot" component of the madonna-harlot equation cannot so easily be reduced to a generic category. This is most dramatically demonstrated by spinsters, who are culturally rejected as nonreproductive women, though it seems ludicrous to associate them, as many did, with harlots. Nor can seduced or raped women (Ruth, Marian) be compared with the prostitutes Lizzie Leigh or Esther, who in turn complicate the raucous prostitute stereotype by turning to this occupation solely for the purpose of feeding their starving children. And where do nonmaternal women fit in this category? Is the childlessness of the infanticidal Hetty Sorrel, the mad Bertha Mason Rochester, the alcoholic Janet Dempster ultimately preferable, given the undesirable offspring (according to genetic theories of the time, diseases such as insanity and syphilis were transmitted only by women) they are likely to produce? Because so many behaviors were indiscriminately relegated to the "harlot" category, both Victorian

16. Alternatively, Edith Honig detects in these writers "a sense [of] rejection of the conventional mothers . . . to whom they felt . . . no intellectual debt" (*Breaking the Angelic Image: Women and Power in Victorian Children's Fantasy,* 14). More conventional is F. K. Prochaska's observation that one of the most effective questions reformists asked of prostitutes was: "Would you like your mother to see how you are going on just now?" (*Women and Philanthropy in Nineteenth-Century England,* 192).

and modern prostitution discourses play a prominent role in my search for answers to these and related questions.[17]

The prominence of the period's middle-class sexual ideology, defined in terms of angels, madonnas, and magdalens, even when its inadequacy to experience was evident, manifests itself in a powerful code of ethics that categorizes deviancy in any form (this includes all women of other classes and races) as fallenness. Fallen characters and the issues they raise function as what W. R. Greg deems "anomalies," and what Mary Poovey calls "border cases," exceptions, in other words, to what is presented as a seamless ideological norm. As Kellow Chesney notes, "Nothing in the literature of the time is more striking than a tendency to lump all unchaste women into one category." Victorian-prostitution theorist William Acton agrees: "many forcible divines and moralists have maintained that all illicit intercourse is prostitution, and that this word is as justly applicable as those of 'fornication' and 'whoredom' to the female who, whether for hire or not, voluntarily surrenders her virtue. According to them, her first offence is as much an act of prostitution as its repetition."[18]

Extending the analogy, what I argue throughout this study is that the term *unchaste,* during the Victorian period, assumes extrasexual connotations. The term expands to incorporate alcoholics and anorexics, the insane, the infanticidal and depressed, and even slave women. This book's central projects are to disentangle the many behaviors relegated, for the sake of neatness and convenience, to the category of "fallenness"; to scrutinize the collapsed boundaries between evangelical, scientific, and ethical rhetoric that characterize the discourses of the period; to complicate critics' (both Victorian and modern) casual or facile use of the term *fallen;* and to consider the implications of assessing all women's behaviors in sexual terms. In her biography of Elizabeth Gaskell, Winifred Gerin's observation that "An injustice so vast in its application, human misery so far-reaching in its

17. Particularly helpful to my study of varieties of fallenness have been those studies aimed at exploring the economic circumstances of, and social attitudes toward, Victorian prostitution. The work of Michael Pearson, Frances Finnegan, Paul McHugh, Judith Walkowitz, Lynda Nead, and Linda Mahood contributed to my understanding of the class component of this subculture. Much of their work was highly suggestive to me in terms of formulating fallenness as a dynamic social and economic paradigm far removed from the static inevitability of low-class immorality.

18. Poovey, *Uneven Developments,* 12; Chesney, *The Anti-Society: An Account of the Victorian Underworld,* 315; Acton, *Prostitution Considered in Its Moral, Social, and Sanitary Aspects in London and Other Large Cities; with Proposals for the Mitigation and Prevention of Its Attendant Evils,* 29.

effects, demanded an answer" reflects the motivation underlying the social-problem literature I discuss. According to Henry Mayhew, "The voice of popular opinion," which is "erected on skeletons and cemented with the blood of women and children," is aptly reflected in the *British Quarterly Review*'s assessment of *Ruth:* "society has decreed that women who have once left the straight paths of virtue shall wander all their days outcast, branded, apart. . . . we believe the *world* is right."[19] Gaskell's Mr. Bradshaw could have phrased it no better himself.

Such an attitude reflects the class issues that in large part *construct* the fallen stereotype even in the process of codifying it. The women characters discussed in this study share a working-class background (or, in the case of slaves, no class at all), a milieu of hopelessness and depravity that precludes a triumph of spirit over oppressive circumstances such as Ada McGrath achieves. Exceptions to this are the middle-class but penniless spinsters and the upper-middle-class "New Women" discussed in Chapter 7, examples chosen to illustrate how even those women ostensibly protected by the period's sexual ideology were instead also victimized by it. Generally speaking, because the lack of education and opportunities limited the likelihood that working-class narratives would enter the literary mainstream, their stories and experiences are told primarily through the middle-class perspectives and values of Victorian writers and critics. Those qualified to write during this period did so from a superior socioeconomic perspective, with the inevitable (though probably unintentional) result that marginalized groups were objectified in terms often irrelevant to their class. All of the writers in this study of social-problem literature seem sincerely motivated to give—not appropriate—voice to those unable to articulate for themselves. Yet, as modern scholarship shows, the disparity between observer and observed created by class inequities creates inevitable gaps in understanding and, thus, in accuracy of representation. Drawing on the work of such social historians as Judith Walkowitz, Mary Abbot, and Françoise Barret-Ducrocq, two of the aims of this study are to distinguish middle-class sexual morality from the working-class standards it attempts to account for and to consider the implications of the Victorian impulse toward culturewide homogenization of moral and ethical values, although not the democratization of economic ascendancy linked with those values.

19. Gerin, *Elizabeth Gaskell: A Biography,* 131; Mayhew, *London Labour and the London Poor,* 4:xxix; review of *Ruth,* in *British Quarterly Review.*

All of the fallen women in this study are judged by middle-class sexual ideology, redeemed (or, as in Hetty's case, condemned) by its maternal imperative, and punished by the literal and metaphorical death or disfigurement of themselves or their children; none of them marries or otherwise achieves social integration. This raises a series of questions: To what extent are these middle-class authors practicing "woman's mission to women" through sympathy for the outcast? Do they participate in the condemnatory policy of their social milieu by exacting a price for deviance? Or do they make a special contribution to the period's fallen-woman discourse through constructing alternative perspectives? Such questions inform my readings of this literature and my considerations of the unresolved ambivalences these writers display toward their characters.

Issues of class disparity are further complicated by the sexual perspective from which an author writes. Victorian male authors were comparatively privileged in relation to their female counterparts by virtue of superior education, economic status, legal and political representation, and professional acceptance; like most men living in a patriarchal society, they enjoyed a privileged position in every respect. Because of this hegemonic privilege, male writers about fallen women lack the experiential perspective integral to a comprehensive understanding of a group from whom they are distanced by gender no less than by economics.

For this reason, male writers—even less-privileged, self-educated ones such as Dickens—write "about" fallen perspectives; women writers, in contrast, write "from" that perspective. As a result, male writers' fallen characters remain one-dimensional, talked about but not developed, objectified in euphemistic terms that fail to establish the social contexts leading to fallenness. Such fallen characters as Dickens's Nancy in *Oliver Twist* and Emily and Martha in *David Copperfield,* George Moore's title character in *Esther Waters,* and Rossetti's sleeping prostitute in "Jenny" acknowledge the existence of this class of women, but the circumstances of and ideological responsibility for their falls remain unarticulated. The significance of these literary portrayals to the aims of "social-problem" literature—that is, raising public awareness with a view toward instituting meaningful change—is thus relatively limited.[20] In such texts as these, the fallen woman was reduced

20. "Social-problem" literature, or "fiction with a purpose," assumed various forms, most typically novels (Gaskell, Dickens, Kingsley, Disraeli), although Wordsworth, Barrett Browning, Thomas Hood, and other poets also addressed these issues. See Robert Colby, *Fiction with a Purpose* (Bloomington: Indiana University Press, 1967); Louis

to a static character type, a figure whose inevitability provoked fear and revulsion rather than active intervention.

Hegemonic privilege is exhibited not only by the predominance of Victorian male writers who address fallen-woman issues but also by twentieth-century male literary critics who assess those writers. To date, I have been unable to locate any book-length study on the topic of fallen women as presented exclusively from women writers' perspectives.[21] Nor have I found studies accounting for those behaviors that, by association and by the intensely suggestive power of the fallen stereotype, result in women's pariah status, even when sexuality is not involved. My book seeks to remedy both these omissions.

A survey of contemporary studies of Victorian fallen women illustrates my concerns on these issues. Martin Seymour-Smith's 1969 *Fallen Women* employs this quaint Victorian term solely for the purpose of discussing prostitutes and their clients and pimps. Far from envisioning the idea of fallenness as multidefined or circumstantial, Seymour-Smith's brief history of prostitution takes as its representative Victorian text the pornographic memoirs of the prurient "Walter."[22] Similarly, Fraser Harrison's *The Dark Angel*, published in 1977, perpetuates the madonna-harlot myth by contrasting an ostensibly seamless respectable sexuality with an unrespectable sexuality; he, too, employs "Walter" as the authoritative voice of Victorian sexual experience. As was true of Dr. William Acton's widely read 1857 *Prostitution*, the woman's perspective is all but erased from such studies.

Eric Trudgill's *Madonnas and Magdalenes*, published in 1976, promises to explore the "origins and development" of Victorian sexual attitudes but devotes only one chapter to the magdalen, a term that here incorporates all forms of deviant sexuality without distinction. Similarly, George Watt's 1984 *The Fallen Woman in the Nineteenth-Century English Novel*, although

Cazamian, *The Social Novel in England, 1830–1850* (London and Boston: Routledge and Kegan Paul, 1973); Monica Correa Fryckstedt, *Elizabeth Gaskell's "Mary Barton" and "Ruth": A Challenge to Christian England;* Aina Rubenius, *The Woman Question in Mrs. Gaskell's Life and Works;* and Sheila M. Smith, *The Other Nation: The Poor in English Novels of the 1840s and 1850s.*

21. Matus's *Unstable Bodies* features women-authored literary texts, but her primary interest is maternal ideology, not varieties of deviance. Matus argues that women's writing offers a discourse no less constructive of female ideology than that of male-authored "biomedical discourse," and that through their writing Victorian women "could alter and influence the way such matters were understood" (13). This insight is central to my study as well.

22. "Walter," *My Secret Life,* 11 vols. (Amsterdam: privately printed, ca. 1880).

offering a series of critical readings, relies on texts selected on the basis of the similarities, rather than the differences, they share. All of the texts Watt discusses are by male authors, with the single exception of Gaskell's *Ruth*.

Sally Mitchell's 1981 *The Fallen Angel: Chastity, Class, and Women's Reading, 1835–1880,* is an important study of sexual fallenness as depicted in "penny weeklies" and other popular presses, though not one focused on women writers or on variations of fallenness. This latter consideration is also true of Amanda Anderson's *Tainted Souls and Painted Faces: The Rhetoric of Fallenness in Victorian Culture,* which was published in 1993. Anderson's explicitly theoretical study, which includes male- and female-authored texts and relies on a more sexually oriented definition of fallenness than what I promote here, is concerned with agency, rhetoric and theory, intersubjectivity, and "the politics of post-structuralism." Also critiquing both female- and male-authored literature is Tom Winnifrith in his 1994 *Fallen Women in the Nineteenth-Century Novel.* Limiting the focus to one genre and incorporating earlier writers on the topic such as Austen, Winnifrith's study is distinguished by its attention to authorial biography as a means of contextualizing the sexual mores found in the literature. Each of these approaches to the problem of Victorian fallenness offers alternative perspectives that are complementary to—though different from—my interest in social history and particularly in varieties and degrees of fallenness as presented exclusively by women writers.

Only one piece of scholarly writing satisfactorily verified my hypothesis that much modern, including some feminist, scholarship perpetuates the madonna-harlot dichotomy by accepting its a priori status rather than delving into the *gaps* left unaccounted for by Victorian sexual ideology. Beth Kalikoff's "The Falling Woman in Three Victorian Novels," which was published in 1987, was revelatory in its transforming "fallen" to "falling," a distinction few Victorians would permit. Kalikoff's article, which applies concepts of fallenness to heroines who do not technically fall—Jane Eyre, Mary Barton, and Maggie Tulliver—demonstrates the power of the stereotype to construct deviant behavior even where none exists.

My literary choices in this study are prompted by a desire to pursue an in-depth examination of women writers of fallen-woman narratives. I make no essentialist claims for privileging female over male writers on these issues, with the important exception that Victorian women writers share with their characters a stigma of fallenness foreign to their male counterparts. Jane Flanders's warning that "To suggest that only women can write sympathetically about women, that men are incapable of authentic representation of female experience, is to restrict the [literature] . . . to autobiography" (a factor Winnifrith employs to advantage) elides several important issues. First, the lack of in-depth studies of women writers on fallen women represents a serious omission in literary history, the very absence of which deserves scrutiny. Second, as Mary Poovey notes, the collapsing of class boundaries among women as a result of sexual leveling places them in a shared position of cultural inferiority. This in itself makes superior the authenticity with which women write about issues affecting women, a dynamic that Josephine Butler demonstrates compellingly in her acute understanding that the Contagious Diseases Acts presented as direct a threat to women in manor houses as to women of the streets. Finally, Flanders's use of the term *autobiography* implies a more direct experiential correspondence than I am suggesting, one that minimizes these writers' literary craft. Deborah Epstein Nord contends, "Associated by gender with the very emblems of poverty, disease, and fallenness . . . women writers had to contend with split identifications: they wrote with the cultural (and class) authority of the writer and with the taint of their sex's role."[23] Clearly, the links joining these writers to their characters and to the issues they raise are far from seamless or uncomplicated, as my discussions of authorial ambivalence will show.

Despite the comparative class privilege that permitted them to write, all the women writers in this study directly experienced the antiwoman sentiment that characterizes Victorian gender ideology. Women writers were often criticized in sexual, rather than literary, terms; self-educated, they were ridiculed for lacking public-school intellectualism. The articulate Harriet Martineau, a woman of formidable intellect and scholarly discipline, found her often controversial opinions met with insults to her spinsterhood and even the hearing impairment that necessitated her using an ear trumpet. Elizabeth Barrett Browning was condemned—"To bless and not to curse is woman's function"—for treating such "unwomanly" topics as rape and unmarried motherhood. Elizabeth Gaskell, a paragon of maternalism, domesticity, and Evangelicalism, was berated by book burners and literary critics alike for her compassion toward the prostitute and for daring to redeem the fallen woman. George Eliot was herself a fallen woman as the common-law wife of George Henry Lewes, while Charlotte Brontë, whose psychosexual insights anticipate Freud by half a century, was labeled

23. Flanders, "The Fallen Woman in Fiction," 98; Deborah Epstein Nord, *Walking the Victorian Streets: Women, Representation, and the City,* 12.

"unregenerate, undisciplined . . . anti-Christian," and rebellious. Deborah Nord's comment that the female "urban spectator"—here, the woman writer on social issues—"cannot necessarily be distinguished from . . . other 'public' women" is true of all these writers: "Unlike the traditional male spectator, who depends on his invisibility and immunity within the crowd, the female spectator must always be both observer and observed, privileged and vulnerable."[24]

Elizabeth Cady Stanton's observation that "woman herself must do this work; for woman alone can understand the height, the depth, the length and the breadth of her degradation" recognizes that the experiential links between women, regardless of class, resonate more compellingly than is possible between men and women.[25] Of course, the period's strict gendered separatism aligns women with women in more material ways through the institutionalized power imbalances that favor men. Women had no political or legal representation, and they were prevented from obtaining the education and skills that would make them economically self-sufficient. Marriage, presented as destiny rather than choice, deprived women of property, child custody, and control over their own bodies. Nonconforming women—criminals, the sexually fallen, widows, spinsters, and other social radicals—should be transported to the colonies, as was Ada McGrath. John Stuart Mill observed that it was all very well for influential men such as himself to speak on behalf of women; however, no meaningful shift in social perspective would be possible until women spoke for themselves. "Women who read, much more women who write," he observed, "are, in the existing constitution of things, a contradiction and a disturbing element"[26]—both conditions necessary for social change.

24. [W. E. Aytoun], "Poetic Aberrations"; review of *Jane Eyre*; Nord, *Walking the Victorian Streets*, 123, 143. See also Barry Faulk, "Spies and Experts: Laura Ormiston Chant and Victorian Professionals." Chant, a social-purity reformer active during the late Victorian period, encountered resistance from the "exclusively male professionals" who argued against women's participation in reformist activities (53). Alternatively, some clergymen promoted the participation of women, warning that men with even the best of intentions often found themselves compromised by opponents who misrepresented their motives.

25. Stanton quoted in Nina Auerbach, *Communities of Women: An Idea in Fiction*, 27. William Thackeray, creator of one of the most notorious fallen women, Becky Sharp in *Vanity Fair*, admits, "When I say that I know women, I mean I know that I don't know them. Every single woman I ever knew is a puzzle to me" (Peter Gay, *The Cultivation of Hatred*, 289).

26. Erna Olafson Hellerstein, Leslie Parker Hume, and Karen M. Offen, eds., *Victorian Women: A Documentary Account of Women's Lives in Nineteenth-Century England,*

To this equation I add women's need to break silences and articulate, as did the Victorian prostitute who told Josephine Butler, "It is *men, men, only men,* from the first to the last. . . . To please a man I did wrong at first, then I was flung about from man to man . . . By men we are examined, handled, doctored," arrested, prayed over, condemned by, and legislated against. Butler observes, "When men, of all ranks, thus band themselves together for an end deeply concerning women, . . . it is time that women should arise and demand their most sacred rights in regard to their sisters." In the terms of modern critics, "Only a challenge to the hierarchy of *sites* of discourse, which usually comes from groups and classes 'situated' by the dominant in low or marginal positions, carries the promise of politically transformative power."[27] Barrett Browning's proposal that "materfamilias" can begin to remedy women's wrongs simply by "looking at them & calling them by their names" aims to realize that promise.

Another aim of this study is to explore a representative sampling of women's writing about fallen-woman issues. It is not my intention to present a comprehensive survey of all available texts that address these issues, nor do I presume to assign positions in the deviance hierarchy to the various behaviors I discuss. Instead, my concern is with the term *fallen woman* itself, which extends beyond the woman who engages in nonlegitimated, or unmarried, sex to incorporate any woman not manifesting the marriage-and-motherhood domestic ideal. The centrality of this ideal, steeped as it is in a thorough sexualization of all aspects of women's lives, is evidenced in cultural attitudes toward slave women, alcoholic and mad women, childless women and mothers of bastards, celibate and sexually responsive women, widows and spinsters, and women forced to work for a living: all are deviant, all are redundant, all require—according to social critic W. R. Greg—transportation to the colonies.[28] I have chosen my primary texts based both on their ability to illustrate these variations on the fallen-woman theme and on their capacity to suggest how open-ended Victorian sexual ideology in fact was.

These women writers' treatments of the fallen milieu directly challenged evangelicals and moralists whose assumptions were promoted by the male

---

France, *and the United States,* provides evidence for these attitudes; John Stuart Mill, *Subjection of Women,* 28.

27. Butler quoted in Janet Horowitz Murray, *Strong-Minded Women and Other Lost Voices from Nineteenth-Century England,* 436–37; Stallybrass and White, *Politics and Poetics,* 201.

28. W. R. Greg, "Why Are Women Redundant?"

medical establishment as scientific "fact."[29] The dominant view decreed that lower-class status, for example, inevitably indicated a predisposition to alcoholism, criminality, and promiscuity, a theory complemented by social Darwinism. In contrast, the women writers discussed in this study argue that lower-class aberrations of all kinds—including murder and prostitution—are *not* genetically class specific, though they are produced by class stratification and power imbalances in society and as such are amenable to change. This shift in focus away from class-based character defects to the significance of environmental influences participates in the discourse of sociological disciplines developed during the Victorian period.

The static "once fallen, always fallen" maxim dictated that a woman need make only one sexual mistake to be branded permanently fallen. The tenacity of this attitude should not be underestimated: perhaps the most dramatic example is George Eliot's Maggie Tulliver in *The Mill on the Floss,* a woman of remarkable intelligence and integrity who suffers vicious social ostracism and death due not to an actual fall, but to only a suspected one. The writers in this study are careful to establish the extenuating circumstances of their heroines' falls, to implicate the male and female characters who variously perpetuate such falls, and to challenge the dictum that the fallen can never rise again. These negotiations are generally problematic, and the resulting denouements sometimes contradictory: some redeemed heroines live out their lives in humble atonement, while others must die. Some women are too good to live; perhaps, Barrett Browning theorizes, "The mother's rapture slew her."[30] Some are too bad to live; Hetty Sorrel's social reintegration is inconvenient to the "good" woman's plot. Others—Lizzie Leigh, Marian Erle—are relegated to a marginal existence as social criminals compelled to work out their atonement through selfless acts.

Literary convention surrounding illegitimate children is similarly varied. Some children are impaired or disfigured (seen in "The Well of Pen-Morfa") or stillborn, while others are as healthy "as if" they were legitimate. In some instances, the child's health seems purchased at the price of the mother's life, as in *Ruth;* for others, the child must sicken and die, as in *Mary*

29. Poovey's *Uneven Developments* provides an illuminating discussion of the often amorphous intersections between medical and clerical rhetoric, two discourse communities striving to assert authority over women's sexuality. See especially chapter 2, "Scenes of an Indelicate Character: The Medical Treatment of Victorian Women" (24–50).

30. Elizabeth Barrett Browning, *Aurora Leigh,* 1.35.

Barton.[31] Sarah Grand provides a striking variation on these conventions by presenting the syphilitic offspring of the chaste Edith and her promiscuous husband as a hideous "speckled toad"; Edith dies of syphilis-induced insanity, while her child lives hidden away in the manor house, bearing grotesque testimony to upper-class hereditary pride and male sexual profligacy.

Along with promoting redemption, these woman writers issue a call for educating young girls. As a central issue in "Woman Question" debates, academic instruction for females was certainly a crucial prelude to women's entering into the professions. The absence of educational and employment opportunities for women reinforced the idea that they belonged at home anyway and that, since only prostitutes could boast economic independence, the illicit propensities of women who worked for remuneration (governesses, seamstresses, factory and mine workers) are by association obvious. Seen through this lens, the moralized economics linking celibate spinsters with promiscuous prostitutes is clarified as the choice between genteel penury (Miss Matty in *Cranford* agonizes over the propriety of her scheme to sell tea) and earning a livelihood by selling sex.

But the sort of education alluded to by the women writers in this study undercuts another tenacious idea: sexual ignorance in women protects their sexual innocence, and the less women know about the taboo subject of sex the purer they will remain. Perhaps nowhere is the power differential between Victorian males and females more clearly seen than in the sexual double standard, which demanded female chastity (a "moral" standard) while promoting the tradition of male sexual activity prior to marriage as necessary to men's health (a "scientific" standard). Dr. William Acton's *Prostitution,* for example, is a treatise that says little about prostitutes but discusses at length the economic (the need to postpone marriage until able to attain middle-class standards of "conspicuous consumption"), physical (men's health is physically damaged by celibacy), and social connotations of men's need for sexual activity prior to marriage.

The idea that "good" (middle- and upper-class) women must be kept sexually pure for marriage in order to ensure legitimate issue for inheritance purposes is echoed even in such evangelical tracts as *The Magdalen's Friend.* Despite public outcry against them, prostitutes were clearly integral to the Victorian social structure. Some clergymen even argued that prostitution was necessary and that it was not for humans to question an institution

---

31. See Loralee MacPike's important discussion of these issues in "The Fallen Woman's Sexuality: Childbirth and Censure."

sanctioned by an apparently utilitarian God "for the greater good." The results of this dynamic are most commonly dramatized by middle- and upper-class males' seduction of working-class girls, whom they subsequently abandon in poverty and disgrace, usually with a bastard child to raise alone and without means (typically regarded by prostitution theorists as the first step to prostitution). In this way, ideologists claim, the purity of respectable women and the sanctity of the middle-class nuclear family are preserved, the sacrifice of lower-class girls and women being a small price to pay for ensuring the dominant culture's perpetuation.

A final distinguishing feature of these woman-authored texts refers back to the idea of silencing and articulation with which I began. What sort of impact resulted from women writers risking their reputations by addressing these unsavory issues? Each text discussed in this study in some way goes beyond the boundaries of social and sexual respectability through more uncompromising and less euphemistic presentations than their male-authored counterparts. This is remarkable in view of the period's tendency to assess women's writing on nonliterary standards, particularly when topics of which "decent" women should have no knowledge were involved. Martineau, for example, clearly articulates the cultural ramifications of the practice of sexual slavery in the American South for such revered Victorian institutions as marriage and motherhood; Barrett Browning extends this analogy by making a convincing case for justified infanticide; Eliot exposes middle-class alcoholism and wife beating; Gaskell's prostitute, Esther, tells her own story; and Charlotte Brontë weaves a complex web of sex, alcohol, bigamy, and insanity. Although such writers prepared the way for Sarah Grand's controversial articulation of the syphilitic consequences of the double standard in her 1893 novel, *The Heavenly Twins,* fin-de-siècle critics, like their Victorian forebears, assessed the author's femininity rather than her literary ability. As Marilyn Bonnell observes, primary credit for the New Woman prototype belongs to Grand, yet that credit was co-opted by literary critics who promoted male-authored treatments while denigrating Grand's "unwomanliness." Thus, Grand's protagonists are still comparatively unknown, while Hardy's Sue Bridehead in *Jude the Obscure* and the works of lesser-known male authors, such as George Gissing's *The Odd Women* and Grant Allen's *The Woman Who Did,* are still the standard citations in discussions of the genre.[32]

32. See Bonnell, "The Legacy of Sarah Grand's *The Heavenly Twins:* A Review Essay." Bonnell argues that Hardy's notebooks reveal he was reading Grand's book during the

The texts I am working with have been chosen with a view toward their relevance to the topic rather than to consistency in genre, an approach that broadens the base of available literary conventions while providing greater variability in treatment of the issues. I share with the writers I discuss a fascination with the intense ideological energy generated by a culture's behavioral anomalies, an energy unmatched by conforming angels in the house. As all of my literary examples demonstrate, the absurd lack of parallelism in the madonna-harlot construct—a woman is either a mother or a whore—collapses when challenged by the "in-between" "border cases" presented in these texts. Subaltern sexuality constitutes a threat that must be managed or, better, repressed and eliminated, the pervasiveness of which is reflected in the images of filth and contagion applied to the period's working classes. Far from anachronistic, the politics linking such attitudes with racism, eugenics, and ethnic cleansing make this a topic peculiarly relevant to our time.

Chapter 2, " 'Marry, Stitch, Die, or Do Worse': The First Step to Prostitution," is a comparison study of two representative fallen-woman texts: Gaskell's novel *Ruth* and Barrett Browning's novel-poem *Aurora Leigh*.[33] Ruth Hilton and Marian Erle share unstable working-class backgrounds, and both become seamstresses, an occupation popularly aligned with sexual falls; both are sexually betrayed and abandoned but bear children that are healthy despite their illegitimacy. Each woman embraces maternity in spite of the circumstances of conception and, accordingly, achieves redemption through motherhood. Such terms as *redemption* and *atonement* signify the centrality of evangelical ideology in fallen-woman discourse; this chapter explores the influence of that discourse through *The Magdalen's Friend,* a magazine typical of the period's social-problem periodicals. My discussion of the needlework milieu further establishes a social context for fallenness, which is caused less by working-class vanity than by middle-class vanity.

The title of this second chapter indicates the grim options available to such women, each one a form of slavery. Working-class marriages often meant endless childbearing, drunken brutality, and grinding poverty;[34] the

---

writing of *Jude the Obscure* and that his narrative was directly influenced by her work with the idea that hereditary influences shape individuals' destinies.

33. The title of this chapter derives from an 1859 speech made by American feminist Caroline Dall on behalf of lower-class women: "Practically, the command of society to the uneducated class is 'Marry, stitch, die, or do worse' " (quoted in Helsinger, Sheets, and Veeder, *The Woman Question,* 2:150).

34. For illustrations of this point, see Hellerstein, Hume, and Offen, *Victorian Women,* 246–47, 279, 301–5.

profession of seamstress was a form of white slavery, while "do worse" indicates prostitution. Death was often the only escape possible from such a dynamic, as the suicidal prostitutes in Thomas Hood's "The Bridge of Sighs" attest. Important issues addressed by these texts include articulation of the differences between seduction and rape; upper-class betrayal of the working class—here, sexual exploitation of virgins by both men and women; the consequences of ignorance in sexual matters, which not only offers no protection for sexual innocence but actually fosters vulnerability; and the inability of the redeemed woman to achieve social integration.

Chapter 3, "The Harlot's Progress: 'Render up your body, or die,'" surveys Gaskell's increasingly radical mediation on behalf of prostitutes. Initially, "The Well of Pen-Morfa" reflects a typically Dickensian approach to the subject: euphemistic and allusive, the nameless fallen woman seems merely part of the local color in the quaint village of Pen-Morfa. But as the "pure" heroine's tale unfolds, it becomes clear that the life experiences of the two women bear a remarkable similarity, raising some interesting questions concerning the relative fates of the pure and the fallen. "Lizzie Leigh" more clearly articulates the protagonist's sexual fall, illegitimate maternity, and decline into prostitution; here, Gaskell effectively employs a biblical interplay between the male characters' Old Testament, angry-God posturing toward the "sinner" and the women characters' Christlike compassion in reclaiming the prodigal daughter.

Esther of *Mary Barton* is Gaskell's most graphic literary treatment of prostitution. Gaskell presents the circumstances leading to Esther's fall in the fuller context of Manchester's starving working-class milieu. Seduced, betrayed, and abandoned with a sickly child, Esther turns to prostitution and alcoholism; her inherent goodness manifests itself in her preventing the sexual fall of Mary Barton, again illustrating Gaskell's signature appeal to compassion. Gaskell's presentation of Esther reflects her assimilation of Victorian fallen-woman discourse, as this chapter's overview of the most prominent prostitution theorists of the time—including doctors, sociologists, clergy, and feminists—makes clear.

Although most often portrayed in urban settings, sexual falls also occurred in more insulated, tightly knit farming communities, making communal culpability a more viable issue than in the indifferent city. Chapter 4, "Am I My Sister's Keeper? Sexual Deviance and the Social Community," considers George Eliot's Hetty Sorrel in *Adam Bede* as a willing participant in her seduction by the aristocrat she dreams will marry her. But Hetty's presentation as opportunistic, vain, and shallow is ultimately inadequate for the degree of "willing suspension of disbelief" required by Eliot's suggestion that Hetty is capable of infanticide. The issues raised by this text lead to an exploration of the options available to women faced with unwanted pregnancies at this time. Hetty Sorrel represents a sexual naïveté similar to that seen in the characters of Marian Erle and Ruth but complicated by an appalling ignorance of social mores. A crucial difference is that Hetty is not redeemed by motherhood, nor is she tempered by tragedy, and she dies never understanding the ramifications of her situation. While this text exposes often disturbing narrative ambivalence, its place in fallen-woman literature is secured by the class issues it raises and by its painful portrayal of the effects of unwanted pregnancy on mother and child while the father's life proceeds unencumbered.

Thus far, the fallen characters I discuss demonstrate sexual impropriety, although none conforms with the hardened stereotype invoked by the term *harlot.* Further complicating this construct in a variety of ways, Chapter 5, "Sobriety and Propriety: 'Her one besetting sin, intemperance,' " surveys a range of aberrant social behaviors in women, behaviors that were by association linked with sexual deviance. These examples demonstrate that the category of fallenness is not limited to women who commit transgressive sexual acts but also includes women who failed to manifest the marriage-and-motherhood domestic ideal in ways other than illegitimacy. Contrary to reigning ideology, the texts discussed in this chapter reveal that such conditions as alcoholism, anorexia, and insanity are not bound by gender or class lines, nor are they necessarily indicative of inherent moral depravity; instead, they are presented as symptomatic of, not responsible for, Victorian social erosion.

Harriet Martineau's "Sowers not Reapers" exposes a range of unsavory cultural tendencies resulting from the industrial milieu. This tale of working-class family life focuses on Mrs. Kay, a victim of habitual laudanum dosing during childhood. As an adult struggling to feed her family, she sacrifices her food portion to her children and relapses into alcoholism and anorexia. Her situation foregrounds the lamentable availability and affordability of gin and opium in working-class communities, replacing food as daily sustenance. Significantly, Mrs. Kay does not fit the sensually depraved stereotype; instead, she manifests the middle-class domestic and maternal ideal in the most self-effacing way possible and dies as a result.

George Eliot's "Janet's Repentance" also addresses female alcoholism in part vindicated by the brutal conditions of Janet's marriage but complicated by her childlessness. Janet's working-class origins are materially improved through her marriage to the middle-class Lawyer Dempster; but his drunken and cruel brutality prevents domestic harmony, and Janet's life becomes a series of beatings dulled by alcoholic stupors. The narrative ambivalence apparent in Eliot's treatment of Hetty Sorrel is evident in her attitude toward Janet as well; rather than examining the life-threatening conditions of Janet's marriage, all of which fell within Dempster's legal rights as her husband, Eliot blames the victim by her insistence that motherhood would correct Janet's aberrant ways.

My final example of alcoholism (although this proves to be but a smoke screen for other "intemperances") is Bertha Mason Rochester, Charlotte Brontë's "madwoman in the attic" in *Jane Eyre*. The narrative provides relatively little information about Bertha, aside from the fact that she is clearly an impediment to the heroine's romantic progress. My discussion aims at uncovering Bertha's story, which is as elusive as if she were a self-willed mute like Ada McGrath. Several characters in Brontë's novel presume to speak for Bertha, claiming her alcoholism, sexual voracity, and violence justify her imprisonment in the attic, but Bertha is never permitted to speak for herself.[35] Her articulations assume the form of animalistic snarls and acts of physical violence, more difficult to "read" than words, perhaps, yet at least as potent with meaning as the other deviant behaviors discussed throughout this study. The Bluebeardian qualities of *Jane Eyre* resonate with the fates of a range of fallen women, deadened aspects of whom are lopped off and imprisoned in metaphorical attics throughout literary history.

Insofar as xenophobic anxieties are aroused by Bertha's foreign heritage —what Jill Matus terms "racially-inflected sexuality"—race adds yet another complication to the period's sexual ideology.[36] "Harem Life, West and East," Chapter 6, discusses travel journals, fiction, and narrative poetry dealing with the subject of slave women's sexuality. Martineau's American and Middle Eastern travel journals provide rare insight into a level of sexual oppression popularly shrouded in erroneous speculation, including the American system of "quadroon connexions" and Middle Eastern "hareems." Her fictional tale of the West Indies, "Demerara," which resulted in Martineau's being nearly lynched while touring the American South, features slaves' articulation of the inevitable erosion of marriage and nuclear-family values resulting from the slave system.

35. Jean Rhys's *Wide Sargasso Sea* (New York: Norton, 1967) remedies this silence by presenting Bertha Mason Rochester's narrative voice and perspective on the events of *Jane Eyre*, giving readers some idea of what Brontë's Bertha might have said, given different ideological circumstances.
36. Matus, *Unstable Bodies*, 14.

Elizabeth Barrett Browning's narrative poem "The Runaway Slave at Pilgrim's Point," one of the period's most powerful examples of abolitionist polemic, addresses such taboo subjects as slavery, interracial sexual relations, illegitimacy, rape, infanticide, lynching, and murder through the slave woman's narrative perspective. This strategy, of course, may be seen as a middle-class white woman's appropriation of the black slave woman's words; it may also be regarded as a writer's employing her international status as a respected poet in the service of a political and social stance to which she was passionately committed. Written for and first published by American abolitionists to promote their cause, "The Runaway Slave at Pilgrim's Point" is a radical contribution to a body of abolitionist literature frequently characterized by the euphemistic sentimentalism that marks Stowe's *Uncle Tom's Cabin.* Insofar as the intellectual, social, and literary interchanges between prominent English and American women formed an integral part of the American abolitionist movement, Barrett Browning's poem, like Martineau's fiction and travel journals, is less an appropriation than a giving voice to an otherwise silenced and misrepresented group of women.

As a prelude to the issues of celibacy and venereal infection (more closely related than is immediately obvious) with which I conclude this study, "The Problem to Be Solved, the Evil and Anomaly to Be Cured," Chapter 7, begins by considering the conundrum spinsters pose to the madonna-harlot ideology. The chapter title, taken from W. R. Greg's infamous transportation scheme as proposed in his 1862 "Why Are Women Redundant?" is suggestive of the fear engendered by women who lack a place—even a place among what Lynda Nead terms "the residuum"—in a culture whose solidarity depends on women's having, and keeping in, their proper place.[37] Greg's associating spinsters—technically, unmarried women without a man (father, brother, or other male relative) to support them—with other candidates for transportation like criminals and diseased prostitutes demonstrates the degree to which proponents of this ideology were willing to go to ensure its seamlessness. Greg's rhetoric arouses evangelical ("evil"), social ("anomaly"), and medical (spinsters are a disease to be "cured") anxieties equaled only by the revulsion exhibited elsewhere against prostitutes.

Although an affectionate and poignant portrayal of this class of women, Gaskell's *Cranford* offers an often distressing view of the pecuniary existence forced on unmarried women unable to, or unqualified for, work. Gaskell's

---

37. Nead, *Myths of Sexuality: Representations of Women in Victorian Britain,* 95.

opening assertion that the village of Cranford is "in possession of the Amazons" suggests a more autonomous lifestyle than is the case. Far from an Amazonian independence, Cranford's widows and spinsters are dependent on the economic decisions men (who are usually absent) make for their provision. Less charitable public attitudes toward such women are demonstrated in Brontë's *Shirley.* For Caroline Helstone, Miss Mann and Miss Ainley alternately inspire pity for their plight and fear of the loneliness and lovelessness integral to the stereotype. Robert Moore, on whom Caroline's future as a wife or spinster depends, is inexorable in his cruel attitude toward spinsters (including his dependent sister, Hortense), demonstrating an almost pathological revulsion for which he is suitably reprimanded by Nurse Horsfall.

Midcentury fears that spinsterhood might actually appeal to some women finds expression in the late-Victorian "New Woman" novel, Sarah Grand's *The Heavenly Twins.* Grand's New Women demonstrate the often lethal effects of angelic ideology on its ostensible beneficiaries (middle- and upper-class women); they also reveal the tenacity of the idea that women of all classes are "always already" fallen, when they "manage" their sexual standards no less than when they do not. As a girl, Evadne Frayling studies the medical books she discovers hidden in the attic, symbolic of other denials of distasteful truths about Victorian sexual ideology. On her wedding day, Evadne learns of her husband's profligate past and, fearing venereal infection, insists the marriage remain unconsummated. Although disowned by her outraged family for thus controlling her own sexuality (as my discussion of spinsters shows, celibacy was no less an aberration than promiscuity), Evadne sees her judgment vindicated by the less cautious newlywed Edith, whose life ends in syphilitic insanity. Despite the social progress implied by the term *New Woman,* the fates of Grand's socially privileged protagonists are not much different from those of midcentury working-class women whose choices were limited to "marry, stitch, die, or do worse."

What happens to fallen heroines once their creators give voice to their experiences? Martineau's slave women and their children are sold on the auction block and never heard of again; Barrett Browning's Runaway Slave is killed by white men, while Marian Erle simply disappears from the narrative. Ruth, Esther, Mrs. Kay, and Hetty Sorrel suffer premature deaths; Janet Dempster, Lizzie Leigh, and Pen-Morfa's nameless outcast devote their lives to serving others. Considering that Brontë's spinsters are little more than targets for ridicule in their community, Cranford's spinsters and widows seem fortunate to be quarantined in their essentially manless circle. Evadne Frayling's crusading spirit compares with Bertha Mason Rochester's in that both persist in articulating the injustices practiced against them; ultimately, however, Bertha's rebellion requires her self-destruction, while Evadne is spiritually diminished to the point of contemplating suicide and enduring a lifelong pattern of depressive episodes. Not one of these characters can be said to transcend the circumstances of her oppression, much less to become a self-actualized individual. What was true of eighteenth-century writers on the fallen-woman theme remains true a century later: "no author has yet been so bold as to permit a lady to live and marry, and be a woman after this strain."[38] Not until a twentieth-century filmmaker revisits the theme of the Victorian fallen woman does such a figure seem to triumph over her trials. Ada McGrath boldly revels in her unconventionality: she is "quite the town freak, which suits." But our final image of Ada—her halting speech and veiled countenance—suggests that the archetype has barely begun to be articulated.

38. Flanders, "Fallen Woman in Fiction," 106.

2

"Marry, Stitch, Die, or Do Worse"

THE FIRST STEP TO PROSTITUTION

We learn from the gracious sympathy thus accorded by the Saviour to the Magdalen that, deadly as was this woman's sin, yet it was not necessarily a sin unto death . . . impurity is not blasphemy. . . . It may lead to that crime. It is not the crime itself.

—"The Accepted Penitent," in *The Magdalen's Friend*

Stitch—stitch—stitch,
In poverty, hunger, and dirt,
Sewing at once, with a double thread,
A shroud as well as a shirt.

—Thomas Hood, "The Song of the Shirt"

THE VERY term *fallen women*, according to Lynda Nead, is in fact a misnomer when applied to the lower classes since it assumes these women had some position of worth from which to fall. Nead argues the label more accurately applies to middle- or upper-class women's sexual falls, although these were considered so rare as to be a contradiction in terms: "only a respectable woman could *fall* from virtue and social status . . . for, according to bourgeois ideology, the women of the undeserving poor were indistinguishable from prostitutes anyway."[1] Indeed, a survey of "Magdalenism" (an umbrella term for various reformist activities) during

1. Nead, *Myths of Sexuality*, 76–77.

27

the Victorian period reveals that lower-class sexual deviance and middle-class reclamation mirrored the culture's broader system of class and moral stratification.

Exceptions to this convention are such fallen-woman characters as Elizabeth Barrett Browning's Marian Erle in *Aurora Leigh* and Elizabeth Gaskell's Ruth Hilton in *Ruth,* who are drawn by their creators as working class only by an accident of birth. Both characters are invested with an "innate" purity and an "inherent" set of middle-class moral values that render them victims of circumstance rather than active agents in sexual deviance. Thus, both are truly "fallen" women, and therefore both must be redeemable and permitted to "rise" again. Such characters represent a special class of fallenness, what Dinah Mulock Craik terms those "who have fallen out of the ranks of honest women without sinking to a lower depth still." Characters such as Ruth and Marian who resist easy categorization arouse middle-class anxieties, like "the fear that respectability is a masquerade, that the individual self is already and inevitably fallen" and that the possibility for the fallen to rise by association implies the possibility for the respectable to fall. This chapter explores a type of fallen sexuality that requires collapsing the class-inscribed morality of the madonna-harlot dichotomy to broaden its definition and to incorporate the idea of redemption. In the words of the Reverend Mr. Benson, "not every woman who has fallen is depraved";[2] put another way, "once fallen, always fallen" is transformed by these writers into "though fallen, yet redeemable."

The intersections of class mores and the pitfalls endemic to the needle-working milieu provide important insights into the issues raised by these texts. Scholar Françoise Barret-Ducrocq, for example, presents a quite different version of Victorian working-class sexuality from that which is popularly assumed. Her 1989 study of London's Foundling Hospital records argues that "What differs from the conventional picture is the motivation and logic of the transgressions described, the evident perception of a specific moral code." The "conventional picture" elides the underlying economic factors that define working-class lifestyles, seen, for example, in the link between crowded living conditions and promiscuity: "proximity alone [fosters] a moral plague every bit as contagious as a disease epidemic."[3]

2. Craik, *A Woman's Thoughts about Women,* 190; Audrey Jaffe, "Under Cover of Sympathy: *Ressentiment* in Gaskell's *Ruth,*" 54; Elizabeth Gaskell, *Ruth,* 350 (future quotations will be cited parenthetically in the text).

3. Barret-Ducrocq, *Love in the Time of Victoria: Sexuality and Desire among Working-Class Men and Women in Nineteenth-Century London,* 4, 19–20.

Often mistaking pragmatism for immorality, conservative reformists focused more on the potential for sexual indecency than on improving working-class standards of living. For example, families shared the same bed (if they had one) because this was their means of keeping warm, not because they were genetically predisposed to incest. But the tendency to privilege decency over utility was insistent: "You may endeavor to impart ideas of modesty and self-respect to a poor girl, and she . . . would gladly practise them if she could; but how is this to be done? She goes home to sleep and undress in a room where there is no privacy of any sort, and where the commonest decencies of life are not observed; . . . and how is she to observe the lessons of modesty you have sought to instill?" These ideas demonstrate Barret-Ducrocq's observation that "received wisdom" assumed working-class sexuality "lacked the basic components of a code of sexual morality," a quality aptly displayed in the teeming squalor of filthy rags, fetid odors, diseased bodies, child-beating mothers, and drunken fathers such as those attending Romney and Marian's aborted wedding in *Aurora Leigh*. The tenacity of this stereotype may explain these authors' investing their working-class heroines with an "inherent" middle-class chastity.[4]

Barrett-Ducrocq observes that "Carnal relations between young people have always been tolerated by the working classes in Western Europe" and that the nineteenth-century's shift in sexual mores was slow to filter down to the lower classes. The practice of premarital sex, traditionally regarded by the community as a ritual marking a couple's engagement, "remained very much alive" among this class and "seems to have kept much of its importance for large numbers of domestics and other working women." F. M. L. Thompson agrees, adding the important qualification that the failure to legitimate consummation among these classes implicated both men and women and that men's "desertion of unmarried pregnant girls" was regarded as no less "sinful" than promiscuity.[5]

Complicating class differences in sexual customs and practices is upper-class seduction of lower-class women, which is a constant throughout fallen-woman literature. Problems arose when working-class women learned that the traditional sexual standards of their class did not extend to higher-class seducers who promised luxuries in return for sexual favors; Eliot's

4. "The Poor and Their Habitations," in *The Magdalen's Friend and Female Home's Intelligencer*, 72; Barret-Ducrocq, *Love*, 33. Also useful is Fryckstedt, *Gaskell's "Mary Barton" and "Ruth,"* chapter 1.

5. Barret-Ducrocq, *Love*, 97–98; Thompson, *The Rise of Respectable Society: A Social History of Victorian Britain, 1830–1900*, 308.

Sorrel is a case in point. Changing attitudes created an entire class of outlaws, demonstrated both in upper-class pathologizing of lower-class sexual mores and in whites' attitudes toward nonwhites' sexuality in colonialist societies. Whether the fallen woman was a white slave (Mayhew's term for Caucasian domestics and needlewomen) or a black slave, her sexuality was assessed by standards foreign to her social milieu. As Laura Hapke notes, the Victorian "horror of sex between people not social equals" is complicated by the persistence of the feudal assumption that "lower-class women are to be had for the taking."[6]

Barrett-Ducrocq compellingly disproves the stereotype of working-class depravity by outlining the disastrous economic effects of the 1834 Poor Law Reform on working-class women. Far from subscribing to the idea that this class of women "long ago ought to have been cared for by the legislature," the reform's "bastardy clauses" denied unmarried mothers any legal or material aid other than the dreaded workhouse, "For it was important to conform to natural law by making a bastard 'what providence seems to have decided it should be: a burden to its mother.'" In other words, women now had no legal recourse against engagements broken after sexual consummation, much less against seducers or rapists of any class: indeed, the bastardy clauses effectually granted men greater sexual license than ever before while shifting the entire moral and economic burden for illegitimate children onto women. Prior to the Poor Law Reform, working-class sexuality did have a logic of its own, and "It is precisely this awareness of a moral code which defined Foundling Hospital petitioners as *respectable* women" (emphasis added). But after the reform, instead of imposing middle-class sexual standards on the working class—if indeed this was the intention—the resulting feminization of poverty set into motion a dynamic repeatedly characterized as "the greatest of our social evils," and prostitution and infanticide became the defining "sins" of the age. William Acton's assertion that unmarried mothers had by definition "taken the first step in prostitution" assumes a moralizing quality, yet studies such as Barret-Ducrocq's reveal that the real issue in this progression is economics. Put another way, "the deflowered virgin loses her economic value: as damaged goods, she is no longer respectably marriageable. Because this status threatens her economic survival, . . . loss of virginity leads directly to death or . . . prostitution."[7]

6. Hapke, "Reflections on the Victorian Seduction Novel," 40.
7. Review of *Ruth*, in *Sharpe's London Magazine,* quoted in Barret-Ducrocq, *Love,* 179; Acton, *Prostitution,* 18; Flanders, "Fallen Woman in Fiction," 102.

Barret-Ducrocq's pointed word choice, *respectable,* emphasizes her claim that the lower classes do have a system of morality, although it may be undetectable to moralists who viewed middle-class standards as immutable and universal. Her observation accords with two ideas important to my study: first, the consensus shared by more progressive prostitution theorists that there exists a clear demarcation between women forced into "casual" prostitution out of economic need (perhaps to support dependent family members) and those whose motivations concern economic greed ("full" prostitution solely for the purpose of earning enough money to open a "legitimate" business, like a tea shop). In other words, although the activity (sex) as well as the goal (money) are the same, respectability and depravity are presented as variables, depending on the woman's underlying motivation—an idea that undercuts "once fallen, always fallen."

The second idea concerns the illegitimate and unwanted (though not always) children of these women. The very fact that a Foundling Hospital petitioner, as an unwed mother, sought a better environment for her child than she could provide was viewed by some as indicative of her integrity and redeemability. Gaskell's and Barrett Browning's fallen women acquire moral stature by their refusal to descend into prostitution and especially by their devotion to their children; neither infanticide nor abandonment is a consideration for them.[8]

Writers of fallen-woman fiction manipulated the prostitution and economics link by recasting the idea that one's class provides the clearest indicator of one's moral standards. According to these authors, morality is a far more complex issue in which even hereditary and environmental factors give way to the notion that "goodness" is a transcendent quality that cannot be tainted by corporeal concerns. The "inherent" morality of lower-class fallen-woman characters aligns itself with the "prostitute with a heart of gold" stereotype, which complicates dismissing these women as merely social deviants. A useful context through which to consider the fallenness these characters represent is Barret-Ducrocq's observation that two basic female-character types emerged from the working-class sexual milieu: first, "the sacrificial victim, unknown, abused by circumstances and exploited by men," and second, "women of the people [who] are seen as

8. The issues are more complex than this: Barret-Ducrocq's study, although intriguing, is limited by only partial access to hospital records and by the absence of comparative studies of other hospitals' records. She presents a far rosier picture of the institution than Martineau, whose critiques of the system's "legalized infanticide" are not addressed or acknowledged, although they were widely debated at the time. See my Chapter 4, "Am I My Sister's Keeper?" for a fuller discussion of this subject.

hard, brutal, and deeply depraved."[9] Marian and Ruth are clearly of the first variety; those women who are instrumental in their falls (including middle- and upper-class characters) are associated with the second variety. Middle-class maternal ideology, believed to be the most effective avenue of appeal by writers promoting reclamation of the fallen, is the factor linking the two types. Hence, contrasting with the nonmaternalism of "women of the people," both fallen protagonists are inherently pure sexual victims, both evince middle-class notions of maternal "instinct," and both remain celibate for the remainder of their lives. A key element of reclamation (although applied differently to middle- and upper-class women), celibacy serves both to expiate illicit *working-class* sexuality and, more important, to delineate a clear separation between maternity and sexuality. While it is true that Gaskell and Barrett Browning view their fallen heroines through a middle-class lens that obscures authentic working-class standards, these writers subvert the stereotype by presenting the boundaries of all classes as permeable and amorphous—in other words, mutable.

Class, then, is no guarantee of morality, nor, argues Harriet Martineau, is one's mode of dress or occupation. In a series of articles written for the *London Daily News,* Martineau critiques "fashionable follies," charging that the fashion industry is responsible for "100,000 deaths a year" due to women's adoption of styles that are hazardous to their health.[10] Hazards include damage to women's skeletal structures by corsets and high heels, the threat of immolation from voluminous crinolines, illnesses fostered by bonnets and bodices that exposed more than they concealed, and hoopskirts that made sitting down or walking outdoors on a windy day positively indecent. Although Martineau's criticism targets women who adopt such styles, a class she regards as participating in their own social oppression by thus presenting themselves as emblems of "conspicuous consumption," her primary concern is with needleworkers. Both consumers and producers, as she points out, suffer health hazards as well as spiritual compromise by fashion standards that are "not very English in taste."

More important, Martineau's recognition that the "height of fashionable folly" in upper-class women results in the "depth of domestic offense" for working-class women participates in an ongoing debate pitting domestic ideology against the economic need for unskilled, uneducated women to

9. Barret-Ducrocq, *Love,* 30–31.

10. Harriet Martineau, "Dress and Its Victims," *London Daily News,* January 13, 1857. See also articles dated June 17, 1856, January 19, February 13, 1865.

work. The "notoriously afflicted and short-lived classes of milliners and shopworkers" whose livelihoods depend on the "fashionable follies" of others, women "who by scores and hundreds sink in sickness, in blindness, in madness, in death, from overwork at the needle": these are the women who pay the greatest price for fashion indulgences. Martineau, who supported herself by needlework during her literary apprenticeship, understood its drudgery and the insufficiency of its remuneration, which is notoriously disproportionate to the time and labor the occupation demands. "Prostitution is fed by constant accessions from starved or overwearied dressmakers," she observes, a profession that regularly sends "a crowd of victims to the hospital, the brothel, the madhouse, and the grave."

Martineau describes the process by which a year's worth of needlework is compressed into several months, as ladies wait until the last possible moment to order their dresses for the social season so as to be as fashionable as possible. To satisfy the demand for immediate turnaround, seamstresses worked sixteen- to twenty-hour days, for weeks and sometimes months at a stretch, in overcrowded, dimly lit rooms. Suffocated by stale air and denied physical activity, even the youngest and healthiest girls deteriorated rapidly. Unhealthy food and drink that aimed at stimulation rather than nutrition fostered nerve damage and liver complaints, spinal deformities, and consumption. Of factory work, the *British Quarterly Review* wrote, "Compared with the drudgery of dressmakers' apprentices it is mere play." More dramatically, Henry Mayhew termed needlewomen a "shamefully underpaid and cruelly overworked class of white slaves." But the tenacity of the negative stereotype is demonstrated in a review of *Ruth* that argues that the protagonist's "martyrlike piety" is inconsistent with Gaskell's "placing her in circumstances where she must very early have been taught the truth."[11] But Gaskell rejects the assumption that all "sewing girls" are or will be sexually promiscuous by remaining focused on the living and working conditions by which they are perpetually exploited.

Further, fashionable ladies were notoriously reluctant to pay their bills, resulting in a "long-credit" system especially damaging to the working class. Shop owners, who had virtually no legal recourse, withheld workers' pay while seamstresses, exhausted, exploited, and grossly underpaid at best, turned to casual prostitution out of necessity. Gaskell's Esther, in *Mary Barton*, recognized Mary's vulnerability as a seamstress's apprentice; the

11. Review of *Mary Barton*; Mayhew, *London Labour*, 4:23; review of *Ruth*, in *Literary Gazette and Journal*.

dangers of walking home late at night unchaperoned after a day of grueling labor include the dismal prospect of returning to a cold, dark, empty house devoid of fire, food, or companionship, posed against the flattery (however false) of a gentleman admirer. Esther observes, "I found out Mary went to learn dressmaking, and I began to be frightened for her; for it's a bad life for a girl to be out late at night in the streets, and after many an hour of weary work, they're ready to follow after any novelty that makes a little change."[12] Both Mary Barton and Ruth Hilton believe their admirers' intentions are honorable; Esther knows they rarely are.

Proving that not all Victorians subscribed to the period's bipolar ideology, the author of *The Greatest of Our Social Evils* observes that "Clandestine prostitution . . . is not to be compared with the open, unblushing, daring prostitution. . . . the greatest number of these unfortunates are drawn into destruction by causes, in which vice and personal enjoyment have scarcely any share."[13] Characters Marian Erle and Ruth Hilton are both seamstresses whose sexual falls implicate the needlework milieu as an exploitative occupation in more ways than one. Although neither Ruth nor Marian becomes a prostitute, their situations demonstrate how the economics of unmarried motherhood—rather than insatiable lust—generally led to some form of prostitution. Like Marian's protection by Aurora, Ruth's timely adoption by the genteel-poor but compassionate Bensons begs Gaskell's question, "What became of such as Ruth, who had no home and no friends?" (34).

E. W. Thomas, noting that "the great majority of professional 'unfortunates' were, previous to their degradation, domestic servants or needlewomen," speculates whether there are "any peculiar temptations connected with their respective callings which will account for the ruin of so many women belonging to these two classes." He agrees that the matter is not moral but economic, and that insufficient remuneration during "the season" and long periods of unemployment "off season" resulted in prolonged exposure to "adverse circumstances." Ultimately defeated by poverty, such women "yielded to the sad alternative of a depraved course, much more sinned against than sinning."[14] Despite his progressive insight, Thomas's rhetoric ("temptations," "ruin," "sinning") demonstrates the discourse's

---

12. Elizabeth Gaskell, *Mary Barton: A Tale of Manchester Life*, 211–12. Future quotations will be cited parenthetically in the text.

13. *The Greatest of Our Social Evils: Prostitution*, 49, 128.

14. E. W. Thomas, "The Great Social Evil, a National Question," in *The Magdalen's Friend*, 101–3.

tendency to cast both fallenness and economics in moral and religious terms.

Traditionally, needlework apprenticeships were purchased for a substantial fee in return for training in the craft and material support during the period of apprenticeship (generally lasting three to five years). In practice, "material support" got short shrift, and apprentices supplied essentially free "slave" labor. Ruth Hilton's apprenticeship was arranged by her guardian and paid for by her parents' tiny legacy; Marian Erle's was arranged by philanthropist Romney Leigh, who in his desire to help Marian escape from her pandering parents failed to consider the profession's associations with prostitution. Distinct from Romney's myopic example, most social critics recognized that the damage to mind and spirit engendered by the fashion industry's exploitative working conditions was more potent than physical debilitation alone.

With her typically acute political insight, Martineau recognizes that such exploitation is the true link between female vanity and prostitution, contrasting with critics who situated sexual vice in working-class imitation of upper-class fashions. Consistent with this stereotype, Esther's (in *Mary Barton*) love of dress, fueled by her earnings as a factory worker, is also exhibited by her niece Mary, suggesting the latter's propensity to fall. Similarly, Hetty Sorrel's love of finery functions, for Eliot, as a sign of moral depravity rather than merely class-inappropriate ambition. In the words of Coral Lansbury, such women are "seduced, not so much sexually as socially" by associating "conspicuous display" (here, stylish clothing) with economic upward mobility and middle-class respectability.[15] Attempting to convey this image, some factory girls literally risked life and limb in order to be fashionably dressed while working; some fainted from tight stays or got their crinolines caught in machinery, proving the ideological claim that fashion was a privilege of the leisure class.

Others, like Esther, whose transparent attempts to appear middle class paradoxically signaled their sexual availability, drifted into an increasingly depraved progression that culminated in prostitution; ironically, these imitative fashions proclaimed not their upward mobility but rather their fallen morality. Patsy Stoneman notes the paradox in John Barton's forbidding Mary to follow her aunt Esther's example by working in a factory: Mary "ends up working for a dressmaker, 'where the chief talk was of fashions, and dress, and . . . love and lovers' . . . the very ideology he

---

15. Lansbury, *Elizabeth Gaskell: The Novel of Social Crisis*, 31.

wishes to avoid."[16] Esther understands the broader implications of this issue: shabby finery may have contributed to her fall, but her acquisition of demure cottons from the pawn shop has the power to transform this soiled "Butterfly" into a respectable housewife (292). This demonstrates that, as an indicator of moral standards, physical appearance was disturbingly inadequate: hence, the period's obsession with regulating working-class vanity.

Such prominent prostitution theorists as William Tait, Henry Mayhew, and William Acton advanced the idea that lower-class sexual immorality was a direct result of "vanity, vanity, and then vanity . . . the love of dress and admiration." Women who "dressed far above their station," continues Acton, those "encumbered with no domestic ties, and burdened with no children" obviously led a "loose life," a description oddly reminiscent of middle-class exhibitions of leisured respectability and conspicuous consumption. *The Magdalen's Friend* claimed that "especially" in girls "the tendency to Vanity needs a constant effort to suppress it."[17] Testimonies by lock-hospital doctors and matrons agreed that lower-class women's self-gratifying pursuit of fashion was the single most prominent cause of Victorian prostitution. Accordingly, some lock hospitals and other penitential institutions enforced strict dress codes in which inmates were required to wear unflattering uniforms and in some instances to cut off their hair. Thus stigmatized in the public eye, these women "announced" their moral status through their appearance as graphically as when they were practicing prostitutes.[18]

The question of vanity reveals other anxieties at work on the Victorian psyche as well. The Bensons' maid-of-all-work Sally, who disapproves of Ruth's love for her bastard child, forces her to cut off her luxurious hair,

16. Patsy Stoneman, *Elizabeth Gaskell*, 77.

17. Acton, *Prostitution*, 20–21, 24; *The Magdalen's Friend*, 44. The tenacity of this idea is reflected in the formation of the 1882 Select Committee of the House of Lords "on the state of the law relating to protection of young girls from artifices inducing them to lead a corrupt life." See Mariana Valverde, "The Love of Finery: Fashion and the Fallen Woman in Nineteenth-Century Social Discourse," 177.

18. Lock hospitals were established to accommodate working-class female victims of prostitution, venereal diseases, and illegitimate maternities. Although a far different type of institution, Brontë's Lowood School for orphan girls in *Jane Eyre* demonstrates the period's concern with women's hair. Brocklehurst is enraged by the sight of one girl's irrepressible curls and orders them clipped off. Such attitudes, like the anorexic diet imposed on the girls, demonstrate the aim of such institutions to manage female sexuality. This was especially desirable for the lower poor classes whose reproduction required repressing rather than encouraging as a function of "nature."

ostensibly to signify her sexual unavailability as a "widow" but in reality as a gesture of penitence for the sensuality such hair represents. But Sally, like Hetty Sorrel's aunt Poyser, surreptitiously admires the young woman's beauty even while disapproving her erring ways and conveys to readers mixed messages: first by regretting her punitive behavior, then by reverently preserving Ruth's tresses in her bureau. The scene is also potent in its suggestion that Ruth's meek compliance—she raises no protest against Sally—indicates her passivity during her seduction: in all her relationships, Ruth is consistently unassuming and self-effacing. The fact that neither Ruth nor Marian exhibits the slightest interest in her appearance thus illustrates another important departure from the fallen stereotype. Like most seamstresses, Gaskell notes, Mason's apprentices "were too sleepy to care for any of the pomps and vanities, or, indeed, for any of the comforts of this world, excepting one sole thing—their beds" (7).

Some women, it is true, entered prostitution by choice, attracted by its comparatively lucrative remuneration for very little work; simply put, prostitution made good business sense at a time when women had few employment options. But others were forced to supplement inadequate incomes from "respectable" jobs to support dependent family members such as children or ill and aged parents. During testimony presented to the Royal Commission on Contagious Diseases Acts in 1871, Josephine Butler asserted that as a "cause" of prostitution, love of dress must be considered in only the fuller context of the working-class experience: "A girl who has no education has a vacant mind, ready to be engaged with trifles" such as fashions and flirting.[19] Reformers such as Butler and Martineau recognized that "working-class vanity" was but a scapegoat for the systematized legal, political, and economic deprivation that marked every aspect of working-class lives. Butler's comment bears a striking resemblance to Martineau's observations that middle- and upper-class women were educated solely for extravagance in dress and obtaining a husband, both "trifles" signifying "vacant" minds. But according to popular thought, upper-class women's clothing represented their innate moral superiority, while the same styles in lower-class women signified their innate moral depravity, a double standard that questions the efficacy of clothing alone to construct a moral identity—as Esther's example proves. What *does* construct a moral identity for women of any class is the primary focus of this book: vanity, at least in the following two characters, is not part of the equation.

19. Quoted in Valverde, "The Love of Finery," 186.

Elizabeth Gaskell's Ruth Hilton is perhaps the quintessential literary example of the seduced fallen-woman character. Gaskell vindicates Ruth of responsibility for her fall, thereby creating a heroine victimized by fate, by society, and by the class, gender, and economic circumstances into which she was born. Ruth also may be said to be a victim of her will—or lack of will—for at the time of her seduction, at age sixteen, she was completely pliable and lacking in judgment. "By gifting her heroine with that much-touted triumvirate of female virtues—ignorance, passivity, and docility," says Suzann Bick, "Gaskell demonstrates that, far from protecting a woman, such traits can actually be the cause of her seduction."[20] Gaskell goes to extremes to present her fallen woman as society's victim, too extreme, argue some critics who regarded Ruth's death after her social atonement as belaboring the point. But Gaskell's literary insight is keen: she knows her audience—the middle class—and she understands that the greatest potential for social change rests with them. A novel that inspires book burnings and is directly associated with midcentury Magdalenism is clearly a novel that has aroused its intended audience from moral complacency.

By presenting sexual fallenness as circumstantial, Gaskell transforms its static inevitability by proving the fallen woman is integral to, not an outcast from, society. According to Susan Morgan, "the whole notion of fallen women assumes . . . that there is no personal history, just an endless repetition of that one defining event."[21] This analysis clarifies Gaskell's somewhat cryptic observations about social conformity at the novel's beginning: "The daily life into which people are born, and into which they are absorbed before they are well aware, forms chains which only one in a hundred has moral strength enough to despise, and to break when the right time comes—when an inward necessity for independent individual action arises, which is superior to all outward conventionalities" (2). Ruth Hilton is "one in a hundred" in three primary ways: her sexual ignorance leads to unwed motherhood but does not result in prostitution; her bastard son inspires not social infamy but social redemption (a model child, he becomes apprenticed to a doctor); and her sexuality, once the clarity of hindsight enables her to manage it, functions as a measure not of depravity but of integrity. Gaskell critiques hypocrisy in the upper-class Bellingham, the middle-class Bradshaw, the working-class Mrs. Mason, and in the community at

---

20. Bick, "'Take Her Up Tenderly': Elizabeth Gaskell's Treatment of the Fallen Woman," 18.
21. Morgan, "Gaskell's Heroines and the Power of Time," 47.

large; but, more important, she creates a heroine "superior to all outward conventionalities," not despite her fallenness but because of it.

Ruth Hilton's background of genteel poverty and traditional rural values —her grandfather was a clergyman, and her parents were farmers—alters drastically when she is orphaned at the age of fifteen. Ruth's legal guardian places her as a seamstress's apprentice in the city and, satisfied he has "done his duty by her" (12), makes clear that he desires no further contact with her. Ruth's rustic background and unchaperoned sexual innocence, combined with an occupation and urban environment notorious for sexual pitfalls, set the stage for her seduction and abandonment as an expectant mother. Ruth's sexual innocence is underscored by the loss of her mother before coming of age: "she was too young when her mother died to have received any cautions or words of advice respecting *the* subject of a woman's life" (44). As a result of these circumstances, notes Coral Lansbury, "In the jungle of Victorian sexual life, Ruth is a predetermined victim."[22]

The novel's opening scene details the exploitative working conditions in Mrs. Mason's shop; instructed to take a short break at two in the morning, some girls fall asleep instantly, others eat standing up, and still others succumb to consumptive coughing, while Ruth—the country girl pent up in the artificial city—longs for a run in the snow. Driven by ambition and professional jealousy, Mrs. Mason makes impossible promises to customers that result in the apprentices' working through the night. Ruth's consumptive friend, Jenny, offers a dubious comfort: "Most new girls get impatient at first; but it goes off, and they don't care much for anything after awhile" (8–9).

Ruth's freshness, as yet unspoiled by the shop's unhealthy environment, prompts Mrs. Mason to take her to the ball as her assistant, thus setting into motion the events leading to Ruth's fall, for it is here Bellingham first sees her. Both the inauspiciousness of this meeting and Ruth's lack of discernment are emphasized by her Brontë-esque dreams: "The night before, she had seen her dead mother in her sleep, and she wakened, weeping. And now she dreamed of Mr. Bellingham, and smiled. And yet, was this a more evil dream than the other?" (18). Mrs. Mason's tangential relationship to Ruth's fall resides in her favoring Ruth because her fresh appearance reflects positively on the businesswoman and in her neglecting to warn her workers against breaches of social decorum that result in sexual snares. Like Ruth's dead mother, Mason is unavailable to guide Ruth in the matters Bellingham's presence represents.

22. Lansbury, *Elizabeth Gaskell,* 58.

But consistent with the text's emphasis on maternal values, Gaskell clearly holds Mrs. Mason responsible for Ruth's fate: "It would have been a better and more Christian thing, if she had kept up the character of her girls by tender vigilance and maternal care" (54). Ruth's loneliness, posed against Bellingham's insistent presence just when she was most vulnerable, emphasizes the inevitability of her seduction. Knowing full well the associations this question will evoke in her readers, Gaskell asks: "What became of such as Ruth, who had no home and no friends in that large populous desolate town?" (34). As a businesswoman who rejects the role of surrogate mother, Mrs. Mason contributes nothing to Ruth's understanding, preferring to assume the worst and dismiss her on the same basis for which she had earlier favored her: appearances, or "keeping up the character of her establishment" (54).

Weighed against days and nights of drudgery (Ruth is at the beginning of her five-year apprenticeship), Mrs. Mason's harsh temper, and Jenny's consumptive illness and death from overwork, Bellingham's urges to walk with him after church seem harmless enough. At twenty-three, the comparatively worldly Bellingham is bored with his privileged lifestyle, but finds "something bewitching" in Ruth's combination of womanly "grace and loveliness" with the "naiveté, simplicity, and innocence of an intelligent child. . . . It would be an exquisite delight to attract and tame her wildness" (33). Ruth is "little accustomed to oppose the wishes of any one—obedient and docile by nature, and unsuspicious and innocent of any harmful consequences" (61). Young, trusting, and pliant, Ruth views Bellingham as one of a series of protectors (first the reluctant guardian, then Mrs. Mason), each of whom has temporarily taken her parents' place. "Tell me everything Ruth, as you would to a brother; let me help you . . . in your difficulties" (41), Bellingham urges. Because Ruth "lacks every quality that would enable her to defend herself," when Bellingham places her in his carriage she trusts he will drive her to the caretakers of her old home as she has asked—as a "brother" would.[23] But when we next see her, he is helping her out of another carriage as a "well-cloaked-up lady" (62), a change in appearance that explains the narrative's elision of a crucial piece of Ruth's history. As Bellingham's mistress, Ruth is still "very modest and innocent-looking" (71), while her behavior toward her lover reflects childlike obedience (she continues to call him "sir") rather than the wantonness typically associated with illicit sexuality. Casting Ruth as the sacrificial victim, Gaskell charges

23. Ibid., 60.

Mason with the "sin of omission" for failing to intervene and Bellingham with the seduction and ruin of a girl who is to him of no consequence.[24]

What one critic terms Ruth's lack of "terrible struggles of conscience" is in fact her deplorable ignorance of sexual matters, which continues long after her seduction.[25] So naive is Ruth that her awareness of her compromised state requires a rude awakening, and it is not until a child slaps her face, shouting, "She's not a lady! She's a bad naughty girl" (71) that a "new idea" (72) ran through her mind. Ruth finally realizes that certain puzzling whispers and unaccountable glances signify that this child's opinion is shared by the community. She now begins the painful process of realizing the gravity of private actions that are open to public scrutiny.

Gaskell negotiates dangerous territory by presenting Ruth's lack of intellectual understanding as complicated by her "instinctual" erotic response to her lover. According to "received wisdom," female sexual response, thought to be latent or nonexistent in "chaste" (good, married) women, was transformed into depraved lust by inappropriate (unwed) sexual awakening. Once unleashed, there was no escaping the inevitable downward progression to prostitution. But Gaskell employs this difficult issue as a vehicle for Ruth's redemption, as she later uses Ruth's illegitimate child: both are transformed into measures of the fallen woman's growth into respectability. Through the character Ruth, Gaskell confronts, rather than avoids, the erotic component of seduction. Patsy Stoneman notes that Gaskell's prelapsarian description of the walk Ruth and Bellingham take to her childhood home is suffused with erotic symbolism.[26] Later, while they are living together in Wales, Ruth wears white dresses while Bellingham crowns her with white lilies, both symbols of purity; yet she is described in the same passage as glowing like a June rose, symbolic of consummated sexuality, while her disheveled, luxuriant hair "seemed to add a grace" (75). Like her foremother Eve, Ruth's eroticized innocence marks her as destined to fall from grace, yet, in Gaskell's version, she is also destined to rise again and to be called "blessed."

When Ruth realizes she has been abandoned by her lover, her response is explosively erotic: she chases wildly after his carriage, throws herself down on the road, writhing in anguish, "her dress soiled and dim, her bonnet crushed and battered with her tossings to and fro on the moorland bed"

24. Fryckstedt, *Gaskell's "Mary Barton" and "Ruth,"* 148.
25. Review of *Ruth*, in *North British Review*.
26. Stoneman, *Elizabeth Gaskell*, 101.

(96). Years later, Ruth unexpectedly meets Bellingham again; alone in her room, listening to the storm raging without—and within—she "threw open the window . . . and tore off her gown; she put her hair back from her heated face . . . the strange confusion of agony was too great to be borne and she cried aloud" (272). She longs to see him and ask him why he left, she calls him "darling love . . . the father of my child!" (273). Sitting on the floor violently rocking herself, Ruth struggles with her maternal duty toward Leonard, her growing sense of personal integrity, and her passion for Bellingham, crying out, "Oh, my God! I do believe Leonard's father is a bad man, and yet, oh! pitiful God, I love him; I cannot forget—I cannot!" (274). Ruth's dilemma concerns, among other things, her urge to romanticize her situation, to sanctify it as an act of love, even while knowing, in retrospect, that it was not reciprocated. Presented as a measure of redemptive growth, once she perceives the differences between love and sex, and legitimate and illegitimate relations, Ruth is able to make choices based on her clarity of understanding rather than on the chaos of her delusions.

Consistent with conventions of fallen-woman literature, because she is ultimately unmarriageable, Ruth's struggle between passion and duty results in her permanent removal from sexual involvement. Once aware that her innocence has been compromised, she, like Marian Erle, becomes celibate and remains so for the duration of her life. Sexual standards became for the Victorians a potent vehicle for differentiating lower- from middle-class standards; to a degree, respectability—for women, at least—was acquired or lost through regulating one's sexuality. Ruth's vulnerability to seduction earlier stereotyped her as low class; now, her management of her desire for Bellingham signals the middle-classness of her standards and anticipates Sarah Grand's fuller articulation of voluntary celibacy as a medium for self-empowerment later in the century, in *The Heavenly Twins*. What *Ruth* demands is a reinterpretation of fallen sexuality as well as of "respectable sexuality," which, like "recuperated fallen woman," seems a contradiction in terms.

Another reinterpretation Gaskell invites of readers concerns Ruth's devotion to her illegitimate child and her refusal to marry Bellingham when they meet again years later, both factors Barrett Browning also employs in her redemption of Marian Erle. Through her pious mothering, Ruth earns the respect of her neighbors, thus proving that it is "possible to rehabilitate a fallen woman who conceived unaware, who repented her fall, and who devoted herself to the welfare of child and society." Ruth's illegitimate motherhood provides "a powerful tool . . . to refashion social

values. For if good women bear and love their sons, might not a bad . . .
woman's love of her son redeem her?" Distinct from the seemingly inevitable
descent to prostitution of other fallen women with illegitimate children,
Ruth vindicates herself through her son: "Leonard becomes not simply his
mother's badge of shame, but rather an agent of growth and reintegration."[27]

Early in the novel, Faith Benson reflects communal attitudes by terming
the illegitimate Leonard a "miserable offspring of sin" (120); but her brother,
the Reverend Mr. Benson, not only saves the lives of both mother and
unborn child (he prevents Ruth's suicide) but also envisions motherhood
as the perfect vehicle for Ruth's redemption. In the words of reviewer J. M.
Ludlow, "Satan sent the sin—God sends the child"; consequently, Ruth
"is made a noble Christian woman by the very consequences of her sin,"
aptly affirming the novel's evangelical underpinnings.[28] But at the same
time, Ruth's prophetic dreams reflect one of illegitimacy's more subversive
aspects. Reflecting the period's concern with the behavioral predispositions
of heredity, Ruth nightmarishly dreams that Leonard is a "repetition of his
father," that he has "lured some maiden . . . into sin, and left her there
to even a worse fate than that of suicide" (163). Ruth's concern is more
dramatically addressed by Barrett Browning's Runaway Slave, in "The
Runaway Slave at Pilgrim's Point," who prevents repetition of the "sins
of the father" by murdering the master's child. During a period marked
by a pronounced rise in infanticides, Gaskell's valorizing the bastard child,
for whom even devoted (though unwed) mothering outweighs paternal
genetic factors, compares favorably with this gruesome alternative, as does
her preventing Ruth's descent into prostitution.

Like the resounding slap that earlier stimulated Ruth's awareness in
Wales, the mature confrontation between Ruth and her former lover dramatizes the moral distance separating them, allowing Ruth to see clearly at
last the futility of her attempt to romanticize their former relationship as
"love." The relationship between Ruth and Bellingham was always inscribed
by money. Just prior to her seduction, Bellingham's arrival is ominously
announced by the "jingling of money" (61); and when he deserts her, she
is left with a fifty-pound note as compensation for her "services." Now,
Bellingham proposes marriage because of the "advantages for Leonard,
to be gained by you quite in a holy and legitimate way" (303). Although

27. MacPike, "The Fallen Woman's Sexuality," 67; Bick, " 'Take Her Up Tenderly,' "
21–22.

28. Quoted in Fryckstedt, Gaskell's "Mary Barton" and "Ruth," 156.

her realization is long delayed, Ruth now sees with painful clarity her unknowing flirtation with paid sexuality, in effect, prostitution, while the difference between their definitions of "love" shows her just how cheapened is the best she had to offer. Bellingham's materialistic emphasis (a disturbing conflation of economics and morality, religion and law, love and sex) only strengthens Ruth's resolve and, when he taunts her legal powerlessness, she makes the break final: "I would submit to many humiliations for [Leonard's] sake—but to no more from you" (300).

Despite the contrast between Ruth's integrity and Bellingham's shallowness, her refusing to marry him was viewed by some critics as a rejection of the moral and social legitimation available only through the father of one's child. For a lower-class mother of an illegitimate child to refuse an upper-class man's offer of legitimation as a "humiliation" was regarded as an aggressive refusal of redemption. But in Gaskell's novel the idea of redemption is reflected in Ruth's growth from passive child not to passive wife, but to responsible woman. Along with sexual discernment and maternal devotion, Ruth's evolution is also, according to Winifred Gerin, "seen in her rejection of Bellingham's proposal."[29] Ruth rightly regards him as a bad influence for Leonard, "Evil would it be for him if I lived with you. I will let him die first!" as well as for herself, "You have humbled me enough, sir. I shall leave you now" (301). Nevertheless, despite the clarity she acquires in retrospect, Ruth makes one final, fatal choice between Leonard and Bellingham that critics still have difficulty negotiating.

Earlier, Ruth was spared the prostitute's fate through the intervention of the cleric Mr. Benson, a man who understands (though underestimates) the limited vision of public opinion and so passes Ruth off as what she is not: a legitimate wife (widow) and mother. But in Gaskell's worldview, a vindication based on a lie is no vindication; Ruth's history must be confronted and accepted by her community in order for social change to occur. When the truth about Ruth's past resurfaces and circulates in the community, she suffers the ostracism Benson sought to prevent. Like the earlier episodes in which Ruth's hair conveys various sexual messages, these events dramatize the "threat of [social] contamination and a fear that middle-class boundaries are alarmingly permeable."[30] However, in an episode demonstrating both personal and communal growth, Ruth regains community respect by nursing during a cholera epidemic, after which

29. Gerin, *Elizabeth Gaskell,* 129.
30. Matus, *Unstable Bodies,* 126.

"many arose and called her blessed" (430). As if this were not enough, although her services are not wanted or needed by the choleric Bellingham, although she employs her compassion in the service of a man she knows to be unscrupulous, although she sacrifices her health, her life, and her responsibility to her son, Ruth Hilton dies as a result of nursing the man who ruined her.

This, then, is the primary point of critical contention. We might well ask why Gaskell creates this extraordinary heroine only to "kill" her out of the text. What is the distinction between a fallen woman's descent into prostitution or rise to social redemption if both lead to disease and death? If we are to interpret death as the greatest sacrifice a sincerely repentant sinner can make, Ruth's death can be seen as an "attempt to regain respectability" in the most extreme sense of the term. For many readers, this narrative sacrifice of Gaskell's most innovative heroine "with a purpose" directly undercuts the force of the novel's social critique.

Although *Ruth* was a controversial novel in many respects, critical opinion on the heroine's death is not so divided. Nina Auerbach argues, "By convention, the fallen woman must writhe in tortured postures of remorse until she dies penitent at the end of her story." Loralee MacPike suggests that "Gaskell spares the world the difficulty of taking Ruth herself to its bosom by leaving it with only the memory of her goodness," while Laura Hapke posits that Victorians' "uneasiness about the sexuality of the Woman Betrayed may well account for the suffering . . . inflicted on her, exacting it as the price of a redemption." Jill Matus simply states, "the symbolic point is that she cannot survive her ex-lover's contagion," whether on a biological, sexual, social, legal, or economic level. Gaskell's contemporaries are only slightly more circumspect: Elizabeth Barrett Browning wrote, "Was it quite impossible but that your Ruth should *die?*" while Charlotte Brontë objected, "Why should she die?" Even Victorian reviewer W. R. Greg, whose ambivalence toward fallenness is recorded in his article "Prostitution," demurred, saying Gaskell "has first imagined a character as pure, pious, and unselfish as poet ever fancied, and described a lapse from chastity as faultless as such a fault can be; and then, with damaging and unfaithful inconsistency, has given in to the world's estimate in such matters."[31]

31. Auerbach, *Romantic Imprisonment: Women and Other Glorified Outcasts,* 151; MacPike, "The Fallen Woman's Sexuality," 65; Hapke, "Reflections," 41; Matus, *Unstable Bodies,* 131; Barrett Browning, letter to Elizabeth Gaskell, July 16, 1853, quoted in Angus Easson, ed., *Elizabeth Gaskell: The Critical Heritage,* 316; Brontë, letter to Elizabeth

Does Ruth's untimely end reflect Gaskell's capitulation to public morality? Has she "given in to the world's estimate," or does this denouement have other implications? Perhaps Ruth's death reflects the author's insight that her fallen heroine would be required to continue proving herself for the rest of her life. There would always be other judgments to satisfy, other gossips to placate, and only through death is she freed of the burden: death is thus a deliverance rather than a punishment. Alternatively, Gaskell's refusing to collude with Victorian expectations of a happy ending forced readers to confront the complex social dilemmas Ruth's character and circumstances represent, without benefit of romanticized palliatives—the same lesson Ruth was forced to learn. More speculatively, the tendency toward suicide shared by all the fallen women discussed in this study—even Ruth attempts to drown herself—is no less effective when the method is passive rather than aggressive.

Stressing the mutability of social dynamics, Susan Morgan argues that "Unless the community is changed by Ruth's story, it remains a personal history," which would clearly undercut the purpose of social-problem literature. Ruth's ostracism in Wales and later in Eccleston demonstrates public scrutiny of socially unsavory private acts; Morgan suggests a similar dynamic may account for *Ruth*'s denouement. Ruth's complex relationship with Jemima Bradshaw, for example, plays out the madonna-harlot script, but by reversing the usual "woman's mission to women" equation: it is Ruth's shift (in public opinion, at least) from harlot to madonna to harlot to martyr that compels the rebellious Jemima to submit to her fate as a domesticated wife. Before Ruth dies, her "private progress" becomes public knowledge, not only through exposure of her past history but also through her roles as mother, teacher, and nurse, all three aspects of the period's transformation of domestic values into philanthropic activities in the public sphere: "Our public realms must take up the values we have relegated to the home. One simple way to describe the plot of *Ruth* is that the fallen woman becomes the angel in the house who then . . . becomes the angel in the town."[32] Ruth of course becomes the "angel in the town," but although her social impact is considerable it is valued only after—and, perhaps, only because of—her death, reiterating the ideology's disturbing links between purity and death.

Gaskell, April 26, 1892, quoted in Easson, *Elizabeth Gaskell*, 317; Greg, review of *Ruth*, quoted in Easson, *Elizabeth Gaskell*, 328.
32. Morgan, "Gaskell's Heroines," 50.

Gaskell condemns both the social hypocrisy that vaguely displaces women's comprehension of sexual decorum onto some "natural" female intuition and the idea that fallen sexuality is a willful and deliberate moral lapse devoid of male responsibility. She exposes the fallacy of class-specific notions of morality and, like many evangelical reformists, regards moral culpability for falls such as Ruth's as a public, social concern. Finally, Gaskell's ambivalence toward the issues this character raises is reflected in her "killing" Ruth in the prime of her life, and in her creating a fallen heroine comparable to Victorian literature's most paradigmatic angels in the house, all of whom are too pure to live in this fallen world.

In a variety of ways, Gaskell's Ruth and Elizabeth Barrett Browning's Marian Erle in *Aurora Leigh* provide the basis for the fallen-woman archetype. Both characters are sexually exploited while young, ignorant, and vulnerable; both are working class yet drawn with an "inherent" moral purity not acquired through birth or marriage; both bear illegitimate children in whom they delight and through whom their social "sin" finds redemption; both are apprenticed seamstresses and thus vulnerable to exploitation on several levels; both refuse marital legitimation; and finally, neither achieves social integration.

An even fuller articulation of the stereotype resides in the two works' points of departure. Distinct from Ruth Hilton, Marian Erle remains subsidiary to Barrett Browning's title character, a narrative positioning that reflects the class issues presupposing sexual fallenness. Further, whereas Gaskell traces Ruth's progress through her increasingly acute discernment in sexual matters, Barrett Browning reveals Marian's growth through her emergence from a girl of "meek words" to a woman who speaks boldly for herself because "she sees clearly . . . / Her instinct's holy."[33] Marian's story assumes three narrative voices: initially, Aurora lends Marian's "meek words" a "fuller utterance," in book 3; then, Marian's letter to Romney, while displaying a greater measure of narrative autonomy, is ominously qualified by Lady Waldemar's insidious prompting, in book 4; and finally, in books 6 and 7, Marian's fullest "utterance" is as a woman whose self-articulation, like her vision and instinct, needs no interpreter or mediator. Like Ruth, Marian evolves spiritually as a result of degrading life experiences; and whereas Ruth's death functions as part of her redemption, Marian's removal from the narrative's final events (simply put, "She was gone" [9.452]) functions

33. Barrett Browning, *Aurora Leigh*, 9.454–55. Future quotations will be cited by book and line numbers parenthetically in the text.

similarly, indicating the impossibility of social integration for the fallen woman despite her "holiness" or "blessedness." This impossibility recalls my earlier observation that the alignments between fallen women and angels in the house are best dramatized by their inevitable deaths no less than by their cultural silencing. Both categories are riddled with a guilt that never can be expiated: for the fallen woman, this represents illicit sexuality, which keeps her perpetually falling; for the angel, this represents the guilt she bears toward the women whose deviance preserves her purity. Both must be silenced permanently, lest the pact of complicity in which they are bound be revealed in all its inequities.

Although with far less contextualizing than Gaskell, Barrett Browning exposes environmental factors that produce unemployed, wife-beating, alcoholic fathers and pandering mothers like Marian's, misguided philanthropists and sterile intellectuals like Romney and Aurora, and promiscuous aristocrats like Lady Waldemar. But a primary difference between Marian and Ruth concerns sexuality. Ruth is an expressly corporeal character, demonstrated by her longing to run in the snow as a palliative for the physical confinement of seamstressing, by her desire for long hikes in the rugged Welsh countryside rather than playing parlor games with Bellingham, and particularly by the wild storm scene when Ruth literally wrestles with her passion for Bellingham and her maternal duty to Leonard. In contrast, Marian Erle is drugged and raped, and is therefore not culpable for her sexual fate; as a result, Marian's almost transcendent victimization demands readers' careful scrutiny of both working-class sexual stereotyping and the cultural silencing required of rape victims.

Marian was "born an outlaw," notes Aurora, and there was "no place for her"; from her first breath, she was "wrong against the social code" (3.845). More graphically depicted than is usual for Victorian social-problem literature, Marian's early influences include poverty and ignorance, vagrancy, and, at times, imprisonment as a result of life "on the tramp"; her father, perennially unemployed, drank and beat his wife, who in turn "beat her baby in revenge / For her own broken heart" (3.869–70). As another "predetermined victim," Marian's cultural vulnerability is her greatest liability, one for which the "counter of this world" (3.872) virtually never allows credit. The parent/child bond, and particularly the mother/daughter bond so central in Gaskell's work, is perverted beyond recognition by the relentless brutality of this lifestyle:

> Father, Mother, home
> Were God and heaven reversed to her: the more

She knew of Right, the more she guessed their wrong:
Her price paid down for knowledge, was to know
The vileness of her kindred . . .

(3.936–40)

The Erle family's poverty, alcoholism, and physical abuse invoke class stereotypes that assume such antisocial behaviors result from the moral depravity endemic to their class. Presented as an anomaly, Marian in her chastity suggests an intelligence belied by her low-browed countenance. While this approach unquestionably redeems the fallen woman, it does so by perpetuating, at least initially, class stereotypes. Whereas most social-problem writing aims to expose economic deprivation as an underlying cause of social deviation, Barrett Browning presents the class and morality link as a priori. The social theory casting low classes as innately immoral and upper classes as morally superior is reflected in Marian's doglike demeanor and Waldemar's social insulation yet also is critiqued through their relative integrity. Barrett Browning acknowledges Marian's mitigating environmental circumstances, but her primary concern—and her greatest strength as a social-problem writer—is to dramatize the immediacy of both victims' and victimizers' perspectives rather than addressing economics in the abstract. She further complicates the class/morality link through a chiasmatic exchange of moral qualities between the characters of Waldemar and Marian, though each retains her class (social and economic) status. Thus does Barrett Browning demonstrate the ambivalence toward the period's ideology of fallenness she shares with all the women writers I discuss.

Marian's education in the "wicked book" of working-class squalor peaks when her mother attempts to sell her into prostitution in order to support the family. When she presents her daughter to the local squire—"He means to set you up, and comfort us" (3.1057)—Marian, whose life experience precludes Ruth's brand of naïveté, reacts with alarmed clarity: "God free me from my mother . . . / These mothers are too dreadful" (3.1063–64). Although to her parents Marian is "not good for much" (3.1022), she clearly has economic value as a sexual commodity, as other white-slave traders later realize.

Parents' sexual exploitation of young girls for economic gain was recognized as a widespread problem particularly resistant to reformist interventions. Few parents would willingly admit to pandering their own children, while those wealthy enough to procure their services had social positions to protect and were hardly likely to admit to the crime. During a period marked by an unprecedented codification of sexual mores—legitimate marriage and parenthood, maternal ideology, and the valorization of the nuclear family—the idea of mothers prostituting their own daughters was a social crime comparable to infanticide. Victorian social worker Ellice Hopkins found girls as young as seven already consigned to lock hospitals for the treatment of venereal disease after their mothers had sold them to "public den[s] of infamy." Outraged by the courts' reluctance to interfere in the practice, Hopkins was subsequently instrumental in instituting protective legislation for such victims later in the century. One social commentator notes, by "Not permitting the eye of power to penetrate into the bosom of families" the resulting "inviolability of the domicile" fosters such perversions of familial ideology.[34] The sanctity of the family thus poses an interesting dilemma: the preservation of privacy so essential to cementing family values also functions to prevent the state's intervention in such antisocial behaviors as prostituting children.

The Greatest of Our Social Evils presents a more melodramatic picture of child prostitution: "What can be more monstrous? . . . [Parents] cry them like common merchandise, display them . . . and suffer [strangers] to touch them, body and mind." The author links the sort of early influence from which Marian escaped with the criminal element: "All these whose parents are thieves and harlots, and who, having always lived in an impure atmosphere, have no idea of a different mode of life. *One cannot say . . . that they have fallen,* for the ladder-step which served them as a cradle is placed below all the others" (emphasis added).[35] According to this line of thinking, prostitution results directly from the perversion of maternal influence, a variation on the theme of the absent mother.

Clearly, Marian's observation—"Both lost! my father was burnt up with gin. . . . My mother sold me to a man last month" (3.1191, 1193)—conforms with this perspective; but Barrett Browning also reflects Victorians' growing awareness of the role of environmental influences in social problems. That Marian's mother should attempt to sell her into prostitution is not surprising to those who viewed such behavior as typical of the class. But the author points out that this woman is also systematically violated, and acts as she has been acted upon: "There's not a crime, / But takes its proper change out still in crime" (3.870–71), suggesting that Marian's behavior is less inbred than environmental. Such assumptions as "morality

---

34. Hopkins, quoted in Prochaska, *Women and Philanthropy,* 210–11; *Greatest of Our Social Evils,* 37.

35. *Greatest of Our Social Evils,* 44, 79.

is systematically linked to the economic factor" reflect the ruling-class tendency to deny responsibility for lower-class degradation.[36] But in Barrett Browning's text, Mrs. Erle's victimization as an abused wife, the alcoholism of her unemployed husband, and their sexual exploitation of their daughter construct a complex system of victimization in which all levels of society are implicated.

After leaving home, Marian meets the philanthropist Romney Leigh, who obtains a needleworking apprenticeship for her in London. As a social activist who should have known better, he places her in a situation notorious for its associations with prostitution, illegitimacy, and suicide in order to protect Marian from her pandering parents. Marian later observes,

> I might sleep well beneath the heavy Seine,
> Like others of my sort; the bed was laid
> For us.
>
> (7.80–82)

Like Ruth, Marian is befriended by a consumptive fellow seamstress, Lucy, who also dies from illness and overwork. As the phrase "marry, stitch, die, or do worse" implies, death seems to be the only viable alternative to prostitution for unmarried working-class women. Despite his philanthropic (if misguided) motives, Romney must be held culpable for his perpetual lack of discernment, demonstrated by his ineffectual gestures toward the lower classes and his remarkably wide-ranging tastes in women. Early in the narrative, the intellectual Aurora refuses Romney's proposal to cement the family fortune through their marriage; he subsequently proposes to her polar opposite, Marian, the ignorant "daughter of the people," again, not out of love or passion, notes Cora Kaplan, but "as a gesture towards the breakdown of class barriers."[37] He then succumbs to the treacherous lamia, Lady Waldemar, whose reputation for promiscuity seems to have escaped Romney's awareness; the image of her "audacious" breasts straining against her tight velvet bodice represents the complete antithesis to Marian's modesty and Aurora's respectability: evidently, Romney's vision of social revolution obscures his perception of this woman's more duplicitous qualities. Indeed, like Brontë's Mr. Rochester, Romney must literally be blinded in order to "see" women's true worth.

36. Jacques Donzelot, *The Policing of Families: Welfare versus the State*, 69.
37. Kaplan, introduction to *Elizabeth Barrett Browning: "Aurora Leigh" and Other Poems*, 7.

Aurora's part in Marian's tragedy is, like *Ruth*'s Mrs. Mason, arguably tangential, though no less effectual. Her reticence concerning Waldemar's unsavory character makes Aurora's culpability another "sin of omission." Aurora's refusal to articulate what she knows is true—an uncharacteristic silence for this writer—has devastating consequences for Marian. Because Marian loves and trusts Aurora and Romney absolutely, Aurora's tacit endorsement of Waldemar, seconded by Romney's assertion that "Lady Waldemar is good" (4.277), results in Marian's confiding in this woman. Aurora's patronizing attitude is best represented in her descriptions of Marian, whose low forehead, wide-spaced eyes, and abundant hair accord with phrenological stereotypes of limited intellect and dim comprehension. Spaniel-like, Marian "had the brown pathetic look / Of a dumb creature" (6.317–18); "Poor Marian, . . . doglike," waits "A-tremble" (4.281–83) for Aurora's greeting, demonstrating Aurora's signature self-aggrandizement and her gross underestimation of Marian's character and intelligence. Aurora's long-delayed admission that she loved Romney Leigh all along casts doubt on the sincerity of her earlier behavior toward Marian (who was, at the time, Romney's fiancée); this is borne out by the speed with which Aurora relinquishes her familial alignment with Marian and her child once Romney reappears. Aurora's early silence regarding Waldemar, her vindictive condemnation of Marian's suspected harlotry, and her final shift away from her "affinity with the 'common woman' " suggest complicity in Romney's social "experiment" resulting in a betrayal of her own sex.[38]

Waldemar, of course, also wants Romney for herself. Although neither Romney nor Marian discerns Waldemar's duplicity, Aurora perceives her as a lamia whose power is as diabolical as it is seductive. Lending a novel variation to the vanity/prostitution link, Waldemar communicates most potently through her clothing. Her influence is so subtly manipulative that Marian is unsure whether this woman articulates words or conveys meaning in some more insubstantial manner:

> *Did* she speak,
>   . . . or did she only sign?
> Or did she put a word into her face
> And look, and so impress you with the word?
> Or leave it in the foldings of her gown,
> Like rosemary smells a movement will shake out
> When no one's conscious?
>
> (6.963–69)

38. Helen Cooper, *Elizabeth Barrett Browning, Woman and Artist*, 177.

This woman's insidious influence as it manifests itself even through the movement of her gown and the scent it wafts through the air presents interpretive difficulties, even for one like Marian, whose primary textbook was the "wicked book" of life "on the tramp." Aurora's perspective on the power of Waldemar's dress has more illicit connotations:

> Those alabaster shoulders and bare breasts . . .
> . . . .
> They split the amaranth velvet-boddice down
> To the waist, or nearly, with the audacious press
> Of full-breathed beauty. If the heart within
> Were half as white!—but, if it were, perhaps
> The breast were closer covered, and the sight
> Less aspectable, by half, too.
>
> (5.619–27)

As with her assessment of Marian, Aurora's motivation must be questioned here too, since Romney is now engaged to Waldemar. But by revealing gossips' comments about Waldemar, who "neither sews nor spins,—and takes no thought / Of her garments . . . falling off" (5.664–65), Aurora establishes the aristocrat's sexual deviancy as common knowledge. But because of her superior class and economic station, Waldemar's profligacy has no particularly damaging effects; in contrast, the very fact that Marian has a child—"Small business has a castaway / Like Marian with that crown of prosperous wives" (6.347–48)—is enough to convict her as a social criminal.

Accordingly, because Marian presents an obstacle to her union with Romney, Waldemar arranges for Marian's emigration to Australia, the standard fate for both deviant and redundant women. Marian may not be susceptible to male seduction, but she is clearly seduced by Waldemar, who

> . . . wrapt me in her generous arms . . .
> And let me dream a moment how it feels
> To have a real mother.
>
> (6.1001–3).

Ironically, Waldemar accomplishes what Mrs. Erle earlier set out to do. Through Waldemar's machinations, enacted by her maid, Marian never reaches Australia, but is instead abducted, drugged, raped, forced into prostitution in "that shameful house," and abandoned to wander across Europe in madness and grief. Of all the women mentors in her life to this point, Marian can rightly claim,

> She served me (after all it was not strange,
> 'Twas only what my mother would have done)
> A motherly, right damnable good turn.
>
> (7.8–10)

Merely on the basis of appearances, Aurora—like Mrs. Mason—assumes the worst about the working-class woman she earlier called sister and friend. She taunts Marian into accounting for her maternity, thereby demonstrating that she is no different from the most pedestrian social hypocrite. But Marian will not be humbled by this sort of moralistic bullying and, in telling her story, reveals a woman transformed by extremes of anguish and joy. What Foucault terms "the transformation of sex into discourse" characteristic of Victorian literature did not extend to the topic of rape, which victims are generally "forbidden to name."[39] Marian rejects both this cultural prohibition and Aurora's accusations:

> No cleaner maid than I was . . .
> . . . no matron-mother now
> Looks backward to her early maidenhood
> Through chaster pulses . . .
> . . . .
> I was not ever, as you say, seduced,
> But simply, murdered.
>
> (6.757–60; 770–71)

Marian is understandably determined to distinguish "murder," or rape, from seduction: "Man's violence, / Not man's seduction, made me what I am" (6.1226–27). Her condemnation of cultural complicity in the rape of working-class women refuses to participate in this violent "dominant tradition." By breaking the silence that generates guilt in the victim rather than the victimizer, Marian gives voice to her oppression and presence to her cultural invisibility:

> We wretches cannot tell out all our wrong,
> Without offence to decent happy folk.
> I know that we must scrupulously hint
> With half-words, delicate reserves, the thing
> Which no one scrupled we should feel in full.
>
> (6.1220–24)

39. Foucault, *History of Sexuality*, 27.

Barrett Browning graphically portrays this taboo subject with violent, grotesque imagery. Marian compares her nameless, faceless rapist to a stinking, corrupted corpse whose "red wide throat" gapes at her like the mouth of hell; already numbed with horror, she need not be sedated by "their damnable drugged cup" (6.121). At last, "Half gibbering and half raving on the floor," she is released by captors who, fearing her madness, realize she is constitutionally incapable of being prostituted.

Critical responses to this episode vary widely. Kellow Chesney argues against the existence of such white-slavery practices as drugging young girls and holding them captive by quoting an Officer Dunlap who, "in all his service . . . had never learnt of such a case. . . . there does not seem to be a single publicised instance of a contemporary brothel keeper being prosecuted for holding girls against their will." Neglecting to account for the likelihood that an imprisoned girl (who was perhaps drugged and naked, typically being deprived of clothing to prevent escape) is clearly not in a position to make her plight known, Chesney states that "some women" probably welcomed the "security" of brothel life, "even counting themselves lucky." Chesney considers neither the absence of legal representation for any Victorian woman nor the complete lack of credibility confronting any woman bold enough to make such charges should she escape captivity. Alternatively, Angela Leighton, referring to William Stead's 1885 exposé of Continental white-slavery and child-prostitution rings, "The Maiden Tribute of Modern Babylon," notes: "If Barrett Browning's account of the rape seems sensational, this is not because it is improbable. The trade in girls to continental brothels may have been exaggerated by Stead in 1885, but it was nonetheless a fact, and he witnessed the use of chloroform. Marian's unconsciousness is not a pretext to prove her innocent, but a truth to prove the guilt of the system."[40]

Like Barrett Browning's Runaway Slave, Marian looks to the inscrutable sky, symbolic of God, for reassurance but receives no response. The very landscape seems to shudder in revulsion at the degradation she represents, as if to say, "Take the girl! / She's none of mine henceforth" (6.1251–52). Compassionate peasants tie the Virgin Mary's image around Marian's neck, but, oppressed by its metaphysical heaviness, she throws it off, saying, "A woman has been strangled with less weight" (6.1258). Anticipating the psychic burden of unmarried motherhood soon to come, Marian in

---

40. Chesney, *The Anti-Society,* 342; Leighton, " 'Because men made the laws': The Fallen Woman and the Woman Poet," 112.

rejecting this symbol of sexual purity signals her awareness that the sanctity of Mary's maternity is forever closed to her. Alternatively, Sandra Gilbert argues, Marian's terming her child "unfathered" stresses "the likeness of his mother, Marian, not only to the fallen woman Mary Magdalen but also to the blessed Virgin Mary."[41] As my examples repeatedly demonstrate, the ultimate paradox of redemption literature is its convention of maternal ambivalence (the absence of positive or realistic role models) posed against the fallen woman's struggle to assimilate the experience of deviant maternity.

Utterly abandoned by God, nature, and humanity, "there I sat, . . . by the road, / I, Marian Erle, myself, alone, undone" (6.1269–70). But Marian is not in fact alone: her subsequent astonishment at learning of her pregnancy mirrors Ruth's quasi-suicidal, then ecstatic, response to this same realization:

> It meant *that* then, *that?*
> . . . .
> . . . it could mean *that?*
> Did God make mothers out of victims, then?
> (7.49, 55–56)

Although Marian describes the horror of waking up to find "bedded in her flesh . . . Some coin of price" (6.679, 681), her subsequent maternity becomes for her, as for Ruth, a vehicle for redemption, while the child represents a more tangible "coin of price" with which she repurchases her sanity. Marian is clearly no longer a woman of "meek words" but one who understands the distinctions between seduction and rape, legitimacy and lawlessness. Marian refuses to participate in the sort of guilt Aurora expects her to assume; she defends her chastity and her baby's innocence by invoking the image of married women whose sexuality and whose babies are sanctified by rings, men, and the Church:

> I have as sure a right
> As any glad proud mother in the world,
> Who sets her darling down to cut his teeth
> Upon her church-ring. If she talks of law,
> I talk of law! I claim my mother-dues
> By law. . . .
> (6.661–66)

41. Gilbert, "From Patria to Matria: Elizabeth Barrett Browning's *Risorgimento*," 204.

Rebelliously, Marian transforms her disgrace into a holy redemption, and her bastard into an angel; she drinks her child "as wine," and in "that extremity of love" she is "Self-forgot, cast out of self" (6.599, 600, 604). Through her anger at the human and divine systems that engender victimization such as hers, Marian's once meek words now carry the power to transform the unutterable into the utterable, the unchaste into the chaste.

A survey of the fates of literature's erring mothers and their illegitimate children reveals that some fallen women were allowed to continue living if they remained celibate by way of compensation. Emphasizing the lack of erotic impulse as the catalyst of her fall, Marian's sexual experience occurred without her consent or conscious awareness and, rather than unleashing increasingly depraved behavior, resulted in voluntary celibacy. Although some associate celibacy with disempowerment, both Marian's and Ruth's celibacy can be seen as their assumption of sexual agency in a culture wherein reproductive autonomy is aggressively obstructed. By refusing to participate in an ideology that outlawed her even while still a virgin and despite the circumstances of her maternity, Marian delineates a space in the social framework for women and children like herself, one that demands redefining the madonna-harlot construct. Along with refusing the role of the penitent bowed with guilt, Marian rejects both legal redemption (through marriage to Romney) and the idea that she has, in Acton's phrase, "taken the first step towards prostitution."

Recalling the unlikely alliance between Ruth and the clerical Benson household, the union between Aurora and Marian, who join to raise the outcast child together, promises to produce an adult who will not carry on the traditions of the paternal order—particularly those by which Marian was victimized. This concern recalls Ruth's fears that Leonard would prove to be a "repetition" of his unscrupulous father, and seeks to prevent the sort of revulsion that drives the Runaway Slave to murder her child. But Aurora's realization that the perfect complementarity of mother and child— "Both faces leaned together like a pair / Of folded innocences self-complete" (7.381–82)—clearly excludes her leads her to in turn exclude Marian for her own "self-completion" with Romney. This realization recognizes that sexual ideology does not necessarily incorporate maternal ideology: the two are, as the writers of redemption literature understood to their advantage, quite distinct issues.

As is true of most fallen-woman literature, the great critical enigma of this text is its abrupt "winding up" of Marian's affairs. When Romney offers to legitimate Marian and child through marriage, Aurora urges her to "Accept the gift . . . and be satisfied" (9.255–56), her word choice—like Romney's proposal—indicating she continues to objectify Marian through upper-class lenses. But Marian's refusal is predictable enough to readers who perceive her differently, that is, as a woman who has always had clear vision and "respectable" standards. "My kisses are all melted on one mouth," she says, "Here's a hand shall keep / For ever clean without a marriage-ring" (9.429, 431–32). Although "I've room for no more children in my arms" (9.428)—of her own, that is—she proposes "To help your outcast orphans of the world" (9.438) once her own outcast no longer needs her. Then "She was gone" (9.452), and that is the last we learn of Marian Erle.

Aurora Leigh is, of course, Aurora's story, to which Marian is ultimately as tangential as Lady Waldemar, although it is through her vicarious participation in Marian's life that Aurora is made deserving (so to speak) of conventional love and marriage. Angela Leighton views Marian's refusal of Romney's proposal as an assertive act, a rejection of male cultural ascendancy that randomly grants or denies legal status to women and children: "she denies the law which he can confer, and rejects the fathering he offers. . . . The law of the father is associated in her memory with the law of violence."[42] This law condemns Marian as a social criminal but does not protect her; in contrast, despite Waldemar's tarnished sexual reputation, her social insulation continues inviolable merely because of her class. The poet contrasts the filthy, diseased masses with the "audacious press" of Waldemar's velvet bodice and bloodred rubies, and is equally critical of both images. Yet the class prejudice evidenced by such phrases as "doglike" and "low-browed daughter of the people" indicates another form of bias not obscured by Aurora's patronage of Marian and the child in Italy. "Conveniently for Aurora," notes Leighton, "Marian has good reason to do without" Romney's brand of loveless legitimation.

The class conflicts among this text's women characters are cited by other critics as well. Helen Cooper suggests the poet "uses" lower-class women such as Marian "to effect her own transformation into subjectivity"; once narratively exploited, "such women . . . then disappear from the poems." Cora Kaplan agrees, noting that for Barrett Browning "self-generated sexuality . . . is permitted to upper-class women"—true of Aurora no less than

42. Leighton, " 'Because men made the laws,' " 113.

Waldemar—but "taints all working-class women."[43] More explicitly than the example of Ruth and Jemima, Marian's function is to promote Aurora's respectable sexuality by sacrificing herself; once that is accomplished, her role is redundant, and she shifts from center stage to silenced invisibility. Both extremes of respectability are as necessary to the ideological equation as the death (or narrative disappearance) of at least one of these women.

Loralee MacPike observes that fallen and thereafter celibate heroines such as Ruth Hilton and Marian Erle "harm no existing family structures" and pose no threat to the social system, making their social ostracism, followed by the disappearance or death of such characters, unnecessarily harsh, even ludicrous.[44] Gaskell attempts to palliate both sides of the issue, first by holding religious rhetoricians culpable for lacking that very Christian compassion capable of preventing and redeeming sexual falls, and second by holding the fallen woman culpable (she must suffer for transgressions) yet worthy of redemption and compassion. Barrett Browning, in contrast, invests her fallen heroine with such compelling dignity that her abrupt disappearance from the text dramatizes her cultural invisibility. Both writers employ controversial denouements to emphasize the unfairness of society's attitudes toward such women, and to demonstrate the impossibility of their social integration. Although I agree with MacPike's observation that Victorian punitiveness toward fallen women is excessive, this excess is not surprising given the primacy of nuclear-family ideology. The very existence of extramarital sexuality and childbirth poses a direct threat to monogamy: hence, ostracism of the deviants, and even relief at their deaths, as the haunting example of Maggie Tulliver in *The Mill on the Floss* so poignantly demonstrates.

By virtue of her raucous education in the "wicked book" of the world, Marian has the perception Ruth Hilton lacked, though this did not save her from prostitution rings, drugs, or physical force, nor does it make her anymore than temporarily indispensable to the "good" woman's plot. Although Barrett Browning objected to Gaskell's avoiding the complex issue of the fallen woman's recuperation by "killing" Ruth, her solution to the question of social integration is in effect no different. The variations in

43. Cooper, *Elizabeth Barrett Browning*, 178; Kaplan, introduction to *Elizabeth Barrett Browning*, 25.
44. MacPike, "The Fallen Woman's Sexuality," 67.

these authors' handling of this issue, dramatically demonstrated by life-or-death denouements, reflects their sometimes ambivalent but always radical negotiation of the madonna-harlot dichotomy. As my next examples demonstrate, redeeming prostitutes, who avoid or otherwise complicate the conditions employed to exonerate Marian and Ruth, proves to be an even more difficult negotiation for these social-problem writers.

3

The Harlot's Progress

"RENDER UP YOUR BODY, OR DIE"

A kind of fatality surrounds her. . . . She is crushed down to
prostitution by the whole weight of society which presses on her.
—*The Greatest of Our Social Evils*

There is perhaps no more telling commentary on the exploitative
character of Victorian society than the fact that some working
women regarded prostitution as the best of a series of unattractive alternatives.
—Judith Walkowitz, *Prostitution and Victorian Society*

*T*HE PROBLEM of prostitution during the Victorian period was of
such proportions as to create what Janet Murray terms "a national
obsession, occupying the minds of prime ministers, journalists, clergymen,
physicians, philanthropists, and social reformers." Statistics vary, with some
sources estimating as many as sixty to eighty thousand prostitutes in
London alone, although it is unlikely that such claims are the result of
reliable statistical methods. The epidemic rise of sexual deviancy during a
period characterized by its codification of respectability posed a disturbing
conundrum for Victorian moralists, particularly when configured as a
factor linking (rather than separating) classes: "Nothing formed so close
a bond between the [Victorian] underworld and respectable society as
prostitution."[1]

1. Murray, *Strong-Minded Women*, 387; Chesney, *The Anti-Society*, 307.

As a prelude to discussing the links between social levels forged by Elizabeth Gaskell's fictional prostitutes, this chapter surveys the principal debates and theories of Victorian prostitution discourse, in the process revealing the period's marked tendency rhetorically to blur the boundaries separating one cultural paradigm from another. As Jill Matus notes, the "authority of science" was invoked to justify social mores, yet the scientific community was itself constructed by the paradigms it sought to analyze: science "depended on cultural assumptions about gender" and can be said to both "reflect and serve ideological needs."[2] Gaskell's characters demonstrate the author's assimilation of this contemporary discourse and also register her unique contribution to that multifaceted debate. As in *Ruth*, Gaskell's appeal on behalf of these protagonists focuses primarily on the maternal ideology so essential to middle-class values, in the process transforming moralists' primary mode of condemnation into a means of redemption. But these characters differ from Ruth in their demonstration of what happens to "such as" the beekeeper, Lizzie, and Esther, who are homeless, friendless, and fallen, and who have children to support. Having "taken the first step" to prostitution, some women have no choice but to continue the descent—in the name, ironically, of maternal ideology.

The very existence of prostitution's deviant subculture challenged those ideologists who studiously avoided what others recognized as a mutual dependence between madonnas and harlots. Questions unanswered by the period's "seamless" ideology include: If women are nonsexual, how is it that some women earn their living by selling sex? How can the image of the down-trodden prostitute riddled with shame and despair be reconciled with that of sexually aggressive women whose livelihood depends on assertiveness, not passivity? More pointedly, since men have sexual "needs" of a frequency "decent" women could not possibly satisfy, would not prostitutes then fill a useful role in maintaining the separate-spheres ideology? The paradox is effectively contained in these words by W. E. H. Lecky on "The Social Function of Prostitution":

> Herself the supreme type of vice, she is ultimately the most efficient guardian of virtue. But for her, the unchallenged purity of countless, happy homes would be polluted, and not a few who, in the pride of their untempted chastity, think of her with an indignant shudder, would have known the agony of remorse and of despair. . . . That one degraded

2. Matus, *Unstable Bodies*, 7, 24.

and ignoble form . . . remains . . . the eternal priestess of humanity, blasted for the sins of the people.[3]

It is but a short step from the interdependence of madonnas and harlots to the Contagious Diseases Acts of the 1860s, which were promoted as the ultimate safeguard of sexual purity and, thus, of national character.

Designed to regulate, not eradicate, prostitution, the Contagious Diseases Acts of 1864, 1866, and 1869 were the official response to an epidemic rise in venereal diseases among the military. The tenacity of sexual double standards is evidenced in the claim that only prostitutes spread venereal disease, not the men who used them, which is an interesting commentary on the ideology of sepsis, and one that oddly elides the issue of infected wives and their genetically damaged children. The acts provided for the arrest, regular speculum examination, and mandatory incarceration for up to nine months of any woman suspected of being a prostitute. This in part explains moralists' objections to fashionably dressed lower-class women, which increased the difficulty of distinguishing decent from indecent women. Men were not similarly examined or monitored on the grounds that such sexual regulation would be humiliating for them. The acts were repealed in 1886 after two decades of debate that succeeded in mobilizing the nineteenth-century feminist movement in England.

Prior to the acts' repeal, the period's prostitution discourse was lively and diverse. A. J. B. Parent-Duchatelet's highly regarded 1836 study *De la prostitution dans la ville de Paris, consideree sous le rapport de l'hygiene publique, de la morale et de l'administration*—a title that underscores, notes Laura Englestein, the "link between health, morality, and state control"—set the tone for subsequent English treatises on the problems and issues of prostitution. The fledgling medical establishment, anxious to assert its scientific credibility, constitutes a primary voice in prostitution discourse, although by today's standards this pseudoscience was a thinly disguised endorsement of middle-class moral ideology. In effect, the influence of physicians such as Tait, Acton, and others was a crucial component of a social milieu in some ways constructed by the very discourse that sought to understand and categorize it. Catherine Gallagher notes that during this period, "The body came to occupy the center of a social discourse obsessed with sanitation, with minimizing bodily contact," and with preventing "bodies from being penetrated by a host of foreign elements, above all

3. Lecky, "Social Function," quoted in Murray, *Strong-Minded Women*, 412.

the products of other bodies." As a result, "*medical* doctors became the most prestigious experts on *social* problems" (emphasis added).[4]

William Tait, in his 1840 study of prostitution in Edinburgh, *Magdalenism,* posits a set of characteristics "natural" to prostitutes, including alcoholism—"the evil is all but universal"—pathological lying or "moral insanity," and thievery. Tait also links "Licentious Inclination—Irritability of Temper—Pride and Love of Dress—Dishonesty and Desire of Property—[and] Indolence" with women prone to sexual falls.[5] But Tait's signature codification of behaviors endemic to prostitutes collapses as a result of his professional association with lock hospitals, penitential institutions designed to cure women afflicted by venereal disease and to prepare them for a reformed lifestyle. Tait gradually realized that the proliferation of "kept mistresses," "private prostitutes," "public harlots," and "sly" or casual prostitutes complicated efforts to determine the extent of prostitution with any accuracy. In other words, Tait grappled with empirical proof that deviance was far too varied and complex to be contained by one category—harlot—alone.

According to Tait's statistics, the majority of prostitutes (662 out of 1,000) were between fifteen and twenty years old, although patients as young as nine were admitted to Edinburgh's lock hospital. Tait questions the capacity of these pubescent (often prepubescent) prostitutes to gratify "that particular passion," but maintains the problem rests with working-class moral depravity rather than with economics or white-slavery and child-prostitution rings. Although historically illuminating, this early study exhibits limitations that are emphasized by the weakness of Tait's proposed "solution": "We must look to the cultivation of the higher sentiments as the most efficient instrument for eradicating the crime," an unabashed promotion of middle-class ideology. Such a solution represents what Stallybrass and White call "an exercise in the accumulation of symbolic capital" promised to those able to differentiate themselves "from the commonality by a sublime translation of popular culture into 'higher' discursive terms."[6] Tait neither addresses how the gap between the two levels is to be bridged nor defines "higher sentiments."

---

4. Englestein, "Morality and the Wooden Spoon: Russian Doctors View Syphilis, Social Class, and Sexual Behavior, 1890–1905," 189; Gallagher, "The Body versus the Social Body in the Works of Thomas Malthus and Henry Mayhew," in Catherine Gallagher and Thomas Laqueur, eds., *The Making of the Modern Body: Sexuality and Society in the Nineteenth Century,* 90.

5. Tait, *Magdalenism: An Inquiry into the Extent, Causes, and Consequences, of Prostitution in Edinburgh,* 51, 55, 113.

6. Ibid., 32, 111; Stallybrass and White, *Politics and Poetics,* 198.

A lesser known study, *The Greatest of Our Social Evils,* written "By a Physician," focuses on the spread of venereal disease, which the writer associates with prostitutes but not with the men who employ them: "public morality becomes ruined, the health of the population becomes affected, armies and fleets are ravaged by a loathsome disease. . . . the evil is one of great magnitude in a military and naval point of view," a perspective central to the Contagious Diseases legislation. But despite the bias demonstrated by this perspective, the writer also poses some insightful questions: "Are prostitutes *necessary?* If necessary, how are *their rights as women* to be protected? If not necessary, is society entitled to suppress them by violent means, compromising *their rights as women?*" (emphasis added).[7] Such questions seem remarkably progressive, although qualified by the comment that perhaps modern reformists should heed Saint Augustine, who viewed prostitutes "as an integral part of the order established by Providence in human affairs" best left alone.

Dr. William Acton's *Prostitution* reinforces the double standard underpinning prostitution discourse by arguing that the problem is a matter of supply and demand. Acton claims that men's "desire for sexual intercourse" is an "ever-present, sensible want," but then claims that "the supply [prostitutes] rather than the want creates the demand." Characterized by a noticeable absence of concern for women's perspective (except for such unsubstantiated assertions as "syphilis has a lesser effect on women than on men" and "use of a speculum to examine women is remarkably free of 'pain or inconvenience' "), this "study" conspicuously lacks scientific validity, but became enormously influential nevertheless.[8]

Contrasting with such pseudoscientific studies, sociological discourse on prostitution concerned itself with the actual conditions of working-class women's lives. Rather than codifying false stereotypes, writers such as Bracebridge Hemyng and Henry Mayhew interviewed prostitutes, needlewomen, milliners, and factory and mine workers and published their stories in the workers' own words. These early social scientists understood the humanizing effects of a narrative approach that acknowledges the silenced subjectivity of what Sheila Smith (taking a cue from Disraeli's concept of "two nations") terms "the other nation."[9]

In contrast, pseudo social science is evidenced by writers such as W. R. Greg, whose "Prostitution" is consistent with Acton's claim that women's

7. *Greatest of Our Social Evils,* 3–4, 197.
8. Acton, *Prostitution,* 114, 69, 92.
9. Smith, *The Other Nation.*

"lapse from virtue" cannot possibly be a result of lust or desire, since women are "by nature" nonsexual and passive. But Greg refines this assumption by equating sexual desire with any other desire, from the gratification of vanity to the desire for luxury. Greg claims that the only desire of which a woman can truly be guilty is the desire to please her man: "They yield to desires in which they do not share, from a weak generosity which cannot refuse anything to the passionate entreaties of the man they love."[10] Greg attributes an astonishing nine out of ten sexual falls to this "weak generosity," thus replacing the "myth" of female sexual response with the "myth" of love and romance. But while Greg's argument evinces some sympathy for women's perspective, it also demonstrates the extremes to which the producers of such discourse were willing to go in order to promote and justify middle-class sexual ideology.

But Greg's perspective avoids accounting for those who are prostitutes by choice, women who dress, live, and eat well and whose health (barring venereal disease) is significantly better than that of their unfallen working-class counterparts. "What the rhetoric of protection obscures," says Deborah Gorham, "is that those whom the reformers sought to protect did not behave as if they saw themselves as passive. . . . it seems fairly clear that the majority of young girls who were prostitutes had not been drugged or physically coerced but had *chosen* to be prostitutes" (emphasis added). Many prostitutes also chose when to quit, generally after earning enough to start a "legitimate" business, such as a tea shop.[11]

The agency implied by Gorham's term *chosen*, however, does not preclude the disturbing fact that, as Walkowitz notes, many women had no other options from which to choose. Interestingly, whether as prostitute or "legitimate" businesswoman, these women posed an economic as well as a moral threat. Contrasting with the idea that rural districts foster sexual depravity, some ideologists linked prostitution with capitalism and urban development: "The prostitute brings to her trade all the active, commercial initiative without which success is unthinkable, an initiative that responds

10. W. R. Greg, "Prostitution," quoted in Murray, *Strong-Minded Women*, 410.

11. Gorham, "The 'Maiden Tribute of Modern Babylon' Re-examined: Child Prostitution and the Idea of Childhood in Late-Victorian England," 364–65. Judith Walkowitz cites a study that corroborates these points: "14,000 out of 16,000 prostitutes indicated they were led away by such allurements as 'nothing to do; plenty of money; your own mistress; perfect liberty; being a lady.' Living in a society where status was demonstrated by material possessions, women sold themselves in order to gain the accoutrements that would afford them 'self-respect'" (*Prostitution and Victorian Society: Women, Class, and the State*, 21).

to competition, demand, and the requirements of the marketplace." A competitive market thus accounts for "the raucous indecency of the prostitute," which, Janet Murray notes, "mocked not only the power structure of female subservience to men, but also the pretense of female sexual ignorance, passivity, and lack of appetite." Demonstrating that class, gender, and moral issues are ultimately reducible to economics, Lynda Nead observes, "The combined associations of cash and the public sphere rendered the prostitute powerful and independent—qualities which were the unique privilege of the white, middle-class male."[12] Generally, women who used prostitution as a temporary means of "getting ahead" understood the futility of trying to survive on factory wages. This in part explains why women rarely returned to the factory (or domestic service or seamstressing) after the sexual falls that left them with another mouth to feed. This issue of female agency—public visibility, economic independence, and, in some cases, sexual aggressiveness—remained an unresolved sticking point in Victorian sexual ideology.

Discourse by proponents of evangelical moral reform presents a similar rhetorical mix. Seeking to disprove "once fallen, always fallen," temperance and missionary reformers such as William Logan encouraged clerical involvement in the reclamation of fallen women. Inspired by the biblical example of Christ's compassion for Mary Magdalen, such reformers mobilized an "army" of their own, resulting in "Midnight Missions" that specialized in tea, cookies, and appeals for repentance, and later more aggressively militant organizations such as the Salvation Army. Clergymen are best suited to reform work, according to Logan, since "no other professional could, without damage to his character, attempt to rescue 'unfortunate females' "; Logan's point is illustrated by the experiences of Prime Minister William Gladstone and journalist William Stead, reformists whose reputations suffered when their philanthropic motives were misrepresented by detractors.[13]

"The Great Social Evil a National Question," a series of articles in *The Magdalen's Friend* in 1862, is typical of this aspect of prostitution discourse. Written by E. W. Thomas, secretary to the London Female Preventive and Reformatory Institution, the series relies both on unexamined assumptions as well as on more progressive ideas such as economic and employment influences. As a result, the author negotiates a fine line between "inherent"

---

12. Englestein, "Morality and the Wooden Spoon," 185; Murray, *Strong-Minded Women,* 388; Nead, *Myths of Sexuality,* 95.

13. Logan, *The Great Social Evil: Its Causes, Extent, Results, and Remedies,* quoted in Linda Mahood, *The Magdalenes: Prostitution in the Nineteenth Century,* 67.

gender standards, such as those promoted by fundamentalist interpretations of the Bible, and the fluctuating social conditions that threatened Victorian cultural stability. Thomas regards men as victimized by female corruption, which he hyperbolically warns will undermine and destroy the British Empire. Oblivious to the glaring lack of parallelism in his theory, Thomas vaguely cites "original sin," poor training of the young, and "society at large" as causes of prostitution.[14]

Although Thomas accepts the usual stereotypes of intemperance, thievery, and vanity, his focus on environmental influences during early-childhood development reveals a more modern tendency to regard criminal or immoral acts as learned behaviors. Like Mayhew, Thomas addresses such problems as employment abuses against working-class women and sexual falls from which female agency is absent, like abduction and rape. However, like Acton, Thomas is more concerned with resolving the dilemma of satisfying men's prodigious sexual drive than with the situation of prostitutes and, like the writer who appeals to Saint Augustine's authority, considers the period of "compulsory celibacy" (required of women; optional for men) preceding marriage as unnatural to "God's arrangements."[15]

A final example of prostitution discourse concerns women political activists, who tended to take a more aggressive approach to moral reform than writing treatises. The evolution of the social sciences provided a broader scope for women's involvement in public issues including temperance, the abolition of slavery, the franchise, and the reclamation of fallen women. Societies such as the Female Mission to the Fallen, established in 1858, regarded themselves as performing a "woman's mission to women"; as a result, the association of sexually respectable women with sexually fallen women had an unprecedented impact on eradicating government regulation of women's sexuality. Not only did women philanthropists participate in running the Midnight Missions and otherwise mobilize by promoting lectures, demonstrations, and rallies to raise public awareness of the Contagious Diseases Acts' legalized double standard; they also, in their zeal to reform, went into brothels to work directly with prostitutes, pimps, and brothel owners. The bravery of women who deliberately disproved the myth of female delicacy—"Mingling with whores on midnight streets was not then for the faint of heart"—was repeatedly tested by prostitutes who "generally laughed in their faces" and by gangs of rowdies who pelted them with rotten

14. Thomas, "Great Social Evil," in *The Magdalen's Friend*, 14, 42.
15. Ibid., 44, 200–201.

food: "Although clergymen cut them in the streets, police arrested them, drunks and profligates assaulted them, and a few were killed in the cause, they persevered."[16]

Josephine Butler, the most famous of these women, made the crucial distinction of insisting that prostitution was a social, not a moral, problem, "for this is not a question of natural vice nearly so much as one of political and social economy."[17] Butler distrusted the political clout of the by-now extremely powerful medical establishment, whose promotion of the Contagious Diseases Acts resulted in an unsavory alliance between state-regulated sexuality and medical interventionist practices. Even from the vantage point of her privileged class standing—according to Lecky's configuration, Butler was of that class whose sexual purity was guaranteed by prostitutes—it was clear to her that, rather than protecting the virtue of sexually "respectable" women, the Contagious Diseases legislation in fact threatened the physical rights of women of all classes.

F. K. Prochaska, in his study of female philanthropy in Victorian England, suggests women's interest in actively reclaiming prostitutes stemmed in part from their concern that the institution threatened "what they believed to be their preserve": legitimate marriage and family. Whether configured as a nationalistic, medical, evangelical, or domestic issue, this interpretation is remarkable for its foregrounding of the very argument traditionally employed to justify prostitution. Those women whose chastity is ostensibly protected by prostitution instead perceive themselves as threatened by its disruption of family integrity as well as by the more material contagion of venereal disease. But women philanthropists also regarded prostitutes as fellow victims in a double-standard system that ultimately benefited no woman, though it exploited some more than others. Reform rhetoric urged women to "promote the purity and morality, the welfare and security of [their] own sex, and especially of the young, the friendless, and the exposed," and succeeded in drawing working- as well as middle-class women together for this cause.[18] Insofar as reform's ultimate goal is the elimination of prostitution altogether, men stood to lose a great deal, whether their exploitation of these women was sexual or, in the cases of pimps, procurers, and brothel owners, economic. These radical alliances between chaste and

16. Prochaska, *Women and Philanthropy,* 192–93, 183.
17. Quoted in Paul McHugh, *Prostitution and Victorian Social Reform,* 21.
18. Prochaska, *Women and Philanthropy,* 184; *The Female's Friend,* quoted in ibid., 186.

fallen, and working- and middle-class, women represent an important avenue through which women sought to manage their own sexuality, rather than having it managed for them.

Magdalen homes, a distinctive feature of "women's mission to women," offered a more humane alternative to the workhouse regimes so unconducive to reform. Removing prostitutes from their degraded environments, providing them with alternative lifestyles and occupations, and keeping mothers with their children were the priorities in such homes. Although none of the fallen characters I discuss would have had access to a magdalen home (which were more prominent during the latter half of the century), the influence of Magdalenism on women's issues in the earlier part of the century is central, as the involvement of prominent women such as Butler, Gaskell, and Christina Rossetti attests. Such activists recognized that, despite the period's ostensible valorization of domesticity, "The misery and vice of prostitution was a reflection of society's disrespect for women and family life."[19]

As this brief overview of prostitution debates reveals, nineteenth-century definitions of prostitution are characterized by what is for twentieth-century readers a confusing elision of degrees and types of sexual fallenness. Lynda Nead notes: " 'prostitute' was the broadest and most complex term within the categorization of female behavior. . . . Definitions of the prostitute and attitudes towards prostitution were multiple, fragmented, and frequently contradictory."[20] A primary contradiction these definitions share is a resistance to the fluidity of sexual standards, posed against reformists' appeals to deviance hierarchies and to the validity of mitigating circumstances. Recent scholarship (for example, Linda Mahood, Lynda Nead, and Judith Walkowitz) on lock hospitals and penitentiaries notes the segregation of experienced "hardened" prostitutes from first-time offenders. Some reformatories admitted the latter over the former in the belief that they were less fallen and more redeemable; others emphasized women's degrees of fallenness by forcing them to wear uniforms and cut their hair.

Such practices complicate "once fallen, always fallen" by exhibiting the fear that even relative "purity" was not strong enough to withstand "contaminating" influences. Clearly, Victorian sexual ideology was heavily invested in promoting a narrowly defined gender system, of which the madonna-harlot dichotomy is the most vivid example. Contemporary

19. Ibid., 204.
20. Nead, *Myths of Sexuality*, 91.

responses to Gaskell's prostitute Esther range from revulsion ("Esther is as hideous as debauchery itself") to rejection (Esther "is no good & does no good to Mary or any body else") to compassion ("Poor Esther is drawn with a fidelity and truth . . . a picture of an outcast under a new and deeply affecting aspect"), aptly illustrating the ideological fragmentation with which Nead is concerned.[21]

Elizabeth Gaskell's fictional prostitutes represent varying degrees of fallenness united by maternal ideology. Gaskell challenges the rigidity of reigning standards through her insistence on the redeemability of prostitutes and in her rejection of the stereotype that couples sexual deviancy with an absence of maternal values. Distinct from the character of Ruth Hilton, who is both sensual and maternal, Gaskell here sharpens the division between sexuality and maternity. This distinction indicates Gaskell's recognition that the privileging of maternal over sexual or moral values is what links the period's ideological factions, thus providing the most strategic position from which to promote reform. "Whatever their differences," notes Mary Poovey, "almost all of the participants in the mid-nineteenth-century battles for social authority assumed and reinforced [the] binary model of difference articulated upon sex," a model based on women's reproductive capacity. As a means of managing ideological fragmentation such as that surrounding prostitution, Jungian analyst Clarissa P. Estes suggests interpreting a story's characters as components constructing an archetype.[22] I employ Estes's analogy in the following discussion by considering Gaskell's prostitutes and those "good" women associated with them as not mutually exclusive types but as interdependent and equally necessary to domestic ideology.

Elizabeth Gaskell's most subtle treatment of deviant sexuality, "The Well of Pen-Morfa," published in 1850, details only briefly the situation of an unmarried mother, a nameless beekeeper whose story is subordinated to that of the central character, Nest Gwynn. Presented as an example of local "color" in this traditional Welsh village, the beekeeper—whose self-imposed silence recalls Ada McGrath—ultimately contributes more to the atmosphere of this story than the heroine. The archetypal women characters in "Pen-Morfa" raise complex issues demonstrating what Victorian feminist theorists such as Josephine Butler knew to be true: that no woman, from madonna to harlot, remained unaffected by the sexual double standard and that, in such a system, one woman's gain always implies another woman's

21. Easson, *Elizabeth Gaskell*, 495, 92, 134.
22. Poovey, *Uneven Developments*, 6; Estes, *Women Who Run*, 80.

loss. This story proves that in quaint Pen-Morfa, no less than in crowded urban centers, the outcast status shared by widows, unmarried mothers, spinsters, cripples, bastards, and the insane is ultimately more normative than the legitimated "angels" of reigning ideology.

According to the narrator, the beekeeper, "stern and severe-looking . . . alone and unassisted," speaks in a "most mournful tone . . . a voice of which the freshness and 'timbre' had been choked up by tears long years ago." Her "story is common enough" in that, once considered the beauty of Pen-Morfa, she had gone "in service" in London and returned a year later, "her beauty gone into that sad, wild, despairing look . . . and she about to become a mother." Adding to her misfortunes, her father dies, leaving her a penniless orphan (there is no mention of her mother, the absence of whose guidance is central to the stereotype), and her child is born deformed. Subsequently, this woman's life is circumscribed by the meager subsistence provided by beekeeping and by the constant care her crippled son requires. Known for tenderly nurturing and for patiently soothing his pain, she otherwise "associated with no one. One event had made her savage and distrustful to her kind. . . . Her sorrow was so dignified, and her mute endurance and patient love won her such respect, that the neighbours would fain have been friends; but she kept alone and solitary."[23] Gaskell's questioning what becomes of homeless and friendless falling and fallen women (in *Ruth*) recalls Acton's prediction that they become prostitutes. The beekeeper's choosing social isolation and a minimal material existence instead of prostitution proves that illicit sexual "awakening" does not necessarily unleash an uncontrollable flood of female desire, as was popularly feared. This fear of nymphomania stems from the ideas that women either become prostitutes to satisfy their lust or that lust results inevitably from the "unnaturalness" of their trade, both fallacies that are disproved by these writers.

The woman's lifelong expiation of her sexual "sins" through self-imposed cultural alienation is further dramatized by the child's insistent reminder of her lack of foresight in that one crucial "event." Readers are lulled by the poignant image of her "crooning some old Welsh air" (244) to her child, only to be rudely awakened by the realization that this "child" is fifteen years old, almost a man, yet must be fed, dressed, and carried about as if he were an infant. Because the degree of physical and psychic

23. Gaskell, "The Well of Pen-Morfa," 243–44. Future quotations will be cited parenthetically in the text.

suffering that marks both their lives seems disproportionate to that "one event" of unchastity, it is tempting to speculate whether venereal disease or a botched abortion caused these birth defects. But, like the implication that prostitution may or may not have been a factor here, such ideas are counterproductive to Gaskell's emphasizing maternal values as a medium for fallen women's redemption. The narrator's account concludes on this depressing, if ideologically suggestive, note: "I hope that woman and her child are dead now, and their souls above" (244).

Despite its brevity, the beekeeper's story creates a pervasive atmosphere characterized by a cosmic indifference to individual pain. With the introduction of Eleanor and Nest Gwynn, her story becomes more than just an example of local color, instead functioning as a striking framework through which to study the situations of sexually "good" women who, no less than their fallen counterparts, find sanctuary only in death. As a widow, Eleanor is effectually redundant, a status partially redeemed through raising her daughter. Like the beekeeper, Eleanor also keeps bees—a traditional metaphor for female domestic economy (in contrast to the absence of legitimate sexual economy in both women's lives)—and lives a frugal, humble life as a single parent.

Character alignments between these two mothers shift to link Nest with the beekeeper. Nest's beauty, like the beekeeper's, is legendary in the district: "Nest knew she was beautiful and delighted in it" (245). When her mother attempts to "check" her daughter's vanity—regarded, as I have shown, as an indicator of one's propensity to fall—the irrepressible Nest dances before her and kisses her mother's lips into silence. The idea that lower-class beauty and vanity signify "loose" standards of sexual morality or, more to the point, upwardly mobile class pretensions, threatened social stability even in a comparatively homogeneous community like Pen-Morfa. Friends of the Widow Gwynn and her beautiful but penniless daughter delighted in Nest's engagement to a prosperous young farmer, while those who were unsympathetic or jealous termed her "saucy," a "flirt," and a "coquette" (246).

But Nest soon learns that her fiancé's enthusiasm for her beauty obscures his more pragmatic standards of value. Wrapped in her Sunday-best cloak (another concession to her high-spirited vanity: it is not Sunday), Nest goes out to fetch water at the town well on a wintery day; distracted by thoughts of her impending marriage, she slips on the ice, becomes entangled in that inauspicious cloak, and suffers a permanently crippling (and profoundly metaphorical) fall. At this point, the story resonates with the beekeeper's haunting presence: beauty such as hers and Nest's sets them apart in the community, earns them praise and attention not accorded their plainer peers, and fuels their understandable ambition to improve their hard peasant lot, the beekeeper by seeking her fortune in London and Nest by marrying well. Both women subsequently fall, one sexually and one socially, and both are rendered permanently unmarriageable as a result. As an added factor to the experiences linking Eleanor, the beekeeper, and Nest, Nest's crippling deformity associates her with the beekeeper's son, a dimension that brings the sequence full circle to construct a composite archetype.

Nest's convalescence is impeded by her growing awareness of her fiancé's waning interest: "by-and-by (ah! you see the dark fate of poor Nest now), he slackened" (249). The otherwise self-abnegating Eleanor confronts the fiancé, Edward, directly—"Put it in words like a man. . . . I ask you whether you and Nest are troth-plight?" (252–53)—and learns at last what the doctor refused to tell Eleanor or her daughter: Nest will be crippled for life. This episode has a particularly unsavory quality to it; not only is it common knowledge that Nest is no longer engaged and that she is a hopeless cripple, but Edward has access to privileged information most unethically provided by the doctor, information that leads him to break off this now unlucrative match. As both the reader and Nest learn, "love" inspired by youth and beauty is not ultimately capable of overriding utilitarian pragmatism; Edward's farm and "deal of cattle . . . makes heavy work, as much as an able, healthy woman can do" (252), a factor that takes priority over such romanticized notions of marriage as Nest has been cultivating. Not only has Nest lost her beauty through her ordeal, but she is now a physical burden rather than a helpmate. Putting aside her pride—"So low and humble was the poor widow brought, through her exceeding love for her daughter" (254)—a distraught Eleanor kneels in supplication before Edward, promising to work in Nest's place: "I've a deal of work in me yet, and what strength is mine is my daughter's" (252); but Edward remains adamant, although guiltily defensive, about breaking his engagement to Nest.

A central paradox in "The Well of Pen-Morfa" is Gaskell's alignment of the sexually fallen beekeeper with the Gwynn women, one a widow, the other destined to be an old maid for whom sexual propriety is not rewarded by the promised social legitimation of marriage. Nest's wild response to her fate in effect articulates the beekeeper's earlier unnamed sufferings: she "cries and moans" alone at night and binds "her sorrow tight up in her breast to corrode and fester there" (255). Like the beekeeper, Nest refuses either to leave the cottage or to receive visitors, she shuns all community, and she rejects the neighborhood children of whom she always had been particularly fond.

Initially, maternal ideology marks a pivotal distinction between Nest and the beekeeper: the former is an embittered spinster whose childlessness is cruelly emphasized by the presence of other women's children, while the latter sustains a crippled bastard child who contrasts unfavorably with the neighbors' healthy, legitimate offspring. But the death of Eleanor inspires Nest to some startling action: she takes "Crazy Mary," the communal scapegoat, to live with her, in effect exchanging her role as dependent child for that of nurturing mother and aligning herself with Eleanor and the beekeeper, all three stigmatized by defective children to whom they are devoted.

Through "Crazy Mary," Gaskell critiques the parish or workhouse system, in which a defenseless victim like Mary suffered abuse. Stallybrass and White note the period's paradoxical attitudes toward the pauper class: the invisibility of the poor, rather than being desirable, instead poses a latent hegemonic threat, and making the "labouring" and "dangerous" classes visible by confining them in institutions or neighborhood ghettos would promote their "transformation."[24] Leaving aside the probability that "transformation" is not geared toward social integration or economic parity, or otherwise breaking down class barriers, increased visibility would be provided through "surveillance by policing" deviant types in a central location. The beekeeper's avoiding such options as baby farms and foundling hospitals and Nest's preferring to care for Mary herself rather than consigning her to the workhouse demonstrate their rejection of the dehumanization created by existing solutions to social anomalies.

"The Well of Pen-Morfa" is a story rich in symbolic female economy that, like *Cranford*'s, persists if not exactly thrives. Providing a variation on the convention of motherless fallen women, Eleanor is the "too-good" mother who must die in order to promote her child's spiritual growth; her love for Nest and compassion for Mary draw these two outcasts together, binding them in a relationship "in her name" (262).[25] The virginal Nest, whose symbolic fall suggests the ideological vulnerability of even "good" women,

24. Stallybrass and White, *Politics and Poetics*, 135.

25. Many Victorian social-problem writers appealed to the idea of "maternal instinct" to vindicate their fallen heroines. See Sherry Ortner, "Is Female to Male as Nature Is to Culture?" (in *Women, Culture, and Society*, by Rosaldo and Lamphere, 67–87 [Stanford: Stanford University Press, 1974]) for a postmodern response to this idea.

is redeemed from an unproductive spinsterhood through nurturing Mary, while the beekeeper, although sexually fallen, is similarly redeemed by nurturing her defective child. Finally, Mary's lack of place among both respectable and unrespectable represents a status she shares with all these characters. Like them, she functions as an inconvenience, an imperfection, and an impediment to "normalcy." Of all the redundant characters in this study, Mary's closest counterpart is Bertha Mason Rochester, with whom she shares a similar cultural alienation. But distinct from Bertha, Mary in her madness is not consigned to the attic but threatened with the workhouse. A later variant on this theme, in *The Heavenly Twins,* finds the site of psychological scrutiny of aberrant women shifted from institutions and garrets to middle-class parlors.

"Lizzie Leigh," another story Elizabeth Gaskell published in 1850, strengthens the links between the characters in "The Well of Pen-Morfa" and the full-blown problem of prostitution in Victorian England's industrialized cities. The tone of this tale is early established in the deathbed scene of James Leigh, a rigid and unyielding patriarch whose last words to his wife—"I forgive her, Annie! May God forgive me!"—refer to the daughter he rejected after her sexual fall.[26] But James dies without asking forgiveness from the daughter and wife he has wronged. His Old Testament angry-God punitiveness contrasts with his wife's Christlike compassion, and Gaskell suggests it is because of Anne's submissiveness that their marriage endured: "Milton's famous line might have been framed and hung up as the rule of their married life, for he was truly the interpreter, who stood between God and her" (206).

"Hee for God only, Shee for God in him" is so uncompromisingly enforced in the Leigh marriage that wifely obedience to a husband's sanctimonious posturing takes precedence over their child's tragic circumstances.[27] For the three years since Lizzie's disappearance, "the moan and the murmur had never been out of [Anne's] heart; she had rebelled against her husband as against a tyrant, with a hidden, sullen rebellion, which tore up the old landmarks of wifely duty and affection" (206–7). Anne Leigh rebels outwardly only after her husband's death, despite her conviction that her duty to her child is paramount. Gaskell's privileging maternal over marital values reflects reform's appeals to maternalism as a vehicle for sexual recuperation. Readers are invited to consider the extent to which patriarchal

26. Gaskell, "Lizzie Leigh," 206. Future quotations will be cited parenthetically in the text.

27. *Paradise Lost* 4.299.

strictures actually foster such "sins" as prostitution by interfering with the mother-daughter bond. Distinguishing sexual from maternal loyalties reveals that Gaskell's challenge to the period's domestic ideology relies on her compelling presentation of a distinctly non-Miltonian women's mission to women.

Anne's appropriation of biblical rhetoric clearly serves to recast the religious underpinnings of the period's sexual ideology. Although Will Leigh attempts to assume his father's uncompromising stance toward Lizzie and his mother, Anne Leigh is curiously liberated by James's death. She promptly moves to Manchester to search for Lizzie, and demands her son's compliance: "I may be dead and gone; but, all the same, thou wilt take home the wandering sinner, and heal up her sorrows, and lead her to her Father's house" (230). Will insists Lizzie is dead, but Anne is equally convinced: "she is not dead . . . God will not let her die till I've seen her once again . . . for God is . . . much more pitiful than man" (212). Asserting matriarchal rule, Anne becomes her own interpreter, adapting the parable of the prodigal son to suit her own situation.

In Manchester, Anne leads a double life: by day, she keeps house for her sons, cooks, sews, and waits, thus fulfilling her proper role in the eyes of society. But by night, she is a vicarious streetwalker, prowling dark alleys, peering from doorways, and listening to illicit conversations for news of Lizzie, determined to "lift up every downcast face till I came to our Lizzie" (211). Anne's convincing assumption of the fallen-woman role, though limited to metaphor, demonstrates the fluidity of sexual boundaries that cannot be contained by visual cues alone.

Eventually, the undaunted Anne's faith pays off in a most unexpected way. Anne's son Will has fallen in love with Susan Palmer, a woman he believes so chaste that knowledge about the "family disgrace"—begun by Lizzie and vicariously perpetuated by Anne—will cause her to refuse him "if she were made acquainted with the dark secret behind of his sister's shame, which was kept ever present to his mind by his mother's nightly search among the outcast and forsaken" (217). But Anne's visit to Susan reveals some unexpectedly material links between the pure and "such as" Lizzie, while their subsequent conversation makes clear the circumstances of Lizzie's fall and its aftermath.

Lizzie's story begins with her father's insistence that she leave the farm and go "into service" in the city while her brothers remain at home. It is certainly odd that a sexually ignorant, socially vulnerable country girl is sent alone to a city merely because, Anne says, "Her father thought I made too much on her . . . so he said she mun go among strangers and learn to rough it" (222). Rough it she does; and when Lizzie later disappears in disgrace, her father disowns her and insists that Anne do the same. Rather than protecting his daughter's virtue, James, threatened by the close relationship between his wife and his daughter, places Lizzie in a situation she is not equipped to cope with and then rejects her when she fails. Further, and particularly significant to Gaskell, he separates mother and daughter at a crucial period in Lizzie's development, in effect paving the way for her "fall," and he keeps them apart after the fall, thus providing the circumstances for Lizzie's further descent into prostitution.

From her nightly wanderings in Manchester, Anne learns that Lizzie lost her position because of her pregnancy: "the master had turned her into the street soon as he had heard of her condition—and she not seventeen!" (223). Anne traces Lizzie to a workhouse, from which Lizzie was discharged following the birth of her child. Anne wails plaintively, "they'd turned her out as she were strong, and told her she were young enough to work—but whatten kind o' work would be open to her . . . and her baby to keep?" (219). What kind, indeed, but prostitution.

According to historian G. M. Trevelyan, the attitude toward "such as Lizzie" shared by her employer and her father is consistent with reigning standards of morality: "The harshness of the world's ethical code, which many parents endorsed, too often drove a girl once seduced to prostitution. And the economic condition of single women forced many of them to adopt a trade they abhorred." Both Trevelyan and Gaskell recognized that these punitive attitudes actually fostered, rather than prevented, prostitution. Lizzie's lack of options is emphasized by her entering the workhouse during her confinement, which Judith Walkowitz describes as a "repressive regime . . . thoroughly unpalatable to any person with the resources to keep out. . . . Only the most vulnerable members of the working class—the old, the sick, unwed mothers, widows, and children—entered the workhouse. . . . Prostitutes only resorted to the workhouse at the time of their confinement or when they were physically incapacitated from carrying on their trade."[28] An added cruelty was that women who entered the workhouse with children were immediately separated from them, a sort of emotional endurance test designed to distinguish the "deserving" from the "undeserving" poor. It is unclear from Gaskell's narrative whether Lizzie went into

28. Trevelyan, *English Social History: A Survey of Six Centuries, Chaucer to Queen Victoria,* 431; Walkowitz, *Prostitution,* 156.

the workhouse as a prostitute, or was forced into prostitution following the birth of her child; the economic difficulties of unwed motherhood, as Acton and others note, suggest the latter is more probable.

Some critics claim workhouses—ironically named, in that those driven to them out of desperation did so out of economic need due to unemployment—were designed more for the purpose of discouraging the able-bodied from exploiting the system than for materially aiding the "deserving" poor. Illustrating the visibility with which Stallybrass and White are concerned, from the workhouse buildings themselves, described as "imposing, dominating, and frightening . . . prisons for the poor" popularly called "bastilles," to the harsh regime within, workhouse inmates were daily reminded of their humiliation as paupers incapable of maintaining themselves. Inmates were forbidden any personal possessions, and further dehumanized by the haircuts and uniforms designed to stigmatize them should they attempt to mix in society outside the institution. The fare was of such poor quality that some inmates chewed the marrow of the old bones they were supposed to be crushing in lieu of more productive employment. In "Lizzie Leigh," Gaskell implies even prostitution is preferable to the workhouse, while Eliot's Hetty Sorrel would rather she and her child both die than resort to this option. "To the authorities," notes Thompson, workhouses "sustained life in physically adequate and morally satisfactorily rigorous fashion. . . . To the poor, . . . [such] punitive conditions" further punished them for their poverty by linking them, in public consciousness, with the criminal element.[29]

At this point in Gaskell's narrative, Susan recalls being followed by a woman who "dropped a bundle" and a note into her arms. With a "bursting sob that went straight to my heart" (224), the stranger instructed Susan to "Call her Anne. She does not cry much. . . . God bless you, and forgive me," and then disappeared. Lizzie's startling behaviors—a country-girl-turned-prostitute who entrusts her child to a total stranger—dramatizes several disturbing considerations. Lizzie is "turned out" of the workhouse after her confinement and, essentially unemployable in any respectable

29. Thompson, *Rise of Respectable Society*, 344, 350. Thompson's comments are corroborated by the three-volume *A History of the English Poor Law*. Especially useful to my study are volume 2 by Sir George Nicholls, covering 1714 through 1853 (published 1898) and volume 3 by Thomas Mackay, covering 1834 through 1900 (published 1900). Both volumes also demonstrate the powerlessness of an orphan like Mary Williams ("The Well of Pen-Morfa"), whose stigma of "craziness" is compounded by her lack of money and family.

trade, has no option other than prostitution. This allows her to support her child, yet—like the workhouse—it too necessitates their separation, as brothel owners, procurers, and clients were little interested in doing business with a girl burdened by a child. Lizzie's plight makes clear the dynamics resulting in the Bridge of Sighs's reputation as a haven for suicidal prostitutes.

Anne recognizes the fabric of the child's clothes as belonging to Lizzie, but her joy in recovering her grandchild is overshadowed by the likelihood of Lizzie's prostitution (Lizzie periodically leaves Susan money for baby Nannie's expenses). Anne says, "Oh, if we could but find her! I'd take her in my arms," to which Susan replies, "for all that's come and gone, she may turn right at last. Mary Magdalen did, you know" (225). Echoing Eleanor Gwynn's devotion to her daughter, Anne tells Susan that, for her part in the drama of her daughter's life, "I'll pray for thee when I'm too near my death to speak words; and, while I live, I'll serve thee next to her, she mun come first, thou know'st" (227). Anne's reinterpretation of biblical ethics not only welcomes the prodigal daughter home but also privileges the magdalen over the madonna.

But tragedy strikes when little Nannie, the binding force of all these characters, dies in a fall. Through this crisis Lizzie, like Anne a mother watching her child from the shadows, is found again: thus, Nannie becomes "the little unconscious sacrifice, whose early calling home had reclaimed her poor wandering mother" (240). The living child is Lizzie's badge of shame; its death or disfigurement signifies the sort of retribution exacted by an unrelenting moral code. But for Lizzie, it is also the means by which she is saved from the "inevitable downward trajectory" from which few prostitutes escape alive.[30] A "guilty, wretched creature," Lizzie wails over her child's corpse "with the fierce impetuosity of one who has none to love her," crooning to herself, "I am not worthy to touch her, I am so wicked" (232–33).

The reunion of mother and daughter, marked by Anne's anxious face reading, suggests but does not specify the degradation Lizzie endured. No longer the "former Lizzie, bright, gay, buoyant, and undimmed," she is now "old before her time; her beauty was gone; deep lines of care, and, alas! of want . . . were printed on the cheek, . . . [which] only made her mother love her the more" (235–36). The idea that Lizzie had no alternative but prostitution to support her child dramatizes the fallen woman's plight while

---

30. Nead, *Myths of Sexuality,* 157.

evidencing her assumption of maternal responsibility.[31] Similarly, Anne's determination to recover her daughter overrides all other considerations, including husband, sons, home, and reputation. We never learn the details of Lizzie's sexual fall, nor are we meant to; instead, readers are led by Anne's perspective, which emphasizes unconditional acceptance: "I never left off loving thee, Lizzie. . . . I'll do ought for thee; I'll live for thee. . . . Whate'er thou art or hast been, we'll ne'er speak on't" (239). Elsewhere, as we will see, Gaskell's concern is to articulate what is here deliberately shrouded in mystery.

Anne takes Lizzie home to the relative moral insulation of farm life, where, like Ruth Hilton, she ministers to any neighbor sick or in need. Now, Anne Leigh "is quiet and happy. Lizzie is, to her eyes, something precious— as the lost piece of silver—found once more," a curious metaphor to apply to a former prostitute. In contrast, Lizzie, now a "sad, gentle-looking woman, who rarely smiles" often sits "by a little grave and weeps bitterly" (241).

Gaskell's understanding of the dynamics of sexual falls is far too acute to suggest that city life equates with sexual depravity while country life protects women's virtue. Such an analogy fails to incorporate factors such as economics, family structure, class and gender issues, or evangelical and moral standards, all of which are acknowledged in her "fallen woman" fiction. But the period's increase in prostitution, fostered by the mushrooming growth of industrial cities and an unprecedented demand for virgins in the white-slave market, created a highly organized system that targeted young female émigrées as its victims. According to Michael Pearson, "No young girl was safe from the procurers [who] waited like vultures" at railway stations, in parks, at boat docks, and outside factory gates and sewing establishments, picking out likely "marks." Deborah Gorham notes that one of the more disturbing explanations for this trend is the "curious and ugly" superstition "that if a man had a venereal disease, he could be cured by having intercourse with a virgin."[32] Trafficking in young virgins proved so

31. See Aina Rubenius's discussion of a review of Parent-Duchatelet's *De la prostitution dans la ville de Paris* in *Westminster Review* (April–June 1850): "filial and maternal affection drive many to at least occasional prostitution, as . . . the only means left to them, of earning bread for those dependent on them for support" (*The Woman Question*, 184).

32. Pearson, *The Age of Consent: Victorian Prostitution and Its Enemies,* 31; Gorham, " 'Maiden Tribute,' " 371. Pearson's comment that "working class girls in the nineteenth century rarely reached puberty until they were sixteen" raises some questions worth exploring (*Age of Consent*, 30). How do we account for this? Is delayed menarche endemic to this class, and if so, why? Are they made weaker by poor diet or stronger by hard work? At what age did their middle- and upper-class counterparts reach puberty?

profitable that procurers invented elaborate schemes to reconstruct girls' hymens, enabling them to practice another "curious and ugly" form of sexual economy.

More relevant to country girls like the beekeeper and Lizzie Leigh, who go "into service" trusting in the legitimacy of the position, "Employment bureaux and even some employers—such as millinery shops—were often recruiting houses for the brothels, advertising jobs that were very different from what the girls expected." Many believed "that they were going into domestic service" only to find themselves stripped and imprisoned in locked rooms, held, tied, or strapped down and raped, sometimes chloroformed to ensure defloration without conflict, as was Marian Erle. Some reformers charged that exploitative "respectable" mistresses of domestics were no less responsible for perpetuating the "great social evil" than professional procurers; as Gaskell's *Ruth* illustrates, employers' indifference constitutes a "sin of omission" no less effective than more aggressive techniques.[33]

Although Gaskell avoids discussing the details of women's falls (at best she associates them with "love" or seduction), it is important to keep in mind the extent to which young girls were sexually preyed upon by those willing to pay as much as one hundred pounds for a virgin. According to Frances Finnegan, working-class girls provided "the source from which prostitutes were most commonly recruited—since poor pay, hard and tedious work and often lonely hours exposed many of them to temptations they were unable to resist."[34] But Finnegan's euphemistic "temptations"—a vague term equally applicable to erotic desire and to material gain—obscures the widespread presence of professional procurers, situating sexual agency within girls' character defects rather than in the sort of white-slavery system Pearson's study exposes. The most problematic aspect of these disparate perspectives on agency results in blaming the victim (who is morally weak and unable to resist temptation) rather than the system's failure to protect the victim from the "vultures" who are prepared to use physical force and drugs to secure virgins' highly lucrative commodity.[35]

Were they made weaker by their infantilizing lifestyle or stronger by "superior" genetics? See also my Chapter 5, which discusses techniques aimed at managing young girls' sexuality.

33. Pearson, *Age of Consent*, 31. See also *The Magdalen's Friend*, 86.

34. Chesney, *The Anti-Society*, 325; Francis Finnegan, *Poverty and Prostitution: A Study of Victorian Prostitutes in York*, 29.

35. Victorian journalist W. T. Stead's scathing indictment of white slavery and child prostitution, "The Maiden Tribute of Modern Babylon" (*Pall Mall Gazette* [1885]),

Elizabeth Gaskell's quintessential prostitute is Esther, in *Mary Barton*, which is her most explicit account of prostitution, although the book was published in 1848, two years before both "The Well of Pen-Morfa" and "Lizzie Leigh." The novel opens with the Bartons and the Wilsons speculating on the fate of Esther, Mrs. Barton's sister. Barton, a pragmatic working-class family man, casts his pretty sister-in-law as a potential prostitute: "Esther spent her money in dress, thinking to set off her pretty face; and got to come home so late at night, that at last I told her my mind. . . . Says I, 'Esther, I see what you'll end at with your artificials, and your fly-away veils, and stopping out when honest women are in their beds; you'll be a street-walker, Esther. . . .'"[36] Barton claims Esther's rebellious response was to take separate lodgings—he denies "turning her out"—and defends his position as necessary to protect his family from contaminating influences. Although Esther is apparently not yet fallen at this point—she "said she was not so bad as I thought her"—her subsequent disappearance suggests the realization of Barton's predictions.[37]

The degree to which Barton is responsible for Esther's fall is debatable; however, his subsequent denunciation of Esther when his wife, Mary, dies in childbirth weakens his credibility: "It was she who had brought on all this sorrow. Her giddiness, her lightness of conduct, had wrought this woe. . . . he hardened his heart against her for ever" (58). In an era noted for its high maternal- and infant-mortality rates and a cultural milieu marked by disease and malnutrition, Barton's punitiveness evidences a skewed

---

"proved to be one of the most successful pieces of scandal journalism" ever written, forcing the passage of the Criminal Law Amendment Act of 1885 that raised the age of consent from thirteen to sixteen (Walkowitz, *Prostitution*, 246). In contrast, parliamentary opponents to age-of-consent legislation argued that upper-class seduction and ruin of working-class women and girls was a time-honored tradition, a kind of upper-class "perk" to be passed on to their sons as it was handed down to them by their fathers. See also Walkowitz, *Prostitution*, 250; and Thompson, *Rise of Respectable Society*, 257–58.

36. Gaskell, *Mary Barton*, 43. Future quotations will be cited parenthetically in the text. Superintendent Dunlap testified that poor working girls were swayed by well-dressed prostitutes, who were "their equal in social standing. They see them dressed in silks and satins; they do not think of the way they get their money. . . ." According to Stead, "many girls fell because of 'the temptation that well-dressed vice can offer to the poor'" (both quoted in Pearson, *Age of Consent*, 33).

37. For more comprehensive discussions of the changes in working-class family structures resulting from industrialization, see also chapter 5, "Family and Society," in Catherine Gallagher, *The Industrial Reformation of English Fiction: Social Discourse and Narrative Form, 1832–1867*; chapter 5, "Elbowed in the Streets," in Nord; *Walking the Victorian Streets*; and Thompson, *Rise of Respectable Society*, 85–90.

perspective—understandably fueled by grief, economic penury, starvation, and his subsequent opium habit—that later leads him to commit murder. Because of rampant infectious disease and the lack of medicine and adequate food indigenous to manufacturing cities like Manchester at the time, Barton is forced to watch first his son and then his wife and infant die, powerless to alter the circumstances.[38] The threat of daughter Mary's sexual fall, the uncertain labor market that keeps them on the verge of starvation, and the abuses he suffers as a result of his efforts to encourage legislation to improve working-class conditions, combined with the insidious presence of gin and opium (more available and affordable than bread), conspire to push Barton beyond the limits of his tolerance. For Gaskell, adverse circumstances foster the criminal element in otherwise law-abiding people, a perspective she applies equally to Barton (a murderer) and to Esther (a prostitute).

His family now diminished to himself and his daughter, Barton's concern is to protect Mary from the sexual threat represented by Esther's "fine-lady ways." Because her father associates beauty with vanity and both with sexual ruin—an inevitable result of women's working in factories and earning enough money to dress above their station—sixteen-year-old Mary acquires a seamstress apprenticeship. As my earlier discussion of the liabilities of this profession indicate, Barton's misguided class consciousness actually steers Mary directly in the path of the sort of sexual situations derogatorily associated with "those sewing girls." Effectually orphaned by her father's opium addiction, Mary is left to fend for herself and falls prey to the middle-class mill owner's son who, she later realizes, "meant to ruin me; for that's the plain English of not meaning to marry me" (160). But unknown to her, and in the absence of both parents' protection, Mary has a guardian angel, one through whose agency she is saved from sexual ruin.

Esther's story establishes the prototype of the prostitute's life merely hinted at in the two stories already discussed. Readers are invited to speculate about the significance of the beekeeper's savage demeanor and crippled child or, like Anne Leigh, to "read" Lizzie's countenance to determine the nature of the life she has led. But Esther tells her own story, "the story of my life is wanted to give force to my speech" (209), an articulation she perceives as integral to preserving the purity of girls like Mary. The streetwise Esther thus becomes a self-appointed guardian of Mary's virtue as John Barton

38. See Fryckstedt, *Gaskell's "Mary Barton" and "Ruth,"* which describes working-class living conditions in factory cities like Manchester as filthy, unsanitary, and degrading.

increasingly detaches from the reality of his hopeless existence. Like each of the fallen characters discussed so far, Esther proves to be necessary to the "pure" woman's plot, and indeed makes it possible for that plot to unfold. But this fallen woman is distinguished from the others not only in her breaking silence about the circumstances of her fall, but also in her unconditional loyalty to and sacrifices for those she loves—qualities not typically associated with the prostitute stereotype.

For example, determined to disrupt Carson's pursuit of her niece, Esther approaches Barton, who earlier "had hesitated between the purchase of meal or opium, and had chosen the latter, for its use had become a necessity with him" (168). Thinking he is being propositioned he "swore an oath, and bade her begone . . . adding an opprobrious name" (169) and pushed her down in the mud. The scuffle results in Esther's arrest and imprisonment for vagrancy. Aina Rubenius notes, "The law allowed prostitutes but did nothing to protect them and was indeed extremely harsh and one-sided in all the cases where they might be involved."[39] The Vagrancy Act of 1824 allowed for the arrest and monthlong incarceration of any woman believed to be a common prostitute who was "behaving in a riotous or indecent manner" in a public place. Although prior to the Contagious Diseases Acts law enforcement tended to be lackadaisical toward prostitutes, the sort of police harassment exhibited in this scene was legal. Esther's being brutally pushed down in the mud by John Barton was interpreted as "riotous" and "indecent" behavior on *her* part, not his. Later regretting his harshness as the drug wears off and the delayed impact of Esther's plea on Mary's behalf registers in his consciousness, Barton now becomes, like Anne Leigh, a vicarious streetwalker: "evening after evening he paced those streets . . . peering under every fantastic, discreditable bonnet, in the hopes of once more meeting Esther, and addressing her in a far different manner from what he had done before" (172). Although Barton never sees Esther again, her brief warning, "Oh, mercy! John, mercy! listen to me for Mary's sake!" (169), serves as a wake-up call alerting him to the sexual threat stalking the only family he has left.

Released at last from prison, Esther is determined to secure protection for Mary, "to that she was soul-compelled" (207). The narrator asks, "To whom shall the outcast prostitute tell her tale! Who will give her help in her day of need? Hers is the leper-sin, and all stand aloof dreading to be counted unclean" (207). Esther repeatedly attempts to break the silence

39. Rubenius, *The Woman Question*, 186, 187.

surrounding the prostitute's experience with varying degrees of success: to John, who refuses to listen and has her arrested; to Mary, who is justifiably confused by the mixed messages Esther conveys during their meeting; and finally to Jem, whose reluctant attention she compels by appealing to his love for Mary.

Although Jem attempts to silence Esther several times during her narrative, she insists, "You must hear it, and I must tell it." Esther describes her love for an officer, "one above me far, . . . so handsome, so kind! . . . and he could not bear to part from me, nor I from him" (209). Esther's involvement with a social superior dramatizes the period's shifting sexual mores: inter-class sexual relationships, which for many working-class women signify not a breakdown in class barriers but exploitation, are unlikely to fulfill these women's expectations that marriage will follow consummation. When his unit was transferred, she went with him to be married: "for, mark you! he promised me marriage," adding pointedly, "They all do" (209). After three happy years together (like Ruth's, Esther's fall was loving and pleasurable), during which time she gave birth to a daughter, Esther continued to believe his "intentions were honorable." As Walkowitz, Barret-Ducrocq, and others have shown, although not exactly encouraged, premarital sex was not stigmatized in this class, at least where eventual legitimation was assumed. But Esther, and many like her, found herself caught between changing sexual standards with no economic or legal recourse against the child's father and with familial support withdrawn.

Although no euphemisms obscure the fact that Esther is now a prostitute, it is significant that the impetus behind her sexual ruin was love, perhaps a step above seduction in the deviance hierarchy: given its duration, theirs was effectually a common-law marriage. Esther's refusal to allow Jem to criticize her lover—"don't abuse him; don't speak a word against him! You don't know how I love him yet; yet, when I am sunk so low" (210)—indicates a continued "wifely" loyalty despite his desertion, which complicates her characterization as a promiscuous woman. Esther's fall results directly from her desire to manifest the period's middle-class romanticized fiction of love, marriage, and motherhood, a standard inaccessible to her by virtue of her class. This is signified by the fact that, in return for her loyalty to him, this lover turned her into a camp follower and prostitute and, as Bellingham did with Ruth, abandoned her with a fifty-pound note for her "services." Esther's unwillingness to implicate this man in her "ruin" despite his clear culpability illustrates W. R. Greg's contention that many women's falls result from false notions of love and loyalty.

The circumstances of Esther's "downward trajectory" further belie that stereotype. After her lover left Esther and the child (he was never heard from again), the child's subsequent illness exhausted Esther's meager resources. Threatened with eviction in midwinter, she "could not bear to see her [child] suffer, and forgot how much better it would be for us to die together; —oh her moans, her moans, which money would give me the means of relieving! So I went out into the street. . . . I've done that since, which separates us as far asunder as heaven and hell can be" (210–11). Like Lizzie Leigh, Esther became a prostitute for the sake of her child; like little Nannie, Esther's child (another Annie) died, despite the extremes to which her mother was willing to go to save her. Gaskell's radical suggestion that even prostitution is justified by maternalism proves that prostitutes "were not rootless social outcasts but poor working women trying to survive in towns that offered them few employment opportunities. . . . Their move into prostitution was not pathological; it was in many ways a rational choice, given the limited alternatives open to them."[40]

The extent to which Esther has been transformed by her trials is suggested not only by her passionate love for her child and grief for her dead sister, Mary, but also by her determined "soul-compulsion" to prevent the sexual fall of her niece. The fallen-woman archetype lends itself with particular force to the women in this novel, literally in the striking physical resemblance shared by Esther, her child, and both elder and younger Marys. This causes a confusion of identity more than once; Mary mistakes Esther for her mother, while young Mary herself is later thought to be a prostitute: "Perhaps . . . thou'rt a bad one: I almost misdoubt thee, thou'rt so pretty" (377). Finally, it is Annie's resemblance to Esther's sister, Mary, that prompts Esther's active intervention in young Mary's life, like the women of Pen-Morfa, "in her name."

The elder Mary Barton is another "too-good mother" who must die, thereby forcing her child into an independence of action she might otherwise avoid. Mrs. Barton is spared the prostitute's fate by legitimate marriage and motherhood, a lifestyle that killed her no less than Esther's life at the opposite end of the sexual spectrum kills her. Interestingly, sisters Mary and Esther are motherless, while the former is sufficiently older than the latter to function as her surrogate mother. Recalling James Leigh, Barton's separating the two women at a crucial juncture in Esther's life participates in the literary convention of dead "angels" and the resulting absence of maternal influence

---

40. Walkowitz, *Prostitution*, 9.

leading to sexual falls. Esther is closer in age to her niece than to her sister, a factor that in a sense permits her a clearer perspective on young Mary's situation than an older and more sexually insulated woman (like the angelic mother) might have. Paradoxically, Esther's sexual experience makes her particularly suited to assume the maternal role with Mary during the most crucial rite of passage of her niece's young life.

Esther clarifies her part in Mary's as-yet-unwritten story by explaining that "I made up my mind, that bad as I was, I could watch over Mary and perhaps keep her from harm. . . . I suppose it would be murder to kill her, but it would be better for her to die than to live to lead such a life as I do" (212). Despite regarding herself as (in Will Leigh's phrase) the "family disgrace," Esther redeems herself by guarding Mary, which by extension positively affects both the Barton and the Wilson families, present and future. However polluted her body by her "leper-sin," Esther is clearly "pure in heart."

Esther's story indeed gives sufficient "force" to her speech to convince Jem that he must act to avert Mary's impending fall. Seeking to rescue Esther in return, Jem urges, "Come home with me. Come to my mother. . . . And tomorrow I will see if some honest way of living cannot be found for you. Come home with me" (212). Though grateful, Esther firmly refuses: "I could not lead a virtuous life if I would. I should only disgrace you" (213). She explains her need for drink, without which memories of the past and horrors of the present would be unbearable: "it is too late now;—too late," a claim verified by the torturous visions dancing around her whenever she is sober, visions of her mother; her child, Annie; her sister, Mary, all dead, all "looking at me with their sad, stony eyes" (213).

Issues of deceptive appearances and misleading sexual identities are again foregrounded during Esther's meeting with Mary. Whereas both John and Jem initially rejected the prostitute's "advances," Mary sees her mother's face and hears her voice: " 'Oh! mother! mother! You are come at last!' " (287). Disguised as a "decent" workingman's wife, Esther's attempts to fabricate a plausible life story result in Mary's misapprehension that Esther lives in material comfort while Mary and her father starve. But Mary's resentment toward her aunt unaccountably shifts to compassion as Esther is about to leave, as if she comprehends her aunt's motivations on some more subtle level. To make amends, Mary attempts to embrace and kiss her: "But, to her surprise, her aunt pushed her off with a frantic kind of gesture, and saying the words, 'Not me. You must never kiss me. You!' she rushed into the outer darkness of the street" (298). Although Gaskell blames Esther's "unregulated nature" (290) and "diseased mind" (291) for this uneven encounter, Mary's lack of perception—she misjudges both Carson and Jem, as well as Esther—demonstrates a different sort of culpability.

Esther's fourth and final appearance occurs at the end of her short life. When Mary learns the truth about her aunt, "Your poor Aunt Esther has no home:—she's one of them miserable creatures that walk the streets" (462), she is anxious to find Esther and restore her to home and family. As a result, like Anne Leigh and John Barton, Jem now prowls the streets, prisons, and workhouses, following the trail of the elusive streetwalker known, because of her once stylish, now garish, clothes, as "The Butterfly." Esther resists being found, but at last comes home of her own volition to die. In the final throes of consumption, she wakes in her old bedroom, wondering if the nightmare of her life has been only a dream: "[But] she knew all was true which had befallen her, since last she lay an innocent girl on that bed. . . . She held the locket containing her child's hair . . . and kissed it with a long soft kiss. She cried feebly and sadly . . . and then she died" (465).

This final image of the penitent prostitute, who comes home to die and whose last thoughts are for the child she believes has gone to an afterlife forever shut against her, crystallizes the elements Gaskell employs to redeem the fallen woman throughout her fiction. Jill Matus argues that the narrative promotes Esther's culpability (she falls because she is vain) and devalues her intervention on Mary's behalf, both factors demonstrating Gaskell's concern for a socially acceptable politics of redemption.[41] It is true that Gaskell repeatedly writes herself into a literary corner by attempting to redeem the unredeemable without compromising middle-class ideals. However, although initially Esther's seduction is social (she likes pretty clothes and is flattered by the attention of a higher-class man), it undergoes several transformations. Seduction is subsequently romanticized as "marital" love, and maternal values lead directly to prostitution, while Esther's persistence on Mary's behalf figures prominently in preserving her niece's chastity. Clearly, Esther's positive influence outweighs her role as social deviant. Although Gaskell's perspective in "The Well of Pen-Morfa," "Lizzie Leigh," and *Mary Barton* is not specifically evangelical (that influence is, however, apparent), her writing resonates with compassion for the magdalen and with the radical insistence that these women are redeemable through their maternalism. Maternal values, as I have shown, are for her to be clearly distinguished from sexual and domestic paradigms. Because the women

41. Matus, *Unstable Bodies*, 72, 74.

characters of all three stories are themselves motherless children, she in effect argues that if maternity is redemptive for sexually pure women then it is doubly so for sexually fallen women.

Gaskell's theme of maternal redemption manifests itself in the bee-keeper's devotion to her crippled son, Eleanor's devotion to her crippled daughter, and Nest's devotion to her developmentally crippled surrogate daughter, "Crazy Mary." In each instance, love is motivated by selflessness and the absence of expectations that love will be reciprocated, an equation from which men and romance are strikingly absent. Women "must love like Christ, without thought of self, or wish for return. You must take the sick and the weary to your heart, and love them. That love will lift you up above the storms of the world. . . ."[42] Such is the quality of Anne Leigh's love for Lizzie, Susan Palmer's for the prostitute's child, and Esther's love for young Mary Barton. What all these women share is the death of "the love of youth," their tainted innocence dramatized by the disfigurement or death of the fruits of such falsely romanticized relations. What they acquire in its place, paradoxically, is the realization of qualities endemic to the sexual ideology that condemns them as outcasts. Thus, "the supreme type of vice" is transformed by Gaskell into "the supreme type of virtue." But what this tidy solution fails to address is the implication that women of all economic and moral ranks may expect no more than the privilege of serving others, an endorsement of the separate-spheres ideology in which women's individual autonomy has no place.

Elizabeth Gaskell's compassionate handling of the problem of prostitution reacts against the moralizing tone of prostitution discourse, her primary concern being the punitive treatment of unwed motherhood. Although Victorian reformers noted the correlation between a period of economic depression and unemployment and a corresponding increase in the number of prostitutes, this fact too was rendered in moralistic terms: "the chances of a woman 'straying from the path of virtue' was intimately linked to her choice of occupation. . . . low wages . . . frequently drove women from 'cruel and biting poverty' to prostitution." But if poverty is the impetus prior to a woman's sexual fall, it is even more so after her fall: "where can she go to? Rejected by all, what means has she for re-entering society? The laws and manners of England favor prostitution, but they afford no protection to prostitutes."[43] The very term *reentering* elides the fact that it

42. Gaskell, "Well of Pen-Morfa," 260.
43. Mahood, *The Magdalenes,* 73; *Greatest of Our Social Evils,* 126.

was the absence of options that led many women into prostitution in the first place, kept them there, and effectively prevented their rising out of the "residuum" to achieve social reintegration.

Based on this sampling of the period's literature and its concern with prostitution as the "greatest" social evil, Victorian gender ideology was clearly at odds with the lived reality of a significant portion of the female population. The idea of female "redundancy," reflected in the literary tendency to "kill off" fallen women and their children, and in the cultural tendency to transport widows, spinsters, convicts, and any other woman who was not an angel in the house, serves as an apt metaphor for the period's desire to sweep inconvenient social anomalies under the carpet. Yet, as my examples repeatedly prove, central to this dynamic of marginalization is the surreptitious fascination fallenness holds for Victorian ideologues. The fallen protagonists I have discussed thus far share a devotion to their illegitimate children presented by their creators as evidence of their redeemability. But seduction and prostitution made up only part of the period's sexual anomalies; and it is the resurgence of infanticide—a problem associated with barbarians and primitives, not the civilized Victorians—to which this study of fallenness now turns.

4

Am I My Sister's Keeper?

SEXUAL DEVIANCE AND THE SOCIAL COMMUNITY

It is too painful to think that she is a woman, with a woman's destiny before her—a woman spinning in young innocence a light web of folly and vain hopes which may one day close round her and press upon her a rancorous poisoned garment, changing all at once her fluttering, trivial butterfly sensations into a life of deep human anguish.

—George Eliot, *Adam Bede*

That intolerable dread of shame, which is the last token of departing modesty, to what will it not drive some women! To what self-control and ingenuity, what resistance of weakness and endurance of bodily pain . . . blunting every natural instinct, and goading them on to the last refuge of mortal fear—infanticide.

—Dinah Mulock Craik, *A Woman's Thoughts*

*F*ALLEN-WOMAN LITERATURE depicts perhaps no more enigmatic figure than Hetty Sorrel in *Adam Bede,* published in 1859, a character Felicia Bonaparte calls "innocently fatal" and I regard as "fatally innocent."[1] Like Mary Voce, the convicted criminal on whom George Eliot based the character, Hetty is presented as a vain and self-centered unwed mother capable of murdering her child.[2] Accordingly, critical responses to Hetty's

1. Bonaparte, *Will and Destiny: Morality and Tragedy in George Eliot's Novels,* 180.
2. Of Mary Voce, executed in 1802 for infanticide, Henry Taft observes that, "though in the most agonising distress, she remained as hardened and impenitent as ever,

92

character generally regard her as an impediment to a union between Eliot's "pet characters," Adam and Dinah, a status she shares with Bertha Mason Rochester and Marian Erle. The ideas that Hetty is unquestionably guilty of infanticide and possesses "no spiritual or physical gifts that will draw the reader's sympathy. . . . Hetty is emotionally insentient" effectively promote the interests of the comparatively deserving Dinah Morris.[3] But Eliot's punishing Hetty by incarcerating her away from the social community, transporting her, and "killing her off" even after she pays her debt to society fails to provide a convincing denouement. Instead, the issues raised by the character Hetty Sorrel throughout the narrative remain unresolved by the novel's conclusion, despite its compelling invitation to accept that they "all lived happily ever after."

This chapter discusses Hetty as a fallen woman situated on a continuum shared by Ruth, who is redeemed by maternal values, and by Esther, who becomes a prostitute because of those same maternal values. Although Hetty submits to her permanently outcast status, this is not sufficient to redeem her from the worst deviance of all: the charge of infanticide. Examining Eliot's presentation of Hetty's fallenness in the context of the options available to unmarried mothers with unwanted children reveals a more insidious manifestation of the period's "great social evil" than the image of garishly dressed prostitutes (or, in this case, dairymaids) alone suggests. The presence of illegitimate offspring produced by the period's deviant sub-culture posed a moral and ethical dilemma: did Victorian society valorize motherhood above all else—as my examples thus far demonstrate—or does illegitimacy's insistent evidence of deviancy prod what Auerbach calls the Victorians' "bad conscience" in some other way?[4]

Hetty Sorrel deviates from literary convention in that she is not redeemed by any of the usual means: celibacy, maternity, transportation, or death. In fact, Hetty's fallenness is distinguished by her apparent lack of "maternal instinct" much more than by illicit sexuality. In 1833, Peter Gaskell defined maternal instinct as "Love of helpless infancy—attention to its wants, its sufferings, and its unintelligible happiness . . . softening, and enriching all her grosser passions and appetites. It is truly an instinct" and as such

---

persisting in denying her guilt" (George Eliot, *Adam Bede*, appendix 2, 589). Taft's assessment ignores the rhetorical disjunction between "agonising distress" and "hardened and impenitent," hardly synonymous concepts.

3. Gordon S. Haight, ed., *Selections from George Eliot's Letters*, 187; Auerbach, *Woman and the Demon*, 174.

4. Auerbach, *Romantic Imprisonment*, 150.

is demonstrated by savage and "intellectual" mothers alike.[5] Measured against these standards, Hetty's fate is predetermined: she is as indifferent to "helpless infancy" at Hall Farm as she is in the wilderness. This raises several pertinent questions: If maternal issues supercede sexual issues, how is this complicated by unwed motherhood? What are the implications of Eliot's challenging the "naturalness" of maternal "instinct"? Since middle- and upper-class legitimacy issues are threatened by lower-class illegitimacy, is infanticide a viable solution to the problem? My analysis considers whether Eliot creates this fallen character merely to condemn her deviance or, alternatively, whether her aim is to investigate the broader cultural problems that coalesce in this unresisting figure.

Catherine Gallagher, in her discussion of Malthusian social thought, notes that the reproducing social body (here, childbearing women) was perceived as simultaneously representing prosperity and heralding its demise, "replacing health and innocence with misery and vice." A character like Hetty Sorrel, whose "bloom of youth is both the prized thing that one wants to 'arrest,' in the sense of fixing forever, and the culprit whose 'arrest' would be necessary to stop the enfeebling process of reproduction," complicates communal prosperity in several ways.[6] As an orphan, Hetty is to a degree superfluous and unaccountable and therefore a threat to the smooth progression of communal roles, a threat realized not only through sexual transgression but also through transgressing class boundaries.

Even further complications are revealed through Malthus's idea that sexual passion is vindicated when its purpose is reproduction.[7] The illicit passion between Hetty and Arthur is configured by her as leading to permanent material luxury and by him as temporary sexual gratification. Hetty vaguely romanticizes sexual complicity with Arthur as "love" leading to marriage, while Arthur—who, "if he should happen to spoil a woman's existence for her, will make it up to her with expensive bon-bons, packed up and directed by his own hand"—is determined to marry within his own class yet equally determined to "secure" as well the lower-class woman.[8] Eliot implies that the "misery and vice" produced by this improperly motivated union results most appropriately in the death of the infant; in Hetty's loss

5. Gaskell, *The Manufacturing Population of England*, quoted in Poovey, *Uneven Developments*, 7.
6. Gallagher, "The Body versus the Social Body in the Works of Thomas Malthus and Henry Mayhew," in Gallagher and Laqueur, *Making of the Modern Body*, 84, 86.
7. Ibid., 88.
8. Eliot, *Adam Bede*, 170. Future quotations will be cited parenthetically in the text.

of beauty, of familial and communal place, and of her life; and in the end of Arthur Donnithorne's apparently weak—because overly privileged—line.

The disparity between Malthusian thought and Victorian maternal ideology—or, alternatively, nature and culture—on this point reveals that, despite the extremely high regard in which reproduction and reproducing women were ostensibly held, there are certain qualifications that supercede even maternal values: the circumstances of conception—whether legitimate or not—and especially the degree to which the offspring can conveniently be assimilated into the existing social structure. The necessity for the death of Hetty's and Arthur's child is early established by her lack of "maternal instinct" and later confirmed by the political clout through which Arthur reduces Hetty's death sentence to transportation. Arthur Donnithorne's actions on behalf of the woman charged with murdering his child may result from his guilty conscience; they may also signal his relief (reflected more broadly in the court's compliance) that the social assimilation of either child or mother is no longer a matter of concern. The capacity of these two individuals to overturn such powerful institutions as the communal and the juridical (both of which are uncharacteristically vindictive in this novel) attest to the tension between individual and collective so integral to the industrial age. Yet, in Malthusian terms, if cultural degeneration results from the misdirected vigor of healthy dairymaids and self-indulgent aristocrats, then the fates of Hetty, Arthur, and their child are necessary for the health of the greater "social body."

Perhaps my dissatisfaction with Hetty's presentation and its critical reception stems from the narrative's binary split between the "analytic narrator" and the "sympathetic narrator," an uneasy alliance resulting in a "disjunction of power and sympathy." Eliot's journal entry on the "History of Adam Bede" records George H. Lewes's influence on her narrative: "Dinah's ultimate relation to Adam was suggested by George, . . . he was . . . so convinced that the readers' interest would center on her, that he wanted her to be the principal figure at the last. I accepted the idea at once, and . . . worked with it constantly in view." However, although "what George Eliot tells us elevates Dinah and condemns Hetty," notes Dorothea Barrett, "what she shows us tends to question Dinah and vindicate Hetty," indicating that Eliot's professed intention was not as unconflicted as her journal suggests.[9]

9. Bonaparte, *Will and Destiny,* 180; Eliot, journal entry dated November 30, 1858, quoted in Eliot, *Adam Bede,* appendix 1, 586; Barrett, *Vocation and Desire: George Eliot's Heroines,* 44.

Aptly illustrating Barrett's point, the novel's epigraph, from Wordsworth's *Excursion,* encourages readers' awareness of those "that prosper in the shade" like the unassuming Dinah but urges "something more" than mere forgiveness for "such . . . as swerved / Or fell."[10] Hetty's tainted life and tragic death resonate with far greater "grandeur" than Dinah's pristine character permits.

The novel also demonstrates this "disjunction of power and sympathy" in its narrative structure. The text's primary emphasis is on the community as symbolized by families like the Poysers, the work ethic as evidenced by Adam Bede, and religious ideology as represented by Dinah; posed against these values, Hetty is a misfit and an outsider in every respect. It is not until Hetty's "Journey in Hope" and "Journey in Despair" (chapters 36 and 37) that the narrator permits any meaningful insight into this character's perspective; yet even that is short-lived, as the focus shifts back to what others have to say about Hetty and away from what she has to say for herself. But despite its brevity, this glimpse into Hetty's experience effectually weakens the united front to which Eliot opposes her character. As Victorian reviewer Anne Mozley notes, Hetty "is less repulsive to us than if we did not see the workings of her mind."[11] The narrative impact of these two chapters shifts readers' sympathy to align with Hetty despite her earlier characterization as shallow and selfish, and despite subsequent events.

As a result, Eliot's bias against Hetty is so pronounced as to weaken narrative credibility. Associated with smiles and dimples, kittens and ducklings, babies and springtime—and, oddly, violence—Hetty's is a beauty "you feel ready to crush for inability to comprehend the state of mind into which it throws you" (127). Hetty has a "false air of innocence" (128), implying that she is sexually experienced; this seems unlikely, although, given her compliance with Arthur's seduction, the suggestion is a potent one. Because its presentation is so overdetermined, this link between violence and infantile sensuality, intended to prepare us to accept Hetty's guilt for infanticide, instead fosters our sympathy and compassion for this social criminal even without the usual redemptive devices.

As a result of this narrative ambivalence, Hetty is a compelling and unforgettable character, particularly in her challenge to "motherhood as

---

10. According to Stephen Gill, "this passage from Wordsworth's . . . *The Excursion . . .* is an account by the Pastor of the lowly people in his charge, whose sufferings have persuaded him of the 'native grandeur of the human soul' " (*Adam Bede,* 593).

11. Review in *Bentley's Quarterly Review,* quoted in David Carroll, ed., *George Eliot: The Critical Heritage,* 94.

the great overriding impulse that need ask no questions about itself."[12] The otherness Hetty represents is ultimately less an individual deviation than a reflection of a major cultural shift—in this case, the demise of the agrarian economy. In light of this broader context, Eliot's case for infanticide is unconvincing as presented, for it suggests that Hetty is failed by—rather than a threat to—her community. Both a symbol of cultural destabilization and an omen for an uncertain future, Hetty Sorrel becomes a convenient scapegoat for societal displacement expressed through blaming the victim. My discussion of Hetty's character considers what Jane Flanders terms the "injustice" of female scapegoating, which becomes "representative of all who are trapped, stereotyped, violated, and unjustly blamed" and of all who are powerless to defend themselves.[13]

An absence of communal responsibility covertly characterizes Eliot's portrayal of Hetty's fall, although the narrative strongly urges readers to situate that fall in Hetty's narcissistic vanity and upper-class pretensions. But Hetty's ambitions are quite guileless, being limited to the symbolic possession of fine lace and white stockings rather than actual power or status: what Hetty really wants is the trousseau, not the sexual responsibility it represents. Like most of the fallen characters in this study, Hetty Sorrel is herself a child, though judged as an adult woman despite her appalling lack of knowledge about sexual and class ideologies. No enlightenment is forthcoming from Hayslope's prominent male citizens: the Reverend Mr. Irwine is Arthur's mentor, not Hetty's (and, accordingly, is politically aligned with upper-class interests); Adam's idea of Hetty is as unrealistic and illusory as Hetty's is of Arthur; and Uncle Poyser believes his responsibility ends with taking the orphaned Hetty into his home. To his credit, Adam understands the unsavory class connotations of Arthur's attachment to Hetty, but his warning comes too late. Arthur understands those connotations as well—"No gentleman, out of a ballad, could marry a farmer's niece" (184)—yet acts against his judgment and Hetty's best interests nevertheless.

Although Eliot presents Hetty's superficiality as a factor central to her fall, this quality is not specific to her character alone. As the deserving lover

12. Auerbach, *Romantic Imprisonment,* 216.
13. Adrienne Rich notes, "The scapegoat is different from the martyr; she cannot teach resistance or revolt" (*Of Woman Born: Motherhood as Experience and Institution,* 278). As critical attention to Hetty's character implies, the capacity of martyrdom to convey political messages is more limited than its dramatic immediacy suggests. Barrett argues that Dinah's martyrlike tendencies reflect a calculated hardness that compares unfavorably with Hetty's victimized softness (*Vocation and Desire,* 45). Flanders, "Fallen Woman in Fiction," 109.

crushed by Hetty's selfishness, Adam values her not for spiritual or moral qualities, but rather for the beauty that sets her apart from Hayslope's other girls. That quality of Hetty's appearance that aligns her with upper-class standards conveniently serves Adam's professional ambition to improve his social rank by becoming Arthur's steward. According to Mr. Casson, landlord of Hayslope's pub, Adam is "an uncommon favourite wi' the gentry. . . . But he's a little lifted up an' peppery like" (61). Adam, like Hetty, assumes "airs" that signify class ambitiousness. Also like Hetty, Adam romanticizes love and marriage (198), yet he too is "hard," uncompromising, and overly proud (514). Adam's response to Hetty's imprisonment is to rush to her side; but once there, he wallows in self-pity, unable to leave his room for mourning "the deepest curse of all . . . *it can never be undone* . . . she can never be my sweet Hetty again" (468). Posed against such monumental issues as life and death, Adam's grief over Hetty's lost virginity demonstrates that this text's interplay between superficial and substantial values is clearly not gender specific.

Similarly, Arthur's attitude is unabashedly shallow: he is "ready to pitch everything . . . for the sake of surrendering himself to this delicious feeling" (178) that Hetty inspires. But after their sexual relations, Arthur asserts he "had not yet seen the woman who would play the lady-wife to the first-rate country gentleman" (484). In fact, he is chagrined by Hetty's marital expectations: "her vision was all spun by her own childish fancy. . . . but Hetty might have had the trouble in some other way if not in this" (358), a particularly disturbing trivialization of Hetty's ruined life and Arthur's role in its tragedy. On this point Arthur is hard and uncompromising, remaining conventionally class bound through the novel's end: although free to do so, he never offers to marry Hetty. The narrator implicates the character flaws of neither Adam nor "that poor young man" Arthur in the events of Hetty's fall, although both exhibit the very traits for which she is condemned. Men like Arthur betray the superiority attached to their social station both by succumbing to the eroticized "power of beauty" of lower-class women and by marrying strictly for wealth or rank rather than for the middle-class value, love. As a basis for marriage, however, the romanticized notion of love so popular during the nineteenth century is a notoriously slippery term of constantly shifting meaning, depending on one's class and gender as well as economic stature or potential.

Hayslope's female community also fails to provide Hetty with the sort of guidance appropriate to sexual rites of passage. Hetty's prettiness sets her apart from the other women in an interestingly class-inscribed way.

According to Mrs. Irwine, "She's a perfect beauty! . . . What a pity such beauty as that should be thrown away among the farmers, when it's wanted so terribly among the good families . . . I daresay . . . she'll marry a man who would have thought her just as pretty if she had had round eyes and red hair" (319), like Dinah Morris, the woman who successively assumes each communal position Hetty vacates, most pointedly as wife to Adam Bede. Distinct from the sturdy look of Hayslope's farmwives and daughters, Hetty's delicate beauty seems destined to be wasted on the sort of farmer or artisan her class limits her to marrying. Even women of her own class regard her beauty as a liability: "That child gets prettier and prettier every day," says lady's-maid Mrs. Pomfret. "The more's the pity. She'll get neither a place nor a husband any sooner for it. Sober well-to-do men don't like such pretty wives" (180).

This cultural distrust of ostentatious display (an interesting variation on Victorian middle-class values) in favor of more utilitarian qualities assumes sexual and moral connotations as well. As my earlier discussion of vanity demonstrated, a lower-class woman's concern with "outward and visible signs of value" implies "some emotional lack . . . that significantly lowers her value on the marriage market," since she cannot simultaneously "be seen" and remain morally vigilant.[14] Eliot participates in the fallenness/vanity stereotype by presenting Hetty's parading in her shabby finery and her petty triumphs over rivals like Mary Burge as evidence of her inherent unsuitability as a "respectable" wife. But recalling Gaskell's Esther, who recognized the power and the importance of appearances, Hetty's behavior is appropriate to a society shaped by class consciousness. As a class—rather than sexual—issue, a love of finery such as Hetty's exhibits ambitions toward social privilege and leisure, a lifestyle particularly appealing to a hardworking farm girl. As the period's concern with well-dressed prostitutes reveals, it is the permeability of class boundaries that underscores Victorians' anxiety about "finery." Middle- and upper-class women's attention to dress signified their respectability; the same attention in lower-class women designated potential or realized sexual fallenness. This leads to the understanding that the well-dressed leisure of one class is possible only through the hard work of the poorly dressed class.

Interestingly, the threat to preserving class stratification posed by lower-class love of finery was stated in sexual, rather than socioeconomic, terms.

14. Nancy Armstrong, *Desire and Domestic Fiction: A Political History of the Novel*, 76–77. See also Valverde, "The Love of Finery."

J. Russell Perkin notes, "Vanity and materialism are shown in this novel to be class privileges; such behaviour has severe consequences for those of the lower orders who adopt it."[15] Despite its rejection of superficial merit, Hetty's community conveys the clear message that her value and worth are measured by her physical appeal alone: "Hetty was quite used to the thought that people liked to look at her. She was not blind to the fact. . . ." (141). Of course Hetty is vain; everything about her environment tells her she has reason to be so. She *is* on display and is thoroughly objectified in varying degrees by everyone in the community from bashful farm boys and the Reverend Mr. Irwine to Adam Bede and, most lethally, Arthur Donnithorne, no less than by Hayslope's women characters.

Hetty's only women mentors are Aunt Poyser and cousin Dinah Morris, neither of whom provides her with the sort of guidance she needs; instead, both are intent on goading her into adjusting to and conforming with community standards. For Dinah, the standard is religion, and for Aunt Poyser it is domesticity. Underpinning both is the maternal ideology that narratively haunts Hetty from her less than nurturing response to Totty and baby animals to her later imprisonment for infanticide. Aunt Poyser has little positive effect on Hetty, which is unfortunate considering she is the most likely person to fill the maternal role for her niece. Aunt Poyser's raison d'être is her consummate domesticity (as distinguished from maternalism), and this is her primary focus with Hetty: "for I've taught her everything as belongs to a house, an' I told her her duty often enough" (201)—"duty" referring to domestic, not sexual, economy. Ironically, the proliferation of highly polished furnishings in the Poyser household—Aunt Poyser's particular vanity—provides Hetty with as many mirrored surfaces as she could wish in which to study her pretty face.

Hetty is in fact not Mrs. Poyser's niece, but Martin Poyser's, which may account for the lack of genuine connection between the two women, while the Poysers' enthusiasm "with regard to Adam" reveals that Hetty is considered less a daughter than a servant or burdensome poor relative: "though she and her husband might have viewed the subject differently if Hetty had been a daughter of their own, it was clear that they would have welcomed the match with Adam for a penniless niece" (143). No one consults Hetty about an arrangement that suits everyone but her; few women of Hetty's mettle would respond enthusiastically to a marriage of

15. Perkin, *A Reception-History of George Eliot's Fiction*, 51.

convenience. Proving yet again the narrative's bias, Mr. Casson observes that Dinah's "kin," the Poysers, "wouldn't like her to demean herself to a common carpenter" (95) like Seth Bede, although Hetty's union with Seth's brother is vigorously promoted. All else being equal—both are nieces, both are orphaned and penniless, both are critiqued for their unconventionality—it would seem that Dinah was simply more valued than Hetty, long before events dramatized that fact.

Dinah's persistence in preferring her factory job some miles away to the domestic circle provided by the Poysers also merits further scrutiny. She chooses a solitary, spartan existence in part for the autonomy it allows her. In contrast, Hetty's position in the Poyser household lies somewhere between disenfranchised relative and maid-of-all-work; more demands are made on her than on hired help, yet her only pay is room and board: "For what could Hetty have been but a servant elsewhere, if her uncle had not taken her in and brought her up as a domestic help to her aunt?" (143). Critical analyses have made much of Hetty's lack of enthusiasm toward little Totty, as if that renders the subsequent infanticide of her own child inevitable; yet Totty is Aunt Poyser's child, not Hetty's, and we might more usefully question why Aunt Poyser is always so anxious to hand Totty to someone else. Even Uncle Poyser, who compares young girls to unripe grain—"they'll make good meal by-and-by, but they're squashy as yit"—defends Hetty on this point: "Hetty'll be all right when she's got a good husband an' children of her own" (201).

Mason Harris argues that the Poysers fail in their "parental responsibility" to Hetty, who remains "childishly dependent" on the communities at Hall Farm and Hayslope—both of whom reject her—through the novel's end: "Mentally she is a child, a case of arrested development, not responsible for her actions, and thus a victim no matter what she may finally do." Thus, her attitude toward the Poyser children is a case of sibling rivalry, and she is experientially aligned with Totty's egocentrism. In a "grim parody" of communal values, Hetty later "denies that she has had a child" just as Uncle Poyser flatly disowns his "fallen" niece. Deborah Gorham's analysis supports this idea, stating that a "wide divergence . . . existed at this time . . . about the significance of the differences between childhood and maturity." The development of middle-class family values resulted in a comparatively lengthened period of children's dependence on their parents, a "process that produced first the necessary conditions for and later the concept of adolescence." Today considered a crucial developmental period, it was then a luxury farming and other working-class communities, who depended heavily on child labor, could ill afford.[16]

Conceivably, Hetty's lack of "maternal instinct" and filial gratitude results from her never having been nurtured herself, although it does not follow that she is a murderess. Mrs. Poyser's utilitarian attitude toward Hetty exemplifies what Harriet Martineau calls "the taking-down system of child-rearing"; Martineau's observation that "a little more of the cheerful tenderness which was in those days thought bad for children, would have saved me from my worst faults, and from a world of suffering" might well apply to Hetty.[17] Aunt Poyser aligns with Dinah against Hetty on another crucial point, although for different reasons: "there was no weakness of which she was less tolerant than feminine vanity, and the preference of ornament to utility" (118). Despite this disclaimer, Aunt Poyser gazes at Hetty's charms on the sly, "fascinated in spite of herself" (128), then turns away "without speaking" (231), conveying some curiously mixed messages to Hetty. Aunt Poyser, motivated by her desire to retain Hall Farm when Arthur inherits the estate, practically pushes Hetty into his arms: "you are very kind to take that notice of her. . . . whenever you're pleased to dance with her, she'll be proud and thankful" (129). As a surrogate mother, Aunt Poyser serves to perpetuate rather than prevent Hetty's fall: it is during that fatal dance that the young couple arrange for the rendezvous that changes all their lives. Later, the Poysers' anxiety over Hetty's "disgrace" concerns the threat it poses to their continued possession of Hall Farm: interest in Hetty's personal state is strikingly absent. This is not to suggest that Aunt Poyser's intentions are anything but well-meaning—she is clearly "anxious to do well" by Hetty—but she does nevertheless fail her by a lack of insight regarding Arthur and by choosing to remain silent about what Gaskell terms "*the* subject" of a young girl's life.

The same is true of Dinah. From her first words about Hetty—"that poor wandering lamb" (78)—Dinah's patronizing attitude reveals her to be as lacking in compassion and sensitivity as Aunt Poyser. Although

16. Harris, "Infanticide and Respectability: Hetty Sorrel as Abandoned Child in *Adam Bede*," 180, 188; Gorham, " 'Maiden Tribute,' " 364, 372. See also Mary Abbott (*Family Ties: English Families, 1540–1920*) and Wrigley and Schofield (*Population History of England* [Cambridge: Harvard University Press, 1981]) whose studies find that the median age for laboring-class marriages circa 1800 was twenty-five for women and twenty-eight for men—considerably older than what has long been regarded as the norm.

17. Martineau, *Harriet Martineau's Autobiography: With Memorials by Maria Weston Chapman*, 1:11.

they are peers, Dinah regards Hetty with a "calm pitying face" (186) and pretentiously calls her "dear child" (187). "The Two Bed-Chambers" scene (chapter 15) poses Hetty's vanity against Dinah's religious fervor, proving how alien are their comparative perspectives. Dinah speaks to Hetty in ominous tones about the doomed path on which she sees her headed, but succeeds only in making her cry: "Why do you come to frighten me? I've never done anything to you" (106). Like Aunt Poyser, Dinah is well-intentioned toward Hetty, yet she is more intent on promoting her own agenda than on appealing to Hetty on a level she can comprehend.

Eliot presents Dinah's public preaching as evidence of her moral superiority, yet Dinah's humiliation of the defenseless Bessy Cranage in front of the entire community suggests otherwise (74–75). Because credible spirituality requires nonsexuality (even more true of a female than a male cleric), Dinah's character is drawn in rather unfeminine terms. Her stride is quick and firm, she mounts the wagon that serves as her pulpit with authority, and she boldly maintains direct eye contact with her audience. But such mannerisms, despite her clerical purpose, do not disguise the fact that Dinah here deliberately presents herself for public viewing, much like Hetty does. Wiry Ben anticipates being converted by this "pleasant-looked 'un," after which he intends to turn the tables and "coort" her (65). Although Dinah's quaint Quaker cap is intended to signal her lack of vanity, it in fact generates great interest among the men in the crowd, who excitedly observe that "the pretty preacher-woman" has "got her bonnet off" (66).

If, on the basis of her clerical intentions, Dinah can be excused for being unaware of the implications of such self-display, then so also must Hetty Sorrel—who really wants only to marry well—be excused. Asked by the Reverend Mr. Irwine, "And you never feel any embarrassment . . . that you are a lovely young woman on whom men's eyes are fixed?" Dinah naively responds, "I've no room for such feelings, and I don't believe the people ever take notice about that" (136). Proving the importance of virginity to the ideology that Eliot both challenges and promotes, it is Dinah's translucent, lilylike features to which Adam Bede is attracted, having been disappointed at learning Hetty's rosiness meant she no longer was his. Accordingly, Adam's connubial "possession" of Dinah results in her rosy transformation while the wayward Hetty dies in pale sexlessness.[18]

---

18. Auerbach's observations on the interchangeability of Hetty's and Dinah's characters are especially insightful *(Woman and the Demon* and *Romantic Imprisonment).* The possibility that chastity may not be detectable by visible means raises an important

Dinah's limited vision is borne out in Hetty's conversion scene following the trial. She repeatedly refers to Hetty as "the poor sinner" (494), although, oddly, Arthur is "that poor young man!" (528). The extreme pressure to confess that Dinah imposes on Hetty's fragile mind and spirit falls little short of Inquisition tactics and is typical of the sorts of confessions required of foundling hospital and workhouse petitioners. The interrogation such petitioners were subjected to, notes Beth Kalikoff, "was a form of cross-examination," not of legal but of moral judgment, true also of Hetty's infanticide trial. Similarly, Dinah pressures Hetty until she breaks, a conversion characterized less by the spiritual glow Henry Taft ascribes to Mary Voce than by a desire to be left in peace.[19]

Dinah describes Hetty's conversion with a quality of self-aggrandizement generally ascribed to Hetty herself: "she is contrite—she has confessed all to me," not to God, and "she leans on me for help" (502); again, not on God. Finally, Hetty "used never to make any return to my affection before, but now tribulation has opened her heart" (502–3); considering Dinah's questionable motives (like Aurora Leigh, she wants the fallen woman's partner for herself), her words evidence an unsavory spiritual ambitiousness. Dorothea Barrett notes, "There is something either unconvincing or unhealthy about Dinah's indiscriminate and forced loving. . . . [Her] decision to love is just that—a decision, not a spontaneous emotional reaction. . . . this seems selfless to the point of masochism but beneath it lurks the egoism of the martyr." Is Dinah an "admirable woman" or a "repressed egoist who unconsciously disguises her egoism as altruism, her sexuality and vanity as religious vocation, and her desire for ascendancy over Hetty . . . as a sincere and disinterested desire to help?" Is Hetty "crucified for the sins of others, not least of women like Dinah who falsify their own, and by extension their gender's true motives and desires?"[20] These

point: if unrespectable women can feign respectability, the implications for respectable women are complex and disturbing.

19. Kalikoff, "Victorian Sexual Confessions," 102. Joseph Wiesenfarth (*George Eliot: A Writer's Notebook, 1854–1879, and Uncollected Writings*) proposes that the model for Dinah's character is John Wesley (xxii). Shared characteristics include a preaching style designed to induce "paroxysms of remorse," conducting "jailhouse conversions," and riding "with condemned criminals to the gallows. . . . Hetty's confession, with its subsequent overtones of psychodrama . . . confirms Dinah's efficacy as a Methodist preacher" (23–27, 159). Mary Voce's confession and repentance, obtained under extreme emotional duress by a contingent of persistent Christians and resulting in her transformation into one who blesses everyone from "the Lord" to her executioner, demonstrates the militancy of such tactics.

20. Barrett, *Vocation and Desire*, 45–47.

are important points that deserve further consideration. Interestingly, the same spirit of ambition condemned in Hetty signifies superior character in Dinah, Mrs. Poyser, Arthur Donnithorne, and Adam Bede. Hetty may be "hard," but Adam and Arthur are inflexibly class bound, and there is no hardness so uncompromising as that of the Poysers, who reject her absolutely when her fall becomes public knowledge. In this text, clearly, vanity is not limited to personal adornment alone.

While I do not suggest that Hetty is entirely without responsibility for her actions, I do think contributing environmental factors are relevant. E. W. Thomas argues that "unfavorable circumstances . . . when the character is being formed" account for the ruin of girls: "Parents and guardians, by neglecting to train the young . . . allow them to grow up with vain notions of themselves, and false ideas as to their happiest course through life."[21] We know little of Hetty's early years, but Eliot's presentation of the static predeterminism of her fall implies this is irrelevant. Yet, Eliot also makes clear that Hetty was left motherless at the onset of puberty to be raised by a pragmatic farmwife intent only on teaching Hetty her "duty." Thomas's remarks reflect an ongoing tension between the individual and the collective, and public and private, that suggests more subtle manifestations of "ruin" than was generally anticipated. The parallels between Marian Erle (her mother "sells" her to the squire) and Hetty (Aunt Poyser's self-interests—however inadvertently—propel Hetty into Squire Donnithorne's arms) demonstrate how indeterminate yet how powerful is the concept of environmental influence.

The Romantic period's celebration of the individual (the time frame of *Adam Bede* is 1799–1807) heralds the demise of agrarian ideology by marking a shift toward individualism and away from community cohesion. *Adam Bede* is noted for its depiction of England's dramatic cultural transition from agrarianism to industrialism, yet the fallen woman is presented as perpetually fallen, a curiously static quality at odds with this text's theme of cultural change. Situated in this context, Hetty's character is a particularization of a broader cultural framework, rather than the "hard and selfish murderess" interpretation the narrative encourages, while her disruption of the community ultimately represents more far-reaching consequences than sexual deviation alone implies. The novel situates Hetty in a period of social upheaval characterized by the tradition of arranged marriages and the "growing ideal of romantic love," by the comparatively relaxed traditional attitude toward premarital sex and the social ostracism of

21. Thomas, "Great Social Evil," in *The Magdalen's Friend*, 326.

illegitimacy increasingly developing from middle-class moral ideology, and by the formerly strict separation of the agrarian class from the aristocracy and the potential for upward class mobility that resulted from the rise of the middle classes. This last category also marks a shift from the sort of feudal mind-set in which aristocrats like Arthur assume peasant women like Hetty are sexual property to the potential for lower-class women to improve their social status by altering their sexual standards. Among this panoply of mixed messages, Hetty Sorrel romanticizes her relationship with Arthur (whose view of marriage is thoroughly pragmatic) and is ostracized from all human community as a result, although it is not inconceivable that she could have married out of her class.

Of laboring-class sexual and marital practices Mary Abbott notes, "Until 1753 a solemn pledge, confirmed by intercourse, amounted to marriage. Parents, who frequently underwrote the enterprise, and neighbours, who had to bear the ultimate responsibility for poor households which came to grief," monitored the progress or advisability of these arrangements.[22] Conceivably, because social change is slow to manifest itself in a village like Hayslope, some variation of this custom (in theory or practice) still exerted an influence during the time frame of *Adam Bede*. What Hetty fails to realize is that Arthur's ideological perspective is quite different from hers; each is bound by the sexual ideology of his or her respective class.

Hayslope's tacitly understood code of sexual conduct is inconsistent with its strict observance of class differences in other regards. Hetty Sorrel's community fails her in that it does not provide her with sufficient knowledge about sexual and class ideologies, and then rejects—rather than helps—her when she breaks the unarticulated rules. Hetty's individualism poses a threat to social cohesion; the community expends no effort to understand her because, in light of the imminent demise of agrarian communities like Hayslope, difference represents change and change generates fear. Although Dinah, too, changes profoundly, her change reinforces conventional values, seen, for example, in her exchanging public preaching for domesticity. Consequently, Dinah's sexual awakening, because legitimate, transforms her into a buxom matron instead of a prostitute, murderer, or nympho-maniac. But blaming the individual rather than broader cultural, political, and economic factors is like treating the symptom and not the disease. As Felicia Bonaparte argues, Hetty is victimized by both "her own nature and the general human condition," or, in other words, by the disparity

22. Abbott, *Family Ties,* 32.

between who and what she is and what her community expects her to be.[23] Thus, Hetty Sorrel may be a convenient scapegoat, but the problems she represents do not go away with her imprisonment, her transportation, or even her death because they are larger than all these factors.

Hetty's culpability, of course, stems from her position as a "border case": she is part of the community, yet her individuality is not fully assimilated by it. Hetty's beauty distinguishes her in a way that fuels her ambitions for a more privileged lifestyle, while her awareness of her beauty's "power" over men provides her with an illusory sense of being in control: "She liked to feel that this strong, skilful, keen-eyed man was in her power, and would have been indignant if he had shown the least sign of slipping from under the yoke of her coquettish tyranny" (143). Hetty's attitude toward Adam is strictly materialistic: "she felt nothing when his eyes rested on her, but the cold triumph of knowing that he loved her. . . . Hetty's dreams were all of luxuries; . . . if Adam had been rich and could have given her these things, she loved him well enough to marry him" (144). Eliot's conflation of erotic appeal with material considerations anticipates—and seems to critique—shifting value systems that culminate in the middle-class romanticization of sexual and economic relationships. But although Hetty's behavior and attitude can be seen as resistance to an unwelcome match, becoming pregnant with another man's child is of course a far more emphatic form of resistance.

The sequence of events leading up to Hetty's trial for infanticide and the biological factors resulting in her imprisonment provide significant insights into the issues raised by this character. Hetty's pregnancy, and her infant's birth and death, are no more convincingly presented as proof of her crime than her "hard-hearted" characterization. While I in no way condone Hetty's alleged behavior, I maintain that it remains alleged, but not conclusively established. Despite the novel's suggestive focus on individual and communal culpability, I detect an overeagerness on Eliot's part to condemn the fallen woman that is not convincingly displaced onto either the deviant or the community.

Worth considering in light of the following discussion is Eliot's narrative complicity in Hetty's fall even as she is clearly "fascinated in spite of herself" (128). Eliot details at length Arthur's struggles with his conscience about the inappropriateness of acting on his desires, while remaining pointedly silent about Hetty's possible introspection. However, this is no indication of moral

---

23. Bonaparte, *Will and Destiny,* 182.

superiority since Arthur always dissuades himself from the resolutions he makes. From their first kiss—"his lips are meeting those pouting child-lips, and for a long moment time has vanished" (182)—to his birthday celebration a month later, we know little except that Hetty now has a secret cache of jewelry, gifts from Arthur that she cannot with propriety wear in public. This has a decidedly unsavory aspect to it, considering that we know something Hetty does not know: she believes "Captain Donnithorne loved her so" (296), which to her mind leads, of course, to marriage. But Arthur has no intention of marrying her, even should a child result from their union. What he calls "love"—"He was getting in love with Hetty" (178)—is in fact sex that he pays for in increments, effectually rendering Hetty Sorrel a prostitute, while she interprets both gifts and sex as promises of marriage.

Although Hetty does not seem to have been coerced into a sexual relationship with Arthur, his accountability for subsequent events resides in the comparative worldliness that could have prevented her fall. He knows what results from upper-class seduction of farm girls, a ruin of the sort hardly repaired by a box of bonbons. He also claims to understand the mind-set of people like the Poysers, "to whom a good name was as precious as if they had the best blood in the land in their veins" (184), a factor he conveniently overlooks while seducing Hetty. Reputation is the code by which Hetty Sorrel lives as well, for despite her relations with Arthur (or, conversely, because of the upward social mobility this relationship signifies to her), personal dignity and communal respect are ultimately more important to her than even alençon lace, although this comprehension comes too late.

At his birthday celebration, Arthur dreads Hetty's tearful response "when he told her what he had to tell her" (330), that is, that their meetings must cease. But as we later learn, far from breaking off with her, he promises to "come again at Christmas, and then we will see what can be done" (365). Thus, Arthur postpones an uncomfortable scene, while Hetty's dreams of marriage, luxury, and social elevation continue unchecked. There can be no doubt of their relations at this point; Arthur worries about a nameless "dread" (pregnancy), but myopically concludes, "It was just as likely to be the reverse" (361). He ponders the fact that "Adam was deceived"—meaning Hetty's virginity is no longer intact—"deceived in a way that Arthur would have resented as a deep wrong if it had been practised on himself" (361). Considering that his actions result in the permanent and irreversible ruin of Hetty Sorrel, in this or any other community, concern for her fate is conspicuously absent.

Hetty's realization of her "swift-advancing shame" (410) occurs "some weeks" after her November betrothal to Adam Bede. The timing is significant because if Hetty were as heartless and mercenary as the narrative encourages us to believe, she would have earlier secured Adam (whom she was well aware was hers for the taking) and insisted on an earlier wedding date in an attempt to present her "great dread" (411) as Adam's child. Further, despite the fact that Hetty earlier seemed to think more of the gifts than of Arthur the giver, Hetty now does not want jewelry or money, she wants marriage: "Reasons why he could not marry her had no existence for her mind" (379).[24] That she undertakes her journey in search of Arthur emphasizes her continued desire to marry rather than to receive material compensation from him. Hetty Sorrel's intentions toward both her fiancé, Adam, and her lover, Arthur, thus reveal not mercenary but rather appallingly naive and misdirected motivations.

Another reason the time frame of Hetty's pregnancy is significant is that it suggests her ignorance of procreative processes. It seems unlikely that Aunt Poyser's concept of telling Hetty her "duty" extends beyond the realm of butter making into issues of sexuality. In this matter, Hetty places her trust in Arthur, whose assumption that the odds of her being pregnant are roughly equal to the odds that she is not is chillingly casual. Though not inconceivable, it is certainly strange that she is pregnant for more than four months without knowing it, particularly since she has clear reason to believe in the possibility. If she truly does not know, if her agreeing to marry Adam is a sincere effort to put the past behind her and go on with her life in a way she knows will satisfy the community and ameliorate her transgression of its moral code, then Hetty Sorrel's innocence is not "false" but fatally misjudged.

What is certainly astonishing and difficult to assimilate is that Hetty is at the very least seven months' pregnant when she leaves Hayslope, ostensibly to go trousseau shopping for her March wedding to Adam. How is it possible, given the close physical proximity of these people who daily live and work together, that no one notices Hetty's condition? Considering the extreme scrutiny under which we know Hetty lives, whether that is Aunt Poyser's severely critical eye or the admiring gaze of the Hayslope community, it

24. Hetty proves not to be a materialist after all: to finance her desperate journey to search for Arthur and to salvage some self-respect, she sells Arthur's gifts, thus avoiding what is to her a fate worse than unwed motherhood—the workhouse or "going on the parish" (see chapters 36 and 37).

is curious that such an increasingly obvious condition went unnoticed, apparently, by everyone, particularly since people she subsequently meets on her journey are immediately aware of it.[25]

But Hetty is not destined to endure strangers' speculative stares for long, as she delivers the child shortly after leaving Hayslope. The abruptness of this event, while jarring, can be credibly accounted for by factors that are also likely to have contributed to postnatal complications resulting in the infant's death. Hetty is barely eighteen when she gives birth, she is herself a child who has not yet achieved physical maturity; and, although earlier described as in "blooming health" (381), the stress and dietary factors alone (and, more speculatively, Arthur's possible aristocratic genetic debasement) could account for a less than hardy infant. On a more ideological level, as Lynda Nead argues, marriage and motherhood were "defined as both social *and* medical norms. . . . Deviation from these norms results in disease and in this way, social deviancy for women is also defined as medical abnormality."[26] For my purposes, disease or abnormality refers to the infant's state of health; the combination of its biological prematurity and social illegitimacy places Hetty Sorrel beyond the sort of redemption accorded other fallen women through maternity. Loralee MacPike's claim that fallen women's maternity transforms shame into redemption reveals that complicity with the maternal mystique to an extent compensates for sexual deviance. But Hetty's situation poses an interesting paradox: her "badge of shame" does not reside in the presence of the child but in its absence, which creates a degree of notoriety Hetty never can live down.

Hetty's child is born prematurely, in February, after only seven months' gestation, circumstances that, even with today's advanced medical technology, seriously diminish the potential for survival. The sheer physical grind of Hetty's "Journey in Hope" and "Journey in Despair" and her wavering suicidal thoughts induce her labor: "The exercise, and the occupation . . . were a stimulus to her" (432), and "she was getting less and less able to

25. One plausible explanation is that Hetty, whether through stress and anxiety or through a deliberate effort to minimize her condition, kept herself in a state of semistarvation, perhaps tending toward anorexia (particularly associated with teenage girls and sexual trauma: willing her body into submission by suppressing its increasing size theoretically "negates" the fact of the pregnancy). This, combined with the mental stress of her situation and the physical stress of pregnancy, would have placed both mother and child at medical risk.

26. Nead, *Myths of Sexuality,* 26.

bear the day's weariness" (435). Without food, sleeping in sheep hovels in midwinter, she looks like a "wild woman" (434).[27] But readers' insight into Hetty's experience is short-lived as the narrative shifts away from her perspective; from now on, her story derives solely from the testimony of strangers at her trial. Hetty remains effectually silenced through the narrative's end, with the important exception of her post-trial confession to Dinah.

Sarah Stone testifies that she took Hetty—a complete stranger—into her home because of "her prettiness, and her condition, and something respectable about her clothes and looks" (477), an interesting commentary on the importance of one's appearance for which Hetty was earlier criticized. Hetty gives birth during the night, attended by only Mrs. Stone, who "didn't send for a doctor, for there seemed no need" (478). When Hetty "got a bit flushed," Mrs. Stone was "afraid of the fever"—puerperal fever, an often mortal affliction of postpartum women during the time *Adam Bede* takes place—and leaves to consult a friend; when she returns, Hetty and the baby are gone. Thus, the possibility of "child-bed fever" or its emotional and psychological manifestation, "puerperal insanity," is hinted at but not medically verified, yet another factor that weighs the evidence against Hetty more heavily. Similarly, the likelihood of complications associated with the infant's prematurity—its chances for survival are slim even without Hetty's abandonment—also remains unaccounted for.

The effect of Mrs. Stone's evidence on both Adam and the reader is "electrical," since it proves "Hetty could not be guilty of the crime—her heart must have clung to her baby—else why should she have taken it with her? She might have left it behind. The little creature had died naturally, and then she had hidden it: *"babies were so liable to death"* (479; emphasis added). Hetty Sorrel is accused of infanticide on the basis of her presumed rejection of the child who symbolizes her ruined life; but why then does she take the child with her? Why not leave it with Sarah Stone? Why not leave it anywhere rather than assume responsibility for it? These are questions that

27. Eliot's reference to the Medusa image anticipates Medusa-faced Maggie Tulliver in *The Mill on the Floss*, a primarily autobiographical character for whom Eliot's sympathy is comparatively explicit. Wiesenfarth records two versions of the Medusa myth of which Eliot was aware: (1) the beautiful princess Medusa (Hetty) was changed into a monster (or social pariah) by the jealous goddess Athena (the carping "world's wife" that destroyed Maggie Tulliver); and (2) Medusa was raped by Poseidan, who (like Arthur) was not held accountable for his crime; instead, Athena punished the victim, Medusa (*George Eliot*, 183). Links between these potent myths, Hetty, Maggie Tulliver, and the sexually fallen Eliot (as common-law wife to G. H. Lewes) are suggestively archetypal.

also complicate the perplexing issues raised by another infanticidal mother, Barrett Browning's Runaway Slave, which I discuss in Chapter 6.

According to the testimony of the next witness, John Olding, Hetty does abandon the infant. Olding sees Hetty wandering about—"she looked a bit crazy" (479)—then hears "strange" animal-like cries. When he finds the child it is dead, and he returns with the constable to find Hetty sitting there crying, "but she never offered to move" (481). Although the effect of Olding's account is also "electrical," it is interpreted as proof of Hetty's guilt rather than as evidence of her traumatized state. The fact that Hetty got up immediately after giving birth to travel by foot, in winter, with no food, shelter, or money and an infant to care for demonstrates either remarkable fortitude or advanced delirium. Significantly, while it is true that she left the child only temporarily (whatever her motives, they remain debatable), her return to what is now a crime scene is not regarded as a point in her favor.

My claim that Hetty's postpartum trauma accounts for her behavior is based in part on the discrepancy between Olding's and Hetty's versions of the infant's abandonment. Olding asserts he was led to the child by its cries, yet, when he locates the infant, he is uncertain whether or not it is alive. Oddly, this strange inability to distinguish living from dead does not undermine Olding's credibility as a witness. According to Hetty, after placing the infant in a hole under a tree, she left in search of food: but "I couldn't go away. . . . I was very hungry, . . . but I couldn't go away" (499). Hetty's instability is shown in her claim that she continues to "hear" the cries of the infant Olding claims was already dead and later in her astonishing denial of having birthed a child at all. That Hetty continues to be a victim of her traumatized mind throughout the trial—as opposed to the sort of belligerence suggested by such phrases as "this pale hard-looking culprit" (477)—is evidenced by her plea, "Dinah, do you think God will take away that crying and the place in the wood, now I've told everything?" (500).

Elaine Showalter presents puerperal insanity (which may be a more aggressive form of what is now called postpartum depression) as a violation of all "Victorian culture's most deeply cherished ideals of feminine propriety and maternal love."[28] Along with its links to severe depression and suicide (Hetty made several unsuccessful attempts to drown herself), puerperal insanity is a "mental disorder occurring within the month after

28. Showalter, *The Female Malady: Women, Madness, and English Culture, 1830–1980*, 57–59.

confinement . . . [in which] the woman evinced 'a total negligence of, and often very strong aversion to, her child.' " Illustrating the nature-culture dichotomy evidenced throughout fallen-women discourse, Showalter observes that "child murder was much more likely to occur in conjunction with illegitimacy, poverty, and brutality. These factors . . . were certainly taken into account by Victorian judges and juries, who were reluctant to sentence infanticidal women to death, and who responded compassionately to the insanity defense generally used in their behalf." This was not, of course, the case for Hetty Sorrel: an insanity—or any other—defense seems not to have been a factor in her case. But whether the historical context is the age of reason or the Industrial Revolution, the period's most powerful institutions—the medical and legal establishments—typically "ignored both the social problems of unmarried, abused, and destitute mothers and the shocks, adjustments, and psychological traumas of the maternal role." The figure of deviance represented by Hetty Sorrel did not spring fully formed out of some genetic anomaly or "moral" aberration, although the narrative treats and presents her as such.

Much has been written about the historical accuracy that characterizes *Adam Bede*. Yet, Hetty's conviction and death sentence are anachronistic according to the legal and social attitudes toward infanticide at this time; the execution of the "real" Hetty, Mary Voce, was in fact an exception to legal custom. Showalter notes that infanticidal women who were committed to prison for life were "more likely to be released than any other group of the criminally insane." Susan Dwyer Amussen suggests a plausible rationale for this tendency: "The unwillingness of juries to convict for infanticide suggests that they saw the choice as the lesser of two evils, and that they were unable to condemn those who did not try to keep their child alive." The "two evils" to which she refers are infanticide and "going on the parish," or public support of both mother and child. While promoting pauper-class infanticide was hardly official policy, it is true that an infant's death and the mother's subsequent disqualification from admission to the workhouse meant two less mouths to feed in an already overburdened system. Not surprisingly, then, "most women accused of infanticide were acquitted," even though convictions were made easy by the law that declared any unattended stillbirth an infanticide.[29]

29. Ibid., 59; Amussen, *An Ordered Society: Gender and Class in Early Modern England*, 114–15. In January 1859, according to *The Magdalen's Friend*, there were 12,353 "illegitimate pauper children" living in the workhouse system: "and thus commences

The court's vindictive interpretation of Hetty's demeanor during the trial—she stares down at her hands with no sign of emotion—further demonstrates its bias against her. Because Hetty's behavior "proves" her guilt, there was "no recommendation to mercy. . . . the sympathy of the court was not with the prisoner: the unnaturalness of her crime stood out the more harshly by the side of her hard immovability and obstinate silence" (482). This evaluation implies Hetty could have defended herself but chose to remain silent, as if she were passively committing the suicide she failed to accomplish earlier. The fact that Hetty's lack of response is not seen as fear, despair, or panic over a situation so thoroughly beyond her control emphasizes that her guilt is a foregone conclusion.

But Hetty's silence is consistent with her apparently passive acceptance of Arthur's sexual overtures, of Adam's marriage offer, of Dinah's aggressive conversion tactics, and of public ostracism. The court's condemnation mirrors society's betrayal of women like Hetty Sorrel and is typical of the categorical denial of legal and political protection to fallen women. The legal system, threatened by the social deviancy that child murder represents, condemns her to death; the Hayslope community, which pities favorite sons Adam Bede and Arthur Donnithorne for their brush with the "little huzzy," ostracizes her; the Poysers, to whom reputation in the community is paramount, reject their own blood relation; and Arthur, through exposing her to sexual experience, unwed motherhood, and illegitimacy, makes her a permanent outcast in any community. As Loren C. Bell argues, Hetty is "a child-woman whose lonely ordeal at last revealed her to be more child than woman—a lost, frightened, hungry child who, after all, had wanted only to return home."[30] Ultimately, those "pouting child-lips" were powerless to speak defensively against the formidable wall of opposition Eliot's narrative constructs.

Hetty Sorrel *is* guilty, not of the sort of aggressive act of violence associated with the term *infanticide* but of temporary neglect and abandonment, the circumstances of which are so tenuous as to render her trial little better than a witch-hunt, a travesty of justice. Hetty's own words suggest the extent of her fatalistic submissiveness: "then the little baby was born, when I didn't expect it; and the thought came into my mind that I might get

---

a continued increasing stream of pauperism; the question becomes one of vast importance to the country" (314). See also Ann R. Higginbotham, "'Sin of the Age': Infanticide and Illegitimacy in Victorian London," 262–63; Acton, *Prostitution*, 204–6; and Matus, *Unstable Bodies*, 187.

30. Bell, "A Kind of Madness: Hetty Sorrel's Infanticide," 87.

rid of it, and go home again" (498). Hetty is unsure what she feels for the baby—"I seemed to hate it" (499)—but the one thing she is certain of is "I longed so to be safe at home." Like Marian Erle in *Aurora Leigh* during her mad wanderings, nightmarishly burdened by unwanted pregnancy and the psychic weight of the Virgin Mary medallion, Hetty struggles under the "heavy weight" of the child "hanging round my neck." Significantly, this least maternal of fallen heroines does respond to her child: "its crying went through me, and I daredn't look at its little hands and face" (499). Evidence of the "maternal instinct" in fallen mothers raises complex and contradictory issues: maternity is promoted as the greatest of all woman's accomplishments, but illegitimate motherhood is as great a perversion of sexual ideology as prostitution, which is why its use as a medium for redemption is so potent. The behavior regarded as worse than either is child murder, which perhaps explains the conflicted quality of a narrative that alternately invites our complicit condemnation of, and our compassionate sympathy for, an infanticidal unmarried mother.

Hetty's last words speak eloquently for her lack of criminal intent. In this final piece of her story, which continues where Olding's left off, we learn of her return to the child, compelled by the cries that exist only in her mind: "I could hear it crying at every step. . . . I don't know what I felt till I saw the baby was gone. And when I'd put it there, I thought I should like somebody to find it, and save it from dying; but when I saw it was gone, I was struck like a stone with fear. . . . My heart went like a stone: . . . But they came and took me away" (500). The stone imagery is consistent with Eliot's characterization of Hetty's hard-heartedness, but the idea that fear prompts her actions differs radically from that of the rebellious intractability by which everyone assesses her.

I have argued that Hetty Sorrel is guilty of infanticide only by association, that is, through the temporary abandonment of her child. I have also argued that the likelihood of Hetty's acting under the influence of puerperal fever or insanity is quite high, considering its prevalence at the time, the medical risks posed by Hetty's physical immaturity and the infant's prematurity, and the extremely stressful conditions she endured before, during, and after the birth.[31] The narrative's presentation of the incoherence and disorientation

31. Traditionally, childbirth was midwife-assisted by attendants who specialized in the birth process only. Male physicians' appropriation of obstetrics (from the seventeenth century onward) and, later, the subsequent shift from home births to lying-in hospitals paralleled a dramatic rise in puerperal fever. Lacking an understanding of sepsis, surgeons went from patient to patient without washing their hands, spreading bacteria

that mark Hetty's postpartum behavior and that continue to characterize her post-trial "confession" clearly supports this interpretation. Hetty acts from desperate compulsion, not informed judgment, resulting in a worst-case scenario—the child dies—while her returning for the child, rather than mitigating her guilt, instead implicates her more fully. What, if any, were Hetty's options? What choices did nineteenth-century unwed mothers have, particularly those with unwanted children? Faced with choosing between the child's life and her own, what could she have done differently? Some consideration of the practices of the time and of the striking resurgence of infanticide during a period characterized by maternalism will prove how limited women's options were and how loosely defined was the term *infanticide*, during both the novel's romantic time frame and the mid-Victorian period in which it was written.[32]

Aside from murder (aggressive infanticide) and abandonment (passive infanticide), abortion, foundling hospitals, and baby farms were the primary means of ridding oneself of unwanted children. Compared with infanticide, abortion seems to have been regarded as the lesser crime. Dr. Lankester, a prominent authority on these issues, notes that in contrast to infanticide, "in the present state of the law, the mother may destroy her infant before birth, and be liable to no consequences under the law," meaning that abortion was unlikely to provoke prosecution.[33] Compared with abortion, infanticide was more closely linked to murder since it involved an *ex utero* human being; then, as now, the point at

---

that proved fatal to newly delivered women. Even through the 1860s, the fatality rate was so high that hospital births became synonymous with maternal death, although empirical medical proof of the existence of sepsis and its connection with puerperal fever was recorded as early as 1795. This affected poor and working-class women primarily: with the outlawing of midwifery and the prohibitive costs of home delivery by a physician, poor women were forced into notoriously dangerous hospital deliveries; "safe" home deliveries were now a privilege of the rich. Although Hetty delivered at home—assisted by a woman of dubious medical judgment—the potential for postpartum complications still existed. Mary Wollstonecraft died of puerperal fever in 1797. See Poovey, *Uneven Developments*, 40; and Rich, *Of Woman Born*, 151–55.

32. *The Magdalen's Friend* notes that in a single year 1,103 inquests of suspicious infant deaths were held in London alone, while some provincial districts conducted as many as 300 such inquests: "That these cases may now be numbered by thousands annually is proved by the recorded number of inquests held on illegitimate children, a large proportion of whom . . . are actually killed by their own mothers, almost as soon as they draw their first breath, while many more are allowed to pine away in want and neglect till . . . death puts an end to their troublous life" (301). See also Hellerstein, Hume, and Offen, *Victorian Women*, 204–5.

33. Quoted in Martineau, *London Daily News*, October 19, 1865.

which one is regarded as fully human is central to reproductive-issues debates.

F. M. L. Thompson notes that abortion was not endemic to the lower classes: among the poor, "it was accepted as a necessary expedient for protecting marriage chances, female employment prospects, or family living standards." But it was also employed by middle-class women for similar reasons and, perhaps, as a means of birth control. According to Hellerstein, "Abortions were available, although they were illegal, highly dangerous and often costly."[34] A woman choosing an abortion at this time was as likely to die from the process as was the fetus. Paradoxically, as an option abortion would have called as much attention to a woman's condition as giving birth to the child; abortionists only initiated the process that took as long as a week to ten days to complete, during which time the woman was basically incapacitated by her condition. Although at this time maternity was fraught with often fatal complications, Hetty's chance of survival was greater in childbirth than in abortion.

"Baby farming," a practice as notorious as abortion or infanticide in that children generally died from the neglect and abuse of unscrupulous guardians, must be discounted as an option as it would have required Arthur's financial help. Considered a relatively humane form of abandonment, baby farms required monetary contributions in order, ostensibly, to ensure adequate care for the infant, although in practice children were likely to disappear or die "unaccountably" soon after. Martineau equates baby farming with infanticide *on the mother's part,* however passive or indirect: "She leaves her infant in hands in which it is sure to die . . . of improper food, drugs, and neglect. The mother knows it will die, and is relieved when it is gone; and she has no pain of conscience, because she could do no otherwise than commit this child murder."[35] This comment is consistent

34. Thompson, *Rise of Respectable Society,* 308 (see also 115–24); Hellerstein, Hume, and Offen, *Victorian Women,* 238.

35. Martineau, *London Daily News,* September 8, 1865. Despite her commitment to responsible journalism, Martineau does not substantiate her sensationalistic claim that women who commit unwanted children to baby farms suffer "no pain of conscience." See also discussions in Matus, *Unstable Bodies,* 158, 182; Hellerstein, Hume, and Offen, *Victorian Women,* 238–40; and Chesney, *The Anti-Society,* 349–53. Of 1871's Infant Life Protection, Matus says, "Regulating baby-farming, as the bill proposed to do, did not address the true causes of infant mortality—women's oppression—and it failed to recognise factors such as ignorance, poverty, seduction, and, above all, the difficulties in the way of unmarried mothers supporting themselves and their children" (*Unstable Bodies,* 167).

with the general discourse of the time in that infanticide—regarded as a women's crime—is as much a matter of passive complicity as of aggressive action.

Another method by which women could dispose of unwanted children was foundling hospitals, although by the turn of the nineteenth century this practice had declined, and would probably have been available only in large cities. Unlike the free-enterprise system of baby farms, such institutions were generally government subsidized and did not require the fees so prohibitive to poor women. Unfortunately, as critics of the practice argue, these charitable institutions often bred punitive attitudes toward the poor, best seen in the penurious environments of such hospitals, the poor-quality care, and the resulting high death rate. Martineau argues that, rather than a "remedy," this "most pernicious class of charity" sanctions sexual immorality by relieving "the unchaste from the burdensome consequences of their sin."[36]

This punitive attitude assumed other forms as well. Some mothers were deterred from applying to foundling hospitals by an admissions process requiring detailed personal histories of their sexual "falls," a practice oddly reminiscent of religious confessionals. Beth Kalikoff discusses the dehumanizing interviews in which petitioners were required to reveal not only the identity of the child's father, but also how many times intercourse occurred and where. Since (in the interest of preserving "good" women's delicacy) the selection committees consisted of men, "The confessions themselves became fictional by-products—eventually documents," such as those examined by Françoise Barret-Ducrocq, "of the erotic process of voyeurism and humiliation in the sexual confession ritual. The questioners, with their rigidly eccentric rules and their tireless desire to penetrate the applicant's . . . secrets, became actors in a public drama of erotic exposure and dominance. . . . Shorn of legal and religious trappings, the ritual exposes a communal sadism."[37] As a result, women deterred from using this system often resorted to the infanticide that foundling hospitals were supposed to prevent.

Designed to counteract this sort of voyeurism by ensuring parents' anonymity, the institution of "turning" or "revolving" boxes offered a

36. Martineau, *London Daily News*, February 13, 1863. Abbott notes, "Thomas Coram (b. 1668) was moved to endow the Foundling Hospital, which opened in 1741, by the sight of dead and dying infants abandoned on the streets and dung heaps of London" (*Family Ties*, 27).
37. Kalikoff, "Victorian Sexual Confessions," 102, 110.

novel alternative: infants were placed in the box from an outside wall, and the box was then turned to admit the child within the hospital. But unfortunately, notes Martineau, unwanted children are not the exclusive province of illegitimacy, resulting in the system's exploitation by parents of legitimate children who simply did not want either the material or financial responsibility of another child: "A very large proportion of the foundlings received at all such institutions, as well as of the infants murdered, are the children of married parents, who thus cast off the trouble and cost of their maintenance." In practice, both the confession or "theater of penitence" and the turning-box systems offered few incentives to women who genuinely sought provision for their illegitimate children. As Kalikoff notes, the system, rather than those in need of its services, was "morally bankrupt."[38]

Martineau's recognition of the considerable influence of economic factors on the "fallen" milieu remains caught between such punitive moralizing as that demonstrated in her infanticide series and Acton's more sobering observation that prostitution is the next step for many women in this position. This leads to a more tangential "option," although it is so only by association. While wet-nursing is not an issue raised in the texts I discuss, lower-class women's breast-feeding the children of middle- and upper-class mothers was a prominent practice of the time. In the event that the mother chose to keep and support her child, wet-nursing was regarded by many as the only suitable alternative to prostitution (where infants were an impediment) or the workhouse (where mothers and children were separated) for unwed mothers needing to earn a living. Hellerstein notes that many unwed mothers, often rejected by both family and employer when most in need of assistance, "could support themselves only as live-in wet nurses," with the result that "their own babies often died of malnutrition and disease." Women striving to sustain both their own and their employer's babies found their own health breaking under the strain. Martineau cautions, "it is not wise that our feelings of pity for the fallen woman should lead us to think of her infant only."[39] This observation at least begins to move beyond

38. Martineau, *London Daily News*, August 8, 1865; Kalikoff, "Victorian Sexual Confessions," 103.

39. Hellerstein, Hume, and Offen, *Victorian Women*, 128; Martineau, *London Daily News*, September 8, 1865. Proponents of the practice argued that wet-nursing relieved upper-class women of the inconvenient burden of breast-feeding, kept lower-class women in the home rather than on the streets, and had the added attraction of suppressing menses (an acceptable means of working-class birth control). Opponents of the practice were concerned about the transmission of low-class tendencies (physical

maternal imperatives to the broader implications of unwanted children and infanticide, concepts of greater complexity than the social management of female sexuality alone can accommodate.

Of the options prevalent at the time, neither abortion nor baby farms, wet-nursing nor foundling hospitals offered viable alternatives for Hetty Sorrel, because of either lack of money, accessibility, or forethought. This leaves only infanticide, which those critics who regard Hetty as "intensely aggressive" agree she is guilty of. But I resist the term *infanticide,* which strongly suggests a violent and deliberate act, in favor of abandonment, a much more passive version of what was actually Hetty's temporary absence from an infant who might have died even had she been there at the time. Such sources as *The Magdalen's Friend* and Dr. Lankester agree that many infant deaths are the result of stillbirths or natural deaths that occur soon after birth. That "infanticide" applies equally to an unattended woman whose infant is stillborn and to an "intensely aggressive" murderer questions the validity of the statistics as well as of the concept itself. Complications caused by prematurity, poor prenatal care, or the mother's physical immaturity could produce such consequences, as would sudden infant death syndrome, a phenomenon that continues to baffle the medical profession. F. M. L. Thompson complicates the already problematic idea of "maternal instinct" by pointing out that the distressingly high rate of infant and child mortality during this period was likely to have fostered a relatively detached attitude in parents, who were hesitant to invest emotionally in at-risk children, at least until their survival seemed likely.[40] Such factors bear considering in regard to Hetty Sorrel, who is ambitious but not mercenary: she easily is led astray, but clearly is not aggressive enough to commit murder, as her passive behavior in other respects suggests.

One of the difficulties in interpreting *Adam Bede* is that it is set during the fin-de-siècle shift away from agrarian ideology, yet its Victorianism is inescapable. Eliot urges readers to apply midcentury attitudes and standards to Hetty's character exemplified in Martineau's claim that infanticide thrives "in the rudest country districts, where the depressed rural class seem to be only half alive in body and mind, and susceptible of animal and devilish

---

diseases and character defects) through the milk to the upper-class infant. The infiltration of venereal diseases into the higher classes was initially blamed on the milk of wet nurses, whose very employment marked them as unrespectable. See also Matus, *Unstable Bodies,* 160–65.

40. Auerbach, *Woman and the Demon,* 174; Thompson, *Rise of Respectable Society,* 123–24.

propensities and notions accordingly." Similarly, an 1859 review of *Adam Bede* flatly states, "she bears a child and murders it. . . . Of course, everyone knows that every sin under heaven is committed freely in agricultural villages." Although modeled after Mary Voce, "a very ignorant girl who had murdered her child and refused to confess," a "common coarse girl, convicted of child-murder," Hetty exhibits a physical appeal and ideological naïveté that undercut Eliot's attempts to establish her criminality or her sexual profligacy. Neither Hayslope nor Hetty fits the rural stereotype, which is why the infanticide episode is disturbing but also unconvincing.[41]

Adrienne Rich observes that infanticide "has always been a form of population control in preliterate societies" and links the subsequent Christian emphasis on paternal legitimacy with the shifting of criminal responsibility for infanticide onto women. Rich's point is aptly illustrated in Martineau's 1845 *Dawn Island,* a tale about a primitive South Seas island culture in which firstborn children were routinely "sacrificed" to appease the gods. Again highlighting the nature/culture conflicts endemic to imperialism, the solution to systematic infanticide resides in the "civilizing" qualities of capitalism: "these children of nature were clearly destined to . . . becom[e] men and Christians by my bringing Commerce to their shores."[42] But how can infanticide be accounted for when it is not displaced onto preliterate or premodern cultures but thrives in mid-Victorian Britain, the bastion of maternal, Christian, and capitalist ideologies?

"Infanticide the Sin of the Age," published anonymously in 1862, attempts to answer this question by applying Darwinian theories to the problem of unwanted children. Insofar as Victorian society consists of individuals who equate concealment of illicit behaviors with self-preservation, the "first law of nature," the "universal prevalence of infanticide" in an age of limited options is precisely a matter of survival. But the writer's laudable nod

41. Martineau, *London Daily News,* September 8, 1865 (see also articles of February 13, September 30, 1863, August 8, October 19, 1865); review of *Adam Bede,* quoted in Carroll, *George Eliot,* 75; Eliot, *Journal* (November 30, 1858), in J. W. Cross, ed. *George Eliot's Life as Related in Her Letters and Journals;* letter to Sarah Hennell (October 7, 1859), in Gordon S. Haight, ed., *Selections from George Eliot's Letters.* See also Perkin, *Reception-History,* 50. Compare such antirural bias with Englestein's analysis, which reflects the claim that urban centers promote vice while rural areas maintain more conservative moral standards ("Morality and the Wooden Spoon").

42. Rich, *Of Woman Born,* 259 (see also chapter 10, "Violence and the Heart of Maternal Darkness"). Rich's discussion of the "psychopathologizing" of infanticidal and nonmaternal women is especially pertinent (263). Harriet Martineau, *Dawn Island: A Tale,* 94.

toward scientific remedies for immorality collapses under the assumption that "debased" and "depraved" women among the industrial poor were capable of committing a crime no respectable woman would consider. The author demands, "do married women murder their offspring? Certainly not. . . . *To the influence of the sin of unchastity*" is owed the full burden of a practice such as infanticide.[43]

But, as Thompson, Matus, and Martineau observe, subsequent exposés of baby farms and related scandals reveal even respectable women were not averse to terminating an infant's life at birth and passing it off as a stillbirth, a tragic and perverse way of managing their sexuality and reproduction, yet often the only one available to them. Such behaviors as unchastity, abandonment, and infanticide are not bound by marital status, class, gender, or economics, yet the stereotype that poses low-class deviance and its resulting illegitimacy against middle-class respectability and legitimacy persists nevertheless.

If the preservation of dominant-class ideology is in fact the fundamental issue underlying fallen-woman discourse, then the period's obsession with sexual management becomes less a moral issue than an economic one. The possibility prompts some disturbing questions: Does the courts' reluctance to convict for infanticide reflect relief at the elimination of superfluous "offspring of sin"? As Susan Amussen points out, is not the parish thus relieved of the expense of another mouth to feed, the foundling hospital of another child to raise? Such ideas anticipate eugenicists' promotion of birth control for the lower classes around 1900 and, later, "involuntary sterilization" of minority races.[44] The fact that Hetty is saved from the gallows and the court's decision overturned by merely a word from Squire Arthur Donnithorne suggests the plausibility that "race suicide" in some instances was highly desirable. "The Victorians could grapple with the problem of crime," notes Ann Higginbotham. "Solving all the problems of illegitimacy, however, would have required rethinking fundamental assumptions about parental

43. "Infanticide," in *The Magdalen's Friend*, 289–91.

44. Of related interest is Thompson's discussion of responses to early attempts to disseminate birth-control information to low-class mill workers in the 1820s and 1830s: "The sense of moral outrage shown by the doctors, and shared by the clergy and much of the middle-class, is of more significance than any practical effect of the birth-control propaganda" (*Rise of Respectable Society,* 76). Many working-class people also resisted this "Malthusian-capitalist ploy designed to attribute all the social evils of poverty and destitution to overpopulation" in these classes, thus diverting attention from government programs for economic improvement (77). The issue is fraught with ambivalence on both sides and on all social levels.

responsibilities, the role of the state, and the allocation of resources." Further, many like Martineau believed aiding unwed mothers "encourages vice. In the end, infant deaths were easier to tolerate than easy virtue."[45]

The "Infanticide" article concludes on a punitive note by complaining that women charged with infanticide are rarely prosecuted because they inspire a "strong and abounding sympathy" in the courts.[46] But despite the rarity of women's conviction for infanticide, no "strong and abounding" sympathy is accorded Hetty Sorrel either by the court or by public opinion, much less by her family, friends, and community. Although Eliot purports to explain this by displacing it on "those stern times" (481) sixty years' previous, the bizarre 1868 case of Hester Vaughan demonstrates that even nine years after the publication of *Adam Bede,* suspected infanticide had the power to generate the lynch mentality. Raped, pregnant, and abandoned, Englishwoman Hester Vaughan emigrated to the United States where she gave birth under brutal circumstances. The infant died, and, when Hester was condemned to death for its murder, American feminists campaigned on her behalf until the charges were dropped. The cases of Hetty Sorrel and Hester Vaughan illustrate exceptions to the period's legal precedents exacerbated by the outcast cultural status they share.

The legal system's power to prosecute women for infanticide regardless of the circumstances surrounding conception and confinement emphasizes the powerlessness of unwed mothers, and suggests the degree to which *orphaned* and *immigrant* unwed mothers in particular were, to paraphrase Martineau, politically invisible and legally nonexistent yet no less subject to prosecution. Reform's Bastardy Clauses, a devastating piece of Victorian legislation, in effect protected "a vile aristocracy, who seduce and ruin more young girls than all the other male population put together."[47] Accordingly,

45. Higginbotham, " 'Sin of the Age,' " 281.
46. "Infanticide," in *The Magdalen's Friend,* 296.
47. Walkowitz, *Prostitution,* 35. A sampling of mother/child legal debates of the time reveals that the primary focus was on the custody and support issues of married women, not unwed mothers. Barbara Leigh Smith Bodichon notes that an unwed mother can claim support from the child's father (until the child is thirteen), providing she can legally prove paternity (at the time virtually impossible, particularly when class issues were involved; few women could afford to hire a lawyer, and the medical technology did not yet exist for scientific proof), while in contrast she was required by law to support her children until they reached age sixteen (*A Brief Summary of the Most Important Laws Concerning Women,* 30). In effect, women were not legally represented at all, although they were directly affected by laws enacted to protect the interests of fathers, husbands, and upper-class males. In Gorham's words, Victorian legislation was

by the conclusion of *Adam Bede*, "that poor young man" Arthur has resumed his place at the head of the community and the perpetual wanderer Hetty Sorrel is dead.

The character of Hetty Sorrel, notes Dorothea Barrett, "became a kind of Frankenstein's monster" for its creator: "Created for a specific and limited purpose, Hetty breaks her confines and threatens to take over the novel. The narrator's lack of sympathy for Hetty defeats its apparent purpose: it wins readers to Hetty perhaps more than a gentler treatment would have done." Alternatively, perhaps Eliot's "apparent purpose" *was* to ensure readers' sympathy for Hetty, but through a means even more radical than the "maternal redemption" employed by other writers: the explicit rejection of maternal ideology. Whether Eliot's primary interest was her title character, Adam, or Lewes's favorite, Dinah, or her desire to reproduce the "gentle thoughts and happy remembrances" of a more tranquil age, continued critical fascination with Hetty Sorrel demonstrates that *Adam Bede* is Hetty's story, her victimization, and her unvindicated mythology. Part of this text's ambivalence stems from the fact that, no less than the Poysers and the Hayslope community, Eliot is guilty of the narrative neglect, abandonment, and metaphorical infanticide of her literary "child." Like Aunt Poyser, Eliot admires Hetty's appeal surreptitiously, only to "turn away" to the ultimate rejection of narrative death; yet, she also invites readers' sympathy for Hetty's victimization. Eliot's ambivalence toward Hetty might be cast as a class issue: "The primary site of contradiction . . . is undoubtedly the low . . . [which is] both reviled and desired." Consequently, the "*political* imperative to reject and eliminate the debasing 'low' conflicts powerfully and unpredictably with a desire for this Other."[48] Like Mary Shelley's "hideous progeny," Hetty is the central force in this novel precisely because she is so vehemently rejected, outcast, and misunderstood. Both Hetty and Frankenstein's creature are individuals posed against the community as threats to its cohesiveness; yet, they are also revealed as psychological entities, and it is this quality that leads us to align sympathetically with the outcast against the community.

A Victorian review of *Adam Bede* captures this quality of innocent transgression punished by an indifferent society far in excess of the crime.

"designed to protect a guardian's right to control a girl's sexuality, rather than to prevent harm to the girl" (" 'Maiden Tribute,' " 363).

48. Barrett, *Vocation and Desire,* 43; Eliot, letter to John Blackwood, February 24, 1859; Stallybrass and White, *Politics and Poetics,* 4–5 (see also 191–93).

According to the reviewer, we are conditioned to accept the "passions and calamities" challenging "a nature lofty enough to cope," but we are not prepared for "a helpless, frivolous, childish creature, inadequate even to understand, much less to contend with, those gigantic shadows, confronted all at once by despair, crime, remorse, and destruction—things with which her soft childlike foolishness and baby character had nothing to do."[49] The setting in motion of such a "grim machinery" leaves us "trembling and appalled" rather than inspired by the "nobler sentiments" of a truly heroic struggle. Such cosmic arbitrariness perhaps resonates in the vast majority of us who, like Hetty, are not of heroic stature. In this sense, Hetty Sorrel, rather than a narratively flawed literary creation, is perhaps the most representative fallen woman in English literature. Ultimately neither a scapegoat nor a martyr, she symbolizes issues with which we all must contend, issues greater than the individual, issues beyond social constructs, issues fundamental to the "general human condition."

49. Review of *Adam Bede*, quoted in John Holmstrom and Laurence Lerner, *George Eliot and Her Readers: A Selection of Contemporary Reviews*, 22–23.

5

Sobriety and Propriety

"HER ONE BESETTING SIN, INTEMPERANCE"

Speaking generally, . . . the causation of insanity . . . is an affair
of three W's—worry, want, and wickedness. Its cure is a matter
of the three M's—method, meat, and morality.
　　—Dr. J. Mortimer Granville, *The Care and Cure of the Insane*

There is a phase of insanity which may be called moral madness,
in which all that is good or even human seems to disappear from
the mind and a fiend-like nature replaces it.
　　　　　　　　　—Charlotte Brontë, letter of January 4, 1848

*A*LMOST WITHOUT EXCEPTION, the term *fallen women* evokes a post-
lapsarian idea of female sexual depravity. While it is true that many
nineteenth-century women, like their infamous foremother, sought knowledge, Victorian sexual falls rarely resulted from education: instead, economic need, sexual naïveté, and ignorance of the broader social consequences of inappropriate sexual unions supplied the most common reasons
for women's falls. Whatever the catalyst, such falls signified women's failure
to conform with a morality that imprisoned them in domestic servitude
as surely as in their pathologized reproductive biology. The women discussed in this chapter are not fallen through illicit sexual liaisons, yet they
were judged so by association. These literary examples of wife beating,
childlessness, female alcoholism, anorexia, nymphomania, and insanity
further complicate the ostensible seamlessness of Victorian sexual ideology.
Distinct from the characters discussed so far, each of these protagonists is

126

married, thus their relegation to the category of "fallen" indicates that legitimate monogamous marriage alone is insufficient to ensure respectability. As my consideration of infanticide demonstrates, the ideological pressure exerted by the madonna-harlot dichotomy (so effectively dramatized by Dinah Morris and Hetty Sorrel) intensified as maternal ideology increasingly supplanted the sexual act as the primary measure of women's social worth. The following discussion more fully articulates some relatively unexpected cultural manifestations of this shift in ideological emphasis.[1]

During midcentury, when Florence Nightingale spearheaded the movement to regulate the nursing profession, a primary criterion for assessing professional nurses concerned their "sobriety" and "propriety." Often, such women proved competent except for that "one besetting sin, intemperance . . . and what this always brings in its train," referring to the sexual promiscuity assumed to link nurses with prostitutes and army-camp followers. Commenting on Ruth Hilton's moral recuperation through nursing, a reviewer of Gaskell's novel reiterates the derogatory image Nightingale sought to change: "the world does not mind what sort of creatures nurses are; they have only to attend on the sick and dying. Character . . . does not matter here."[2] Women like Gaskell and Nightingale tackled a formidable stereotype by rejecting the nurse/prostitute link while promoting the associations between nursing and maternalism, itself a vexed alliance, yet one useful for helping to legitimate a now respected profession.

Yet, as my investigation of the status of women in other arenas reveals, such rhetorical focus on morality evades the always-present economic factor. As was true of prostitution, at least part of the period's resistance to legitimating the nursing profession stems from the economic threat posed by women participating in the marketplace. Whether women were remunerated for sex (prostitutes), healing (nurses), or for "white-slave" labor (factory and mine workers, domestics, seamstresses), their intrusion into the masculine realm of capitalism was cast in moral, and even religious,

---

1. Social-purity movements such as the Women's Christian Temperance Union aimed specifically at male alcoholism, arguing, "If men would stop spending their wages on drink and coming home to be useless fathers and husbands or worse, women would be better able to provide themselves and their children with good and healthful lives" (Virginia Sapiro, *Women in American Society*, 433). Alcoholism was assumed to affect women only indirectly; the literary examples discussed here indicate otherwise, relying instead on another association: that "intemperance and prostitution were indissolubly linked" (Barret-Ducrocq, *Love*, 13).

2. Françoise Basch, *Relative Creatures: Victorian Women in Society and the Novel*, 119; review of *Ruth*, in *Eliza Cook's Journal*.

terms. In the words of one social critic, nurses "must be an order, working for the love of God and man, not a class, working for their livelihood."[3] Thus is yet another employment option for women rendered unrespectable by the cash nexus.

Interestingly, nurse characters in Victorian women's literature sometimes promote the profession's links with alcohol though not with sexual impropriety. Mrs. Horsfall, Charlotte Brontë's caricature of a tipsy yet competent nurse in *Shirley*, seems little designed to evoke readers' sympathy for female alcoholism, much less for women professionals. Although elsewhere Brontë champions the causes of governesses (in *Jane Eyre*), teachers (in *Villette*), and bluestockings (in *Shirley*) whose gender alone excludes them from the world of productive work, she in some respects holds Mrs. Horsfall up for ridicule and scorn.

From her bestial name to her masculine habits—"she took her dram three times a-day, and her pipe of tobacco four times"—Mrs. Horsfall is formidable.[4] She eclipses even the town harpies: "she was no woman, but a dragon. Hortense Moore fell effaced before her; Mrs. Yorke withdrew—crushed: yet both these women were personages of some dignity in their own estimation, and of some bulk in the estimation of others. Perfectly cowed by the breadth, the height, the bone, and the brawn of Mrs. Horsfall, they retreated to the back-parlour" (526). Mrs. Horsfall nurses the wounded Robert Moore, whose invectives against spinsters and unattractive women are consistent with his cavalier attitude toward Shirley and Caroline. Most appropriately, Robert falls to the mercy of Mrs. Horsfall, "a sort of giantess his keeper" who "taught him docility in a trice." The brawny nurse tosses her manly patient about as if he were a child and cuffs him when he is "bad." Moore complains, "that woman" is a "dram-drinker," to which the doctor responds, "they are all so. . . . But Horsfall has one virtue . . . drunk or sober, she always remembers to obey *me*" (527). In the medical profession, as in other realms, women's submission to male authority outweighs even their adapting masculine behaviors like drinking. Arguably, the fact that alcohol was regarded as medicine for the sick and believed to "fortify" otherwise healthy people as well may account for the propensity of nurses to develop a drinking habit. Whether the stereotype extends to male physicians is well worth exploring.

3. "Hospital Nurses as They Are and as They Ought to Be."
4. Brontë, *Shirley*, 526. Future quotations will be cited parenthetically in the text.

Victorian ideologists might further argue that, removed from the do-mestic sphere so central to engendering and preserving feminine delicacy, women like Horsfall become masculinized, they are "unwomaned" through their contact with base biological functions. Yet, this does not neces-sarily signify sexual impropriety. Brontë's characterization avoids linking Mrs. Horsfall with the sexual deviation associated with the nurse/prostitute/ camp-follower stereotype; as a result, Mrs. Horsfall's "propriety" is in effect no more questionable than that of *Shirley*'s other women characters. Aptly illustrating this project's broader claims about the period's generic concept of fallenness is Mary Poovey's observation that all nurses were lumped together "into a homogeneous mass, distinguished only by its varieties of failings."[5] As the remainder of this discussion will show, other literary examples of women, their addictions, and the falls associated with them prove far less amusing than the parodic Nurse Horsfall because far more representative of a damaging sexual ideology.

Along with middle-class assumptions that working-class women were by definition promiscuous persisted the idea that promiscuity led to prostitu-tion and alcoholism, a progression many believed stemmed from sensuous self-indulgence. As I've shown, Elizabeth Gaskell scrutinizes this stereotype through the character of Esther in *Mary Barton*, whose promiscuity and drinking are not prompted by sensuality but by poverty, grief, and despair. Esther details the events of her fall, from her ill-fated affair with a soldier ("He promised me marriage") to his abandonment of Esther and their child; from the child's illness to Esther's "casual" prostitution in order to buy medicine; and from the child's death to Esther's complete demoralization as an alcoholic trading sex for gin. According to the stereotype, the down-ward progression to prostitution Acton predicts will result from unwed motherhood often culminates in alcoholism: "these miserable women," argues W. R. Greg, "ply their wretched trade with a loathing and abhorrence which only perpetual semi-intoxication can deaden. . . . gin alone enables them to act." Greg's implication that the degradation of their "trade"—not sensuality—is what leads prostitutes to drink is an idea Gaskell employs

---

5. Poovey, *Uneven Developments,* 174. In terms of her participation in the professional (rather than domestic) realm, Horsfall's age in a sense removes her from ideological expectations. Although women were measured against an angelicized ideal from the cradle to the grave, there was a point at which they could legitimately (if grudgingly) be excused from the domestic sphere. Redundancy promised some liberation to women hardy enough to resist intense social pressure.

to vindicate Esther. She further courts readers' sympathy for Esther by characterizing her as sensitive to the deleterious effects of her habit on the respectable Wilson household: "I could not lead a virtuous life. . . . I should only disgrace you. . . . I must have drink. Such as live like me could not bear life if they did not drink. It's the only thing to keep us from suicide. If we did not drink, we could not stand the memory of what we have been, and the thought of what we are, for a day. If I go without food, and without shelter, I must have my dram."[6]

But despite her presentation of extenuating circumstances, Gaskell in part allows the drunken-prostitute stereotype to prevail by not explaining a fact of which she was clearly aware: for many people like Esther (John Barton, for instance, who prefers opium to "meal"), not only was gin far cheaper and more readily available than bread, but it also numbed one's hunger pangs better and longer. Thus, alcoholism, like prostitution, among the poor and working classes was generally more a matter of economics than of sensuous self-indulgence or inherent moral depravity. According to Brian Harrison, "The hordes of prostitutes and drunkards in Victorian England were not psychological aberrations but the products of a particular socio-economic structure," a claim Martineau illustrates in "Sowers not Reapers." But Harrison also extends this reasoning to the privileged classes, whose excesses are signified by the fact that gout rests were standard furniture in "respectable" homes or establishments.[7] Harrison's comments highlight a primary contradiction in Victorian social ideology: sensual self-indulgence, in terms of fashionable clothing and illicit sexuality no less than of addictive habits, signifies moral depravity in the lower classes while being a privilege and right of the upper classes.

But what about women who, although poor and working class, fulfilled their roles as wife and mother to the point of self-annihilation? Women who manifested the domestic ideal, whose every waking moment was a self-negation, women who were all this and also alcoholic? A case in point is Mrs. Kay in Harriet Martineau's 1843 "Sowers not Reapers," a story that details the sufferings of the poor who are exploited for their labor, adversely affected by such arbitrary legislation as the Corn Laws, and economically devastated by natural disasters like drought and poor harvests. Social writer

6. Greg, "Prostitution," 452; Gaskell, *Mary Barton,* 213.
7. Harrison, *Drink and the Victorians,* 355, 41. Gout is an illness resulting from excessive consumption of alcohol and rich foods. See also Thompson, *Rise of Respectable Society,* 319–20.

Henry Mayhew's account of working-class women's alcoholism serves to perpetuate, rather than disprove, the stereotype Martineau aims to subvert: "Thousands of our felons are trained from their infancy in the bosom of crime. . . . Many of them are often carried to the beershop or gin-palace on the breast of worthless, drunken mothers." A literary portrayal of a "respectable" working-class woman alcoholic is rare indeed, and Martineau's distinctly sympathetic presentation of Mrs. Kay is at least as daring and radical as Gaskell's portrayal of Esther's inherent integrity.[8]

Mrs. Kay's dedication to her family is paradigmatic; after working all day at her domestic chores, she wanders through the drought-stricken fields at night with her sister, Mary, looking for water while her children sleep. She is worried and nervous, often "nearly unable to walk."[9] Worn out with watching, "Fear and fatigue had overpowered her, and she could only lean, faint and sobbing, against the rail" (15). Her fragility could be explained as nervous exhaustion or, more vaguely, "female delicacy"; the possibility of alcoholism, presented only later in the book, seems quite out of character with Mrs. Kay's impeccable performance of her feminine role.

Neighbors notice she is often "poorly" and "droops sadly" (20) and, despite the faminelike conditions, has little appetite. Family members, who stand to benefit from Mrs. Kay's uneaten portion, seem only mildly curious about her mode of sustenance. Mr. Kay claims her flurried behavior and tendency to be withdrawn result from inadequate sleep, thus deflecting attention away from what turns out to be a fatal condition. A later episode dramatizes the (probably well-intentioned) complicity of family and neighbors alike. When Mary Kay and Chatham witness Mrs. Kay leaving a gin shop, their response to the sight proves it is a common one: Mary will pretend not to have seen her, while Chatham's "She shall have mercy from me;—more perhaps than from those who are answerable for her falling and

---

8. The Corn Laws were a series of protective tariffs designed to stabilize Britain's agrarian economy, which was undermined by the importation of lower-priced foreign grain. As a result, people had to rely solely on English grain, which benefited the farmers but forced the poor classes to choose between food prices they could not afford or starvation. The Corn Laws were rescinded in 1846. Mayhew, *London Labour,* quoted in Armstrong, *Desire and Domestic Fiction,* 182. Stephen Blackpool's drunken (though childless) wife in Dickens's *Hard Times* conforms with this stereotype. In these instances, both Dickens and Mayhew elide the economic aspects of alcoholism, relying instead on the depraved values "endemic" to the working classes. See also Harrison, *Drink and the Victorians;* and Hellerstein, Hume, and Offen, *Victorian Women,* 235–36.

9. Martineau, "Sowers not Reapers," 13. Future quotations will be cited parenthetically in the text.

sinking as she does, poor soul!" (52) prepares us to accept that Mrs. Kay's dilemma is rooted in something other than character weakness. Subsequent events reveal that "those who are answerable" applies less to family and community than to broader social structures. Most significant in terms of my discussion is that here is one example of fallenness that refuses to participate in blaming the victim.

According to Brian Harrison, several factors contributed to the prevalence of alcoholism during the nineteenth century, a primary one being, simply, thirst: in both town and country, "drinking water was unsafe and scarce, and . . . it was natural . . . to rely increasingly on intoxicants." Hospitals gave patients alcoholic drinks rather than tainted water, and throughout the century many people believed "water should not be drunk until purified with spirits." Physicians prescribed alcohol as a pain killer and anesthetic, to soothe crying babies (the origin of Mrs. Kay's habit), and to "fortify" childbearing and lactating women. Alcohol was believed to protect one against everything from polluted air to rancid food. "For doctors," notes Harrison, "alcohol was a godsend, in that it actually created several of the diseases it was supposed to cure. . . . many patients . . . had difficulty in abandoning in health the alcohol which their doctors indiscriminately prescribed for them during sickness." Socially, drinking houses and gin shops offered a cheap and effective palliative for the deprivations of working-class homes that often lacked food, light, and heat: "To denounce the drunkenness of the nineteenth-century slum-dweller surrounded by warm and cheerful drinkshops and by a culture which justified their use [is] unreasonable . . . the environment acted as a constant incentive to the behavior under condemnation."[10] The social circumstances Harrison outlines suggest that Mrs. Kay's alcoholism is hardly anomalous.

But although Martineau typically dramatizes the reverberating effects of political economy on individual lives, she does not trivialize Mrs. Kay's condition as merely an extenuating circumstance of an arbitrary economic system. Instead, she exposes the long-range effects of culturally sanctioned "medical" practices resulting in alcoholism and even death. As the strain of her double life takes its toll, the formerly mild-mannered Mrs. Kay quarrels with her neighbors, her hands shake uncontrollably, she grows increasingly temporally confused, and she often weeps for hours. Mary's urging Mrs. Kay to take her medicine "from the dispensary" (121) in order to regain her health is weighted with irony. The subsequent confrontation between Kay

10. Harrison, *Drink and the Victorians*, 37, 41, 355.

and his wife concerning her "problem" reveals how insidious this seemingly innocuous medical practice proved to be.

Kay, like Chatham, regards his wife's drinking as a logical result of the hard life his family is forced to lead, and blames himself for economic inadequacies and for his insensitivity toward her. She allows this is true (his lack of emotional engagement with her, even during this crucial scene, is disturbing), but admits that the problem runs far deeper than contemporary economics: "O, it began long and long ago. When I was weakly as a girl, they used to give me things, and that was the beginning of it all. Then when I grew weakly again, it seemed to come most natural, especially because it was cheaper than bread, and the children wanted that" (124). Mrs. Kay presents a compelling enigma: here is a woman alcoholic, made so not by a failure of will, sensuous self-indulgence, or sexual deviation, but because the habit innocently instilled in childhood by her parents provides a solution to economic dearth in adulthood. Mrs. Kay finds herself unable to effect any positive change in her family's desperate situation—with one exception. She empowers herself, in a most perverse and self-destructive way, by refusing to eat and by fortifying herself with gin. Tragically, this occasional solution to short food supplies becomes a habit that renders her incapable of ingesting any food at all. Although not typically associated with alcoholism, anorexia's effects are similar in that the prolonged refusal to eat becomes addictive, resulting in the inability to eat. Thus, in Mrs. Kay's case, not eating is as deeply ingrained a habit as the gin. As her only source of "nourishment," gin leeches her body of nutrients until she literally starves to death. By the time Kay confronts her, it is far too late to alter the process.

Given the length of Mrs. Kay's addiction, Kay's confrontation is oddly delayed: "So, often when you have pretended to have no appetite, it was for the children's sake and mine. Well, I half thought so all the time" (125). The narrative does not clarify why her debilitation continued unchecked and unchallenged until it became irreversible. Everyone seemed to agree tacitly to acknowledge her downward progress euphemistically to each other but never to her. When Kay encourages her to give up her habit (otherwise, he threatens to tell their children the truth about her alcoholism), she agrees to his terms; but her admission that she would gladly die and free them all from her burdensome presence proves to be more prophetic and realistic than Kay's cheerful bravado.[11] Whereas Esther regards drinking as suicide

11. Charlotte Davis Kasl notes, "Women suffering great emotional pain think of dying as a welcome relief from struggling through one more day. Fantasies of suicide become

prevention and thus the lesser of two evils, Mrs. Kay knows alcohol causes a slower death, but death all the same.

Significantly, Kay seems less interested in his wife's well-being than in protecting the morals of their children. But Mrs. Kay has already proved her maternal devotion by refusing passively to witness her children starve, and by making the ultimate sacrifice of her own life. She gives them her share of food, while Kay does not. But an even further mark of her integrity is the fact that, although alcohol is part of her own childhood experience, easily available, affordable, and socially condoned, she does not expose her children to a habit that may enslave them, even, or especially, to assuage their persistent hunger. In other words, she takes the cheap gin so they may have the "dear" bread, and believes her life worth the sacrifice; judging by her husband's attitude, she does just what her culture expects of her. As a result, Mrs. Kay's sufferings and subsequent death symbolize the feminine ideal taken to its logical extreme: self-annihilation.

Kay's apology to his wife for his past behavior reveals he contributed to her fall in ways other than economic dearth and insensitivity. He promises, "no more thoughts of cruel joking, or of Mrs. Skipper" (126), referring to his flirtation with a neighbor who is, by cruel irony, the town's bread-baker. Comparing Mrs. Kay with Mrs. Skipper reveals the former's inability to feed her family sufficiently, even by starving herself, and the latter's capacity to feed Mrs. Kay's children *and* her husband. This is not to suggest illicit conduct between Mr. Kay and Mrs. Skipper, but rather to invite consideration of the effect of this woman's buxom, bouncing healthiness, aptly symbolized by the nourishing loaves she bakes, on the listless, unsexed Mrs. Kay. Witnessed silently through the lens of starvation and alcohol, the banter between her husband and her neighbor is a "cruel joke" indeed.

Kay keeps his promise to his wife, as she does to him, although she achieves sobriety only to die. Her last words warning against the consequences of wives living too long in abject poverty sharpen Martineau's focus on economics and maternalism and their links with female alcoholism, family breakdown, and capitalist exploitation. "Sowers not Reapers" concludes with Kay singing his dead wife's praises to their children and with Martineau questioning agricultural and economic systems that engender

---

a central part of addiction for many women, for knowing that one can commit suicide brings a feeling of control" (*Women, Sex, and Addiction,* 205). The idea of control is central to anorexia as well.

such tragedies among hardworking, "decent" people. This "tale for the people" conveys its political protest through the potent medium of maternal ideology, which by definition cuts across class lines. As the following considerations reveal, the juxtaposition of motherhood with the fallen habit of drinking and the silent rebellion of anorexia raises much broader issues than Martineau's localized context suggests.

Women's participation in the industrial workplace posed a child-care problem that challenged gender and class hierarchies—configured by some, inevitably, as a moral issue. A common practice among factory and other working-class women was the dosing of babies with alcohol or laudanum (a tincture of opium in alcohol). Case studies collected by the 1843 Children's Employment Commission describe factory workers who, in order to work uninterrupted, gave their infants "Godfrey's" or "Anodyne" cordial (a special strength of laudanum for children) to make them sleep. Other testimony revealed that working mothers routinely accustomed their infants to alcohol or laudanum "at the breast," not because the child was ill, "but to compose it to rest, to sleep it." As a result, such infants typically slept six to eight hours at a stretch, became thin with enlarged heads and joints, and were listless and "vacant" during the approximately four years of steady dosage. Once the laudanum was discontinued, and "if they get over the seasoning" or survive withdrawal, they "generally begin to come around" just in time to begin working in the factories and mines themselves.[12]

Demonstrating yet again the period's ambiguous attitudes toward working-class infant deaths, chemists (that is, druggists) testified that a child's "accidental" death from overdose and malnutrition was rarely investigated: "many infants die by degrees, and . . . no inquest or other inquiry is made."[13] Given the prevalence of such practices at this time, it seems reasonable to conclude that, having been routinely dosed as a child for "weakliness"—an umbrella term covering such typically inconvenient childhood behaviors as whining, crying, weaning, and teething—Mrs. Kay's adult alcoholism was inevitable.

The malnutrition resulting from poor-quality food and from appetite-suppressing addictive substances leads to the more modern concept of anorexia. During the Victorian period, anorexia was associated with mental or "nervous" illnesses initiated by such "moral causes" as psychological stress and poverty. According to one Victorian doctor, "the unceasing,

12. Hellerstein, Hume, and Offen, *Victorian Women,* 236.
13. Ibid., 237.

and . . . the hopeless struggles of the poorer and middle classes for a bare existence necessarily predispose the brain to a diseased action." Mrs. Kay starves out of economic necessity, becoming "weak, sexless, . . . voiceless [and] unwomaned." Contrasting with the period's "diseased brain" diagnosis, Susie Orbach proposes that such eating disorders begin "as sane and mentally healthy responses to an insane social reality": in Mrs. Kay's case, the tragic lack of nourishing food in the foremost industrialized nation in the nineteenth-century world.[14] That anorexic women "can feel good about themselves only in a state of permanent semistarvation" emphasizes Mrs. Kay's dangerous acquiescence to the motherhood mystique. For what is the twentieth-century's "beauty myth" if not an avatar of the Victorians' self-abnegating domestic ideal?[15]

Martineau demonstrates that alcoholism and eating disorders are not "moral" diseases: they afflict respectable working-class women, women who are mothers, women who literally would rather die or, worse, become "fallen" through alcohol, than shirk their maternal duty. Martineau's complicating Mrs. Kay's alcoholism with an eating disorder reflects her prophetically acute understanding of what we now know is almost exclusively a women's disease. Whether the result of Victorian poverty and malnutrition or of an obsession with emaciated thinness amid the plenty of modern industrialized nations, anorexia bears eloquent testimony to the institutionalized regulation of women's sexuality and the silent rebellion of eating disorders that links both centuries ideologically.[16]

14. Quoted in Showalter, *Female Malady,* 29; Naomi Wolf, *The Beauty Myth: How Images of Beauty Are Used against Women,* 197; Susie Orbach, quoted in Wolf, *Beauty Myth,* 198.

15. One of the more striking examples of the women/poverty/neurasthenia nexus concerns "lactational insanity," the "delirium of poor mothers who nursed their babies for long periods in order to save money and to prevent conception; it was caused by malnutrition and anemia" (Showalter, *Female Malady,* 54). The grotesque image of maternity presented by "lactational insanity" and by laudanum-addicted infants reduces the working-class breast to a medium of death rather than sustenance. Lactational insanity also resulted from wet-nursing for wealthier women, a way of earning money at the expense of one's health and, often, that of one's own children.

16. Later in the century, imprisoned suffragist who refused to eat were force-fed, ostensibly "for their own good" but in fact to silence the powerful political messages conveyed by their behavior. Similarly, the "rest cure" denied psychologically distressed women (like Virginia Woolf) physical activity while forcing them to eat copious amounts of food. Such "cures" resulted in a weight gain of as much as thirty to fifty pounds before women were pronounced submissive enough to be released. Modern research reveals that many eating-disorder patients are victims of sexual abuse (rape, incest). As a response to such violation, the starving body loses not only its sexual appeal,

The sexual components of anorexia presented Victorian ideologues with intriguing dilemmas concerning female psychology and biology. Side effects include loss of interest in sexuality, cessation of menses and thus infertility, and emaciation (reverting to a preadolescent flattening of the exaggerated breasts and hips of the hourglass figure admired by Victorians): the power of female biology was prodigious indeed if women could revert from adulthood to girlhood at will. Accordingly, sexual precocity was believed manageable by deliberately delaying menstruation in girls as long as possible. Accepted methods included sexual segregation to eliminate "temptation"; cold showers and avoidance of feather beds, compelling the young to redirect their energies from "self-abuse" to coping with discomfort; avoidance of novels—widely believed to convey indecorous ideas to otherwise innocent minds—and animal flesh (traditionally associated with male sexual virility, some regarded meat as an inappropriate food for women); and wearing drawers. There were two schools of thought concerning underwear: proponents claimed more coverage promoted greater modesty, while opponents argued that drawers' close proximity to females' sex organs served to keep girls in a constant state of arousal. Lowood, the all-girl boarding school in Brontë's *Jane Eyre,* is an example of the concerted effort to keep young girls sexless through malnutrition and physical discomfort. According to one authority, delayed menarche was "the principal cause of the pre-eminence of English women, in vigour of constitution, soundness of judgement, and . . . rectitude of moral principle."[17] Clearly, the power of female reproductive biology was such that the nation's very morality, no less than its status in world politics, depended on its management, as the extremism of the madonna-harlot polarization demonstrates.

The protagonist in "Janet's Repentance," one of George Eliot's *Scenes of Clerical Life,* which was published in 1858, departs distinctly from the example of Mrs. Kay. Janet Dempster is not poor or working class (as a

---

but also sexual function, leaving the victim unsexed and therefore safe (theoretically) from the threat of further violation.

17. Dr. E. Tilt, quoted in Showalter, *Female Malady,* 75. Carol J. Adams discusses the "intersection of feminist and vegetarian insights," arguing that there is an ideological link between the sexualization of the female body and animal flesh and blood; both are similarly appropriated by patriarchal societies for mass consumption (*The Sexual Politics of Meat: A Feminist-Vegetarian Critical Theory,* 4). See also chapter 5, "The Management of Female Puberty," in Deborah Gorham, *The Victorian Girl and the Feminine Ideal* (Bloomington: Indiana University Press, 1982), and Matus's discussion of nature and culture, which foregrounds some of the imperialist considerations against which English women's "pre-eminence" was measured (*Unstable Bodies,* 36–40).

milliner, her mother was poor but genteel, a situation improved by Janet's marrying out of her class), nor was she habituated to alcohol as a child. Janet's marriage to the prosperous, middle-class Lawyer Dempster seemed to promise all a Victorian woman could ask, all, that is, as Eliot repeatedly reminds us, except children. Janet's comparison with Mrs. Kay, with the crucial added component of her childlessness, provides a contrasting perspective on female alcoholism unmitigated by maternalism, poverty, or wandering husbands that Martineau thought necessary to a credibly sympathetic presentation of a "respectable" female alcoholic.

Janet is unusual among Victorian literary heroines in that her mother is not only still alive but also her strongest (albeit ineffectual) ally. Janet is loved and admired by her neighbors, who question her wifely loyalty to a brutal, loutish tyrant with a prodigious capacity to drink. But Eliot's focus is on Janet's "fall" and redemption, not on Dempster's alcoholism or abuse. An important link between Janet Dempster and the "vain notions" of other fallen women concerns her aura of dignity, a pridefulness that detractors interpret as a lack of humility. It is this quality that initially leads Janet to internalize the abusiveness of her marriage, even to the point of developing an alcohol habit of her own rather than admitting to the brutality of her husband; as a result, with increasing frequency, "she wasn't fit to be out."[18] Her uncompromising dignity enrages Dempster, who is infuriated by her refusal to break under his violence: "she was not to be made meek by cruelty" (335). Janet's behavior in this regard functions as a grotesque realization of the "suffer and be still" standard; but it is ultimately her idiosyncratic self-respect and capacity for endurance that enable her to survive when faced with the choice between life and death. While many Victorians regarded dignity and pride as interchangeable with vanity, Eliot's narrative recasts the stereotype by crediting Janet's subsequent recovery to this same self-valuing quality.

The extent to which the Dempster marriage parodies the nuclear-family modality is evidenced by their time spent together. A bearable night for Janet is one in which Dempster is so drunk he passes out; an increasingly rare morning is one in which he is not hungover at the breakfast table. But a more typical scene is Dempster lurching through the door, raging and cursing, looking for the one person over whom he legally exerts physical power: "Cruelty, like every other vice, requires no motive outside itself—

18. Eliot, "Janet's Repentance," 273. Future quotations will be cited parenthetically in the text.

it only requires opportunity. . . . And an unloving, tyrannous, brutal man needs no motive to prompt his cruelty; he needs only the perpetual presence of a woman he can call his own" (334–35).[19] The relationship between Janet and Dempster dramatizes Brian Harrison's observation that "drunken husbands were often stung by the wife's silent or open reproach into the wife-beating for which Englishmen were notorious abroad."[20] In one scene, Janet—fortified by wine in anticipation of Dempster's mood—regards him expressionlessly as he begins the beating that has become a routine occurrence: "Her wide open black eyes had a strangely fixed, sightless gaze, as she . . . stood silent before her husband" (284). Janet's failure to respond or otherwise defend herself offers chilling commentary on the degree of her degradation, and indicates that her drinking habits have become as routine as Dempster's beatings.

To a degree, Eliot raises the issue of wife abuse only to perpetuate its silencing. Her focus on maternity and religion, represented by the combined forces of Janet's mother, Mrs. Raynor, and the Reverend Mr. Tryan, infantilizes Janet, caught as she is by ideologies that demand her wifely loyalty and silent obedience. This complicates readers' engagement with the legally sanctioned threat to her life this marriage in fact is, and raises these questions: To whom is Eliot appealing in this narrative? What exactly is she critiquing? And what is she promoting?

Two major turning points lead to Janet's "repentance." The first, her meeting Mr. Tryan, produces a confusing mix of comfort and anxiety: "There is a power in the direct glance of a sincere and loving human soul, which will do more to dissipate prejudice and kindle charity than the most elaborate arguments" (331). The threat Tryan poses is that of change at a time when she is already "afraid of arriving at a still more complete contraction of her former ideas" (332). Janet's life, however painful, at least has the comfort of familiarity, and she remains in her dull round of nights

---

19. Eliot's point is variously illustrated. Sally Mitchell notes that women of all classes were property, whether of a father or a husband; upon marriage, the husband assumed all her property and earnings. He could "lock her up . . . beat her at will" with impunity since legally she had no separate existence (*The Fallen Angel: Chastity, Class, and Women's Reading, 1835–1880*, xi); Bertha Mason Rochester, whose powerlessness as a wife is tripled by her madness and her foreignness, presents another disturbing example. Mitchell further notes that rape was "impossible within marriage," an issue Jane Campion addresses in *The Piano*, while a woman who attempted to control her own body (like Evadne Frayling in Sarah Grand's *The Heavenly Twins*) "interfered with the property rights" of both husband and father (xi).

20. Harrison, *Drink and the Victorians*, 46–47.

contending with Dempster, "impossible to brave without arming herself in leaden stupor" (333), and days that bring no respite to aching bruises and dulled senses.

Eliot contradictorily vindicates Janet of all responsibility for this failed marriage: "do not believe that it was anything either present or wanting in poor Janet that formed the motive of her husband's cruelty," only to remind us again that "Janet had no children" and "mighty is the force of motherhood! . . . If Janet had been a mother, she might have been saved from much sin" (334). Brian Harrison notes, "the under-employed middle-class housewife is more likely than fully employed members of society to become an alcoholic; frequent were the nineteenth-century tales of concealed intemperance above stairs." The problem of "nothing to do" was universal among middle-class women; but Eliot presents Janet's childlessness—itself a lack of meaningful employment—as a factor that outweighs spousal abuse in her alcoholic "fall." The implication that children would either compensate Janet for a brutal marriage or repair the damage between husband and wife is curious, considering that children would provide Dempster only further opportunity for abuse.[21] In the meantime, Janet's alcohol habit is increasingly apparent to her neighbors; she looked "more miserable than ever . . . she was scarcely ever seen . . . she had not seemed like herself lately"; she was "out of health," had headaches, and was often "so strange" (336). Like Mrs. Kay, Janet admits to thoughts of suicide, but "I can't kill myself; I've tried" (339). Her dignity is wearing thin, but her spirit is not yet quelled, as the following scene reveals.

Janet's second major turning point occurs during another of Dempster's drunken, abusive scenes. To this point, she has endured outwardly and rebelled only inwardly (by drinking and by turning to her mother). But the process so subtly begun by Tryan's earlier glance now propels Janet into a radical paradigm shift from which she emerges quite a different woman: "for the first time in her life her resentment overcame the long-cherished pride that made her hide her grief from the world. There are moments when by some strange impulse we contradict our past selves—fatal moments, when a fit of passion . . . lays low the work of half our lives" (340). The "work" refers to Janet's determined internalization of suffering, a quality she shares with

---

21. Ibid., 305. According to Basch, the nineteenth-century husband had not only "complete control of his wife's assets and person," but also "unlimited rights over the children." A father "could sequestrate the children, punish them, take them away from their mother, entrust them to a third person of his choice, . . . and refuse their mother the right of visit" (*Relative Creatures,* 22).

Mrs. Kay, characterized by rigid endurance and threatened by the prospect of change. Dempster beats her and threatens to kill her, which in fact appeals to Janet at this point. After locking her outside in the snow (she is barefoot, clad in only a thin nightdress), he leaves her to contemplate the likelihood of freezing to death. Something stirs in her, and a new life begins; in effect, she metaphorically gives birth to herself: "Life might mean anguish, might mean despair; but—oh, she must clutch it, though with bleeding fingers; her feet must cling to the firm earth that the sunlight would revisit, not slip into the untried abyss, where she might long even for familiar pains" (345). The childless Janet's desire to live, which "made her recoil from suicide," contrasts with Mrs. Kay's desire to die despite the support of family, friends, and neighbors, despite her valiant triumph over alcohol, and despite the children left motherless by her death.

Having chosen life, Janet also has chosen sobriety. The most significant influence on her "repentance" is Mr. Tryan, who proves to be both an ally in suffering and her strongest supporter. Janet confesses her alcoholic fall to Tryan, describing how her love and devotion to Dempster were repaid by brutality until she learned how numbing and comforting wine could be. But there is no comfort more inspirational to her than Tryan's own story, which is particularly relevant to this study of variously fallen women abandoned by variously accountable men.

Tryan describes his reckless youth of drinking, gambling, and sexual debauchery, during which he formed "an attachment" with Lucy, a girl well below his "station": his admission that "I never contemplated marrying her" (359) recalls the stories of Esther, Ruth, and Hetty Sorrel. Abandoned and ruined, Lucy turns to prostitution, then suicide. Tryan's remorse for his part in her emphatically permanent fall makes this his life's major turning point and is the source of the "power of the direct glance" that earlier conveyed to Janet a "fellowship in suffering" (331). Having devoted his life to religion and charity, Tryan now anticipates his impending death from consumption with patient resignation, praying only to live long enough to ensure Janet's "redemption." Thus, as the prostitute Lucy makes possible Tryan's redemption, so also does Tryan's repentance culminate in Janet's, creating intriguing links between male sexual responsibility, female fallenness, class and economic disparity, and an ideology that engenders self-destructive behaviors.

Janet's final scene with Dempster, who is dying after a drunken accident, compares significantly with Tryan's last moments. Integral to Janet's repentance is her forgiveness of Dempster and, hoping to tell him so, she watches over his deathbed. Not until the moment of death does he open his eyes: "Could he read the full forgiveness that was written in her eyes? She never knew; for, as she was bending to kiss him, the thick veil of death fell between them, and her lips touched a corpse" (388). This morbid image is consistent with the entire tenor of their marriage. The neck he once caressed became the throat he throttled, and the lips she once kissed now symbolize the deadness of love, life, and spirit. Janet, who has relinquished alcohol, constantly confronts its availability since Dempster's physician regularly doses him with, of all substances, alcohol. Janet's self-effacing humility, evidenced by her patient nursing of her tormentor even during her own healing crisis, recalls Gaskell's Ruth, whose final cruel irony was to die as a result of her compassion for the man responsible for her sexual fall. Unlike Ruth, however, whose redemptive death is a hollow victory, Janet lives on to redeem herself through adoptive motherhood and a life devoted to philanthropy.

Contrasting with Dempster's, Tryan's final moments are weighted with a curious quality of eroticized spirituality. The magnetism between Tryan and Janet deepens as they give each other strength for the trials each must ultimately endure alone: death and sobriety. Tryan comforts her with assurances of God's love, saying, "Let us kiss each other before we part" (410). This kiss between soul mates signals a spiritual consummation that sustains the widowed Janet through the remainder of her long life: "She lifted up her face to his, and the full life-breathing lips met the wasted dying ones in a sacred kiss of promise." Although the rhetoric here is highly spiritualized, Eliot's pronounced anxiety over Janet's childless state strongly implies that Janet, but for Tryan's untimely death, could have been redeemed maternally as well as by religion, sobriety, and the love of a good man.

The spiritual wedding of Janet and Tryan sustains both during their respective "dark nights of the soul" and prompts Janet, now in a sense twice-widowed, to adopt children. Thus, "Janet in her old age has children about her knees, and loving young arms round her neck" (412); no longer is she marked by the "fatal blank" (402) of the childlessness associated with Dempster. Janet, who never remarries, merits Eliot's praise for thus filling in the "fatal blank" with other women's children, while her profound victories over alcohol, abuse, and suicide are comparatively downplayed. Although she is a woman of remarkable courage, strength, and integrity, Janet's only true scope for action resides in (surrogate) motherhood. The point seems belabored, particularly since the Dempster marriage is a mockery and alcoholism and physical abuse significantly reduce the potential for conception and for Janet's carrying a child to term; the atmosphere of the Dempster household is hardly conducive to family values.

Further, religious and maternal rhetoric shifts readers' focus at every significant narrative turning point. For example, "Mammy" Dempster daily witnesses the drunken brutality of this marriage yet remains determinedly silent. She neither aligns herself with Janet nor reproves her son for his unmanly behavior. Her own marriage a failure, "the husband was too careless," and her "mother's heart . . . weighed down by a heavier burthen," all her care has produced a loutish brute of a son: "no hope remains but the grave" (297). Neither Mammy Dempster nor Mrs. Raynor, who was widowed before the birth of her only child, Janet, evidences accepted patterns of wifehood or motherhood. Janet's lack of a suitable role model makes Eliot's obsession—or, perhaps, her parody of Victorian culture's obsession—with "the fatal blank in her life" all the more curious. But despite the insistent emphasis on maternalism, Janet's participation in this ideology, though delayed, is on her own unconventional terms. She chooses to be surrounded by children, but children *who are not her own;* she chooses to remain single and childless, parenting only, in a sense, vicariously. This parallels Eliot's personal choices as well: she also chose to mother another woman's (Mrs. G. H. Lewes's) children rather than bear her own. Whether the gesture satisfied the ideologues of either Victorian society or the fictional town Milby is debatable.

Unique among fallen-woman heroines, Hetty Sorrel and Janet Dempster demonstrate that Eliot's contribution to the literature consists of protagonists who arouse readers' sympathy *despite* the absence of maternal redemption. Perhaps Eliot's perspective is best understood as a challenge to "compulsory" motherhood, an idea as ludicrous as that linking childlessness with fallenness. "Janet's Repentance" also challenges the middle class's ideological investment in lower-class immorality by demonstrating that alcoholism and wife beating are not class specific. Françoise Basch contends, "When, in 1856, J. W. Kaye drew the public's attention to the legal impotence of the ill-treated wife, he drew a distinction between the refined, verbal, emotional and usually private torture by bad middle-class husbands, and the blows and cruelties . . . inflicted by bad husbands in the less privileged classes."[22] But this distinction proves to be a false one, in fiction no less

---

22. Basch, *Relative Creatures*, 48.

than in real life. Mrs. Pryor, in Brontë's *Shirley*, was so brutalized by her alcoholic, abusive husband that she relinquished maternal responsibility in the interest of self-preservation by leaving her child, Caroline, behind when she fled for her life. Reunited years later, Caroline recalls the traumatization of being locked up by her father in the attic alone, without food, for days at a time; his returns from such absences were marked by drunkenness and physical abuse. That these horrific scenes depict a middle-class, not lower- or working-class, family is all the more striking for its illustration of maternal ideology perverted by a patriarchy derailed by substance abuse.

Other Victorian accounts of these issues focus primarily on either the politically unrepresented lower classes or on the upper class, whose wealth permitted legal action and public visibility (the cases of Lady Caroline Norton, for example).[23] The dearth of accounts of middle-class family strife implies that this class had no such problems; both "Janet's Repentance" and *Shirley* suggest otherwise. According to Erna Hellerstein, "conflict in marriage could erupt, in all social classes, into extreme discord and even violence. The relative powerlessness of women in marriage left them vulnerable to physical and sexual abuse, as contemporary accounts of domestic violence, incest, and adultery illustrate. . . . though court and prison records show that women, too, could resort to alcohol and violence under economic and personal stress."[24] Scholarship on women's responses to cultural powerlessness reveals their tendency to internalize oppression through such addictive and suicidal behaviors as Mrs. Kay's anorexia and alcoholism, and Janet's drinking and enduring years of physical abuse. But examples such as these are difficult to verify statistically, since cases of middle-class wife beating or working-class anorexia are not likely to have been recorded in Victorian court and prison records.[25] Responding to publisher John Blackwood's advice to "soften" her presentation of the unpleasant issues raised in "Janet's Repentance," Eliot says: "Everything *is*

23. On the lower classes, see Martineau, *London Daily News*, September 8, 1853.
24. Hellerstein, Hume, and Offen, *Victorian Women*, 123–24.
25. According to Carole J. Sheffield, this is still true today: "Crimes of violence against females (1) cut across socioeconomic lines; (2) are the crimes least likely to be reported; (3) when reported, are the crimes least likely to be brought to trial or to result in conviction; (4) are often blamed on the victim; (5) are generally not taken seriously; and (6) are not really about sex." Further, since "sexual violence is not 'nice,' we prefer to believe that nice men do not commit these acts and that nice girls and women are not victims. Our refusal to accept the fact that violence against females is widespread on all levels of society strongly inhibits our ability to develop any meaningful strategies directed toward the elimination of sexual violence" ("Sexual Terrorism," 8–9).

softened from the fact so far as art is permitted to soften and yet to remain essentially true. The real town was more vicious than my Milby; the real Dempster was far more disgusting than mine; the real Janet alas! had a far sadder end than mine, who will melt away from the reader's sight in purity, happiness, and beauty."[26]

But what of those women who resist being silenced and made invisible by refusing to "melt away," women whose aggressive, chaotic presence threatens the delicately balanced gender system? The subculture of female violence to which Hellerstein refers is powerfully dramatized by the character of Bertha Mason Rochester. *Jane Eyre,* an incisively psychological novel, lends itself to an archetypal analysis in which its two primary women characters—Jane and Bertha—not only share certain qualities but also are necessary to the realization of each other's destinies. Although my primary interest here is Bertha, Jane's behavior in the red-room scene in chapter 2 provides the text's strongest link between the two women and insanity. Locked in the red room for rebelling against the Reeds' tyranny, the orphaned Jane shares her outcast status with the immigrant Bertha, who was imprisoned in the attic at Thornfield at about this time. Superstitious, fainting, hair wild, and blood hot with rage, Jane screams, "Unjust!—Unjust!"[27] Jane is incapable of Helen Burns's passive submissiveness; rejecting Helen's angelicism and inevitable death, she rebels as Bertha does and in consequence is "locked away" at Lowood. Brontë early establishes this link to discourage interpreting Bertha as merely an impediment to Jane's progress, and to encourage seeing her as a crucial avatar of Jane's character that must be not relegated to the attic but fully acknowledged. This is further emphasized, as Beth Kalikoff observes, by Rochester's terming both Jane and Bertha "imp" and "fiend," suggesting he regards them in a similar light. "To grasp such a tale," says Clarissa P. Estes, "we understand that all its components represent a single woman's psyche . . . undergoing an initiatory process." This novel's "tension between parlor and attic, the psychic split between the lady who submits . . . and the lunatic who rebels" reveals the Victorian urge to domesticate every aspect of women's lives from sexuality to insanity.[28] At Lowood, Jane serves an apprenticeship under Helen Burns and Miss Temple, learning how to

26. Eliot, letter to Blackwood, June 11, 1857, quoted in Haight, *George Eliot: A Biography,* 235.

27. Charlotte Brontë, *Jane Eyre,* 49. Future quotations will be cited parenthetically in the text.

28. Kalikoff, "The Falling Woman in Three Victorian Novels," 360; Estes, *Women Who Run,* 80; Gilbert and Gubar, *Madwoman in the Attic,* 86.

manage her "restlessness." At Thornfield, learning what Bertha can teach her about submission and rebellion is the task Jane must accomplish before she can assume married middle-class respectability.

The term *middle class* here refers to the sexual and marital values promoted by this novel as well as economic status. Kalikoff observes that Jane's ambition is to achieve conventional "security and status" through marriage. As a child, she "identifies [materially] with the Reeds" and, given the choice between Lowood and poor relatives, chooses the former, admitting, "I was not heroic enough to purchase liberty at the price of caste" (57). Later, Jane's role as governess serves as a "perpetual rehearsal" for her role as a middle-class wife, which she can assume only after Rochester understands her "moral" worth. Until then, notes Kalikoff, Rochester treats Jane differently from women of his own class: he "pursues" the former, but "courts" the latter.[29]

The paradigmatic "madwoman in the attic," Bertha is unlike other fallen women in this chapter in that she does not internalize her oppression through a self-destructive habit like alcoholism. Insanity could be construed as a form of internalization; however, I am basing my distinction between internalization and externalization of oppression on the idea that conditions such as alcoholism, anorexia, and suicide involve some element of choice, at least in the initial stages. In contrast, the degree to which mental illness is manageable by the individual will alone is debatable. Whether Bertha's suicidal leap is an act of insanity or rational will remains indeterminate. Bertha's inclusion in this discussion of female alcoholism results from her link with the alcoholic nurse Grace Poole and from the questionable validity of Rochester's charges that Bertha not only drinks but also is promiscuous and insane. As the narrative reveals, the first charge is untrue and the second unsubstantiated, rendering the third highly suspicious in light of Rochester's transparent motives, his legal power over his wife, and the unsavory alliance between a man of social consequence and the "medical men" whose salary he pays.

Ensconced in her attic domain and thus parodically elevated on a domestic pedestal, Bertha represents womanhood gone berserk; she is ultimately uncontrollable, which mocks Rochester's social and sexual potency, an idea reflected in his gypsy-woman masquerade, his physical maiming, and the loss of the estate that marks him a gentleman. Because Bertha refuses to be silenced, because her chaos presents Rochester with the constant threat

29. Kalikoff, "Falling Woman," 359–60.

of eruption and exposure, because she rebels through external aggressive behaviors, the "medical men" label her "mad." Far from weakening her, locking up this deviant fuels her desire for vengeance, even at the cost of her own life; for, whether internalized or externalized, the price of female rebellion is generally imprisonment and death, metaphorically or literally.

Grace Poole, a far more sinister alcoholic nurse than the boisterous Mrs. Horsfall, absorbs the consequences of Bertha's behavior for Rochester and sanitizes them for public view. Grace is "an able woman in her line, and very trustworthy, but for one fault—a fault common to a deal of them nurses and matrons—*she kept a private bottle of gin by her,* and now and then took a drop overmuch" (452). Jane Eyre regards her as "that living enigma, that mystery of mysteries" (232), which is exactly the image that the staff at Thornfield Hall is paid to promote. Grace Poole's "dram habit" provides a palpable explanation for her eccentric practice of always sewing "alone" in the attic and for demonic laughter, deadly fires, and other unexplained irregularities. At best, the character Grace Poole deflects the real source of Rochester's public embarrassment, as does, in another sense, the presence of Adèle Varens, Rochester's "ward."[30] At worst, though to Jane's ultimate benefit, Grace's alcoholism provides Bertha with the opportunities for aggressive action that function to save Jane from the sexual fallenness Rochester represents.

Jane is irresistibly drawn to the third floor, which she describes as "like a corridor in some Bluebeard's castle" (138). She has indeed stumbled into a Bluebeardian domain peopled with women variously implicated in Rochester's colorful sexual past: Bertha, his wife, and Grace, her nurse; Mrs. Fairfax, who censors Grace when she becomes careless, as she later censors Jane for the carelessness of falling in love with a married man; vain, sexually precocious Adèle, who bears an uncanny resemblance to her mother, Rochester's French mistress, Celine Varens; and finally, Blanche Ingram, who is likened to the young Bertha (332) and thus presents Rochester with the opportunity to repeat past mistakes. "I saw he was going to marry her," notes Jane, "for family, perhaps political reasons; because her rank and connexions suited him" (215), the same motivations that

---

30. Adèle is "not my own daughter," claims Rochester. She is "a French dancer's bastard" (329). Although it can refer to a legitimate connection, the term *ward* can also connote illegitimacy. Since Rochester is duplicitous and resists sexual accountability, it is probable that Adèle is the daughter of Rochester and Celine Varens. Either way, her presence at Thornfield Hall is curious: Why does he not send her away to school? Similarly, why not eliminate Bertha's threatening presence by sending her away?

prompted his marriage to Bertha fifteen years previously. While Blanche reigns in the drawing room, Jane and Bertha, separated only by an attic wall, pace "backwards and forwards," striving against the psychic imprisonment and outcast status they share. Gilbert and Gubar note, "Bertha not only acts *for* Jane, she also acts *like* Jane," and it may be said of both women that "the restlessness was in my nature; it agitated me to pain sometimes" (141).[31]

Jane's comprehension of her adversary/ally Bertha is limited to the partial knowledge afforded by disembodied voices ("a snarling, snatching sound, . . . A shout of laughter, . . . [a] goblin ha! ha! . . . a canine noise, and a deep human groan" [238–39]) and later by Rochester's self-serving version of her story. Jane does not initially regard Bertha as victimized, nor does she see herself as a potential victim of this Victorian-age Bluebeard. But later, the link between Bertha's madness and Jane's restless agitation finds expression in her defense of Bertha: "Sir, . . . you are inexorable for that unfortunate lady: you speak of her with hate—with vindictive antipathy. It is cruel—she cannot help being mad" (328). Bertha's story resonates with Jane's memories of injustices in the red room, and Jane gradually understands that Bertha, like the remains of Bluebeard's wives, bears witness to that tendency in Rochester that may be not quite murderous yet is clearly not in women's best interests. Like the key to Bluebeard's secret charnel house that will not cease bleeding until its truth is known, Bertha's presence is insistent, for all Rochester's attempts at concealment. It is not until both Jane and Rochester fully acknowledge, if not exactly vindicate, Bertha that past impediments give way to future unions.

In the absence of Bertha's narrative voice, Jane's dreams of babies and children anticipate the burden of dependency presented not only by this character but also by Jane's psychic alignment with her. Jane's movements are "fettered" by this child, yet "however much its weight impeded my progress, I must retain it. . . . the child clung round my neck in terror, and almost strangled me" (310). The suggestion that Bertha's belligerence might stem from fear of imprisonment (true of the ten-year-old Jane) unexpectedly aligns the two women in a shared vulnerability and powerlessness.

Like the period's "taking-down" system of child rearing, treatment of the insane was cruel and punitive, aimed at containment rather than cure. Rochester says, "Since the medical men had pronounced her mad, she had, of course, been shut up" (335), an incarceration that at times includes

---

31. Gilbert and Gubar, *Madwoman in the Attic,* 361.

physical restraints, no treatment for her condition, and only a drunken nurse for company. Considering the power differentials separating male from female experience at this time, "we can see how men could deliberately invoke the masculine powers of Victorian medicine and law to disarm, discredit, and confine women who refused to suffer and be still."[32] That Bertha is a prisoner in her own home while her husband toys with Blanche Ingram in the drawing room or with Jane Eyre in the parlor, and the illegitimate Adèle has the run of the house, presents a disturbing image of the darker aspects of patriarchal ascendancy.

Bertha has not even the dubious legitimation of wifehood, as the locals assume she is either Rochester's "bastard half-sister" or "cast-off mistress" (320; see also 452). Marilyn Kurata notes the unparalleled stigma attached to even the idea of insanity; like sexual fallenness in its many forms, the taint is never fully eradicated, which functions to keep a woman like Bertha as isolated socially as she is physically. The suggestion that Bertha may be afraid and vulnerable—behavior not inconsistent with her enraged outbreaks—undermines Rochester's claim that it was Bertha who "dragged" *him* "through all the hideous and degrading agonies which must attend a man bound to a wife at once intemperate and unchaste" (334; his prodigious catalog of adulterous affairs on 338–39 provides an illuminating comparison here). Those most subject to "wrongful confinement," notes Kurata, were women "who refused to submit to the authority and control" of their husbands: "the powers of law and medicine could be—and were— invoked by vindictive men to permanently disable, disarm, and discredit sane, but rebellious, women."[33] This opens up the possibility that Bertha's "malady" may be less insanity than political impotence.

---

32. Marilyn J. Kurata, "Wrongful Confinement: The Betrayal of Women by Men, Medicine, and Law," 43–44. According to Showalter, Victorian treatments for female insanity included injecting ice and ice water into the rectum and vagina, and applying leeches to the labia and cervix; performing clitoridectomies; and employing such mechanical restraints as "manacles, chains, fetters, hobbles, gyves, leather muzzles . . . gloves . . . [and] sleeves, handcuffs, muffs, body straps, stocks to prevent biting, strong-dresses, strait-waistcoats, coercion-chairs, strongchairs, and crib-beds. Noisy women were silenced with the brank, or 'scold's bridle' " (*Female Malady*, 31). Brontë's text does not disclose whether Bertha's "malady" caused her to be subjected to such treatments, but we do know Rochester has Bertha placed in restraints to prevent her nocturnal wanderings (see chapter 27).

33. Kurata, "Wrongful Confinement," 48, 64–65. Helen Small notes, "Rochester's account of the moral degeneration of his Creole wife is remarkably close to his confession of his own activities in the years after she is officially declared mad" (*Love's Madness: Medicine, the Novel, and Female Insanity, 1800–1865*, 174).

Rochester consistently denies responsibility for Bertha, as did the Reed family with Jane. In both instances, the middle-class characters are as uncompromising in their stance as the outcast characters—one an immigrant and one an orphan—are rebellious in theirs. But despite her "pigmy intellect" (334) Bertha is capable of periods of lucidity, and it would be a mistake to underestimate her understanding of the implications of Jane's presence at Thornfield Hall. Her profoundly symbolic setting fire to Rochester's bed and rending Jane's bridal veil demonstrate that Bertha is clear on this point long before Jane, and perhaps even Rochester, are.

Jane's first sight of Bertha, whom she dehumanizes as "it" and likens to that "foul German spectre—the vampire," is obscured by her sleep-drugged senses. "It" seems to be dressed in a shroud, its features "fearful and ghastly, . . . a discoloured . . . savage face, . . . red eyes and fearful blackened . . . lineaments" (311). Bertha places Jane's bridal veil on her own head, where it at least legally belongs, before ripping it to shreds, perhaps less an act of insanity than of impotent rage against her adulterous husband. In a movement remarkably deliberate and collected for one presumed to be in an incendiary rage, Bertha gazes out the window, then stands by Jane's bed: "I was aware her lurid visage flamed over mine, and I lost consciousness; for the second time in my life . . . I became insensible from terror" (311–12). Recalling Tryan's probing glance when Janet Dempster was most lost to herself, Bertha's presence symbolically rends the veil of deception dividing Jane from her best perceptive insight. Jane first fainted in the red room at Gateshead when she was terrified by her own delusions. Her subsequent loss of consciousness at Thornfield Hall indicates she is not yet capable of discerning dream from reality or desire from truth. Clearly, Bertha represents a kind of knowledge and psychic stamina that Jane lacks.

Following the aborted (because bigamous) wedding, Rochester's confession of the deception he has been practicing on Bertha, Blanche, and Jane also serves as the narrative's only version of Bertha's story; given her imprisonment at his command, this is a particularly disturbing example of women's silencing and misrepresentation. "Bertha Mason is mad," he states, "and she came of a mad family; idiots and maniacs through three generations!" (320). According to Sally Shuttleworth, "received wisdom" decreed that "not only were women more prone to insanity than men, they were also more responsible for hereditary transmission." Further, Elaine Showalter observes, "since the reproductive system was the source of mental illness in women, women were the prime carriers of madness, twice as likely to transmit it as were fathers," a configuration that supports the idea that female sexuality is by nature chaotic and requires regulation.[34] Illustrating these ideas, Bertha's brother, Richard—who forces Rochester's confession, defends Bertha, and actively prevents Jane's sexual fall—is not associated with madness. But although Mason's response to his sister's condition is distinctly aggrieved, Bertha's violent physical attack on him complicates his seeming blamelessness. What role, if any, did he play in this arranged marriage? As the Mason son and heir, what did he stand to gain by this alliance? While he may be culpable even indirectly for Bertha's fate, Mason's timely appearances serve to remind readers that there is more to Bertha and her story than Rochester's skewed account implies.

According to Rochester, "Her mother, the Creole, was both a madwoman and a drunkard! . . . Bertha, like a dutiful child, copied her parent in both points" (320). His attitude is consistent with scientific theories that "emphasized the hereditary disposition to madness and the congenital inferiority of the insane": "insanity thus represented an evolutionary reversal, a regression to a lower nature," a theoretical justification for the foregone conclusion that women (and foreigners of any color) are an inferior class.[35] Interestingly, this is the first indication that it is Bertha who drinks. Does this mean Grace Poole's alleged "dram habit" was just a deliberate fabrication to divert attention from Rochester's secret? If so, why is alcohol accessible to Bertha, whom the "medical men" have diagnosed insane? Finally, how can Bertha's shrewd watching for opportunities to escape her nurse (it is during Grace's drunken stupors that Bertha roams Thornfield Hall) be explained if *she* is the alcoholic? The boundaries between sanity and insanity, and alcoholism and sobriety, are deliberately collapsed here in the service of Rochester's self-aggrandizing justification for his own sexual promiscuity.

Brontë's adding cultural issues, which implies a deviant brand of sexuality, to this already complex mix encourages readers' sympathy for the beleaguered Rochester at the expense of the beleaguered Bertha. In light of Bertha's foreign origins, Rochester's version of her story reveals several unsavory facts about this arranged marriage. Bertha's family is wealthy, and

34. Shuttleworth, "Demonic Mothers: Ideologies of Bourgeois Motherhood in the Mid-Victorian Era," 36; Showalter, *Female Malady*, 67. Showalter notes that some explanations for the statistically higher incidence of insanity in women include women's comparative longevity, making them "less likely to be discharged as cured," and the "feminization" of poverty. Illustrating the period's signature reduction of economics to morality, "Women were the majority of recipients of poor-law-relief," and thus "more likely to be committed to institutions" (*Female Malady*, 54).

35. Showalter, *Female Malady*, 104, 106.

thus this marriage serves the dual purpose of enriching the disinherited Rochester with her dowry and enhancing the Masons' social status through its link to English landed gentry. Of the latter consideration, Rochester, seeking to obscure the reciprocal terms of this agreement, claims he has been duped by the Masons: "Her family wished to secure me, because I was of a good race" (332), "good race" being equated with cultural ascendancy.[36] Rochester was himself used as a medium of exchange through his family's machinations, admittedly just cause for resentment, although Bertha should hardly bear the full burden;[37] her resentments for similar treatment are not even a consideration here.[38]

Britain's state-of-the-art psychiatric methodology—practiced almost exclusively by male physicians on female patients—was a "source of national pride," composing a sort of "Great Exhibition of insanity."[39] The epidemic proportions of female neurasthenia at this time provide a disturbing reminder that Victorian Britain's colonialist mentality was as prevalent at home in gender issues as it was abroad in racial issues. This is symbolized in the colonization of Bertha by Rochester and his army of "medical men" as well as by St. John Rivers's efforts to "colonize" Jane before colonizing Indian "heathens" with Christianity.

Eugenicists' attitudes being grounded in what Shuttleworth calls "breeding anxiety," it is appropriate that Bertha has no children, since "madness [is] the mark of the impotent and unfit, the sign of social, intellectual, and

36. "Race" has class connotations for Jane as well: she calls herself a "revolted slave" (46) and believes Aunt Reed dislikes her because she is "not of her race" (48). This novel's conflation of "race" with "class" is suggestive of imperialist attitudes toward women and of classist attitudes toward race. Small observes, "The language of colonialism (heathen passions subject to the control of an imperial reason) sets up a racial model of psychology which will be explored more literally through St. John later" (*Love's Madness,* 168), seen both in the thwarted alliance between Rivers and Jane and in Rivers's compulsion to cool India's "heathen passions" with his frigid brand of Christianity.

37. According to Rochester, his father did not wish to divide the estate and settled it all on the eldest son. Father and brother "provided" for the disinherited Rochester through the arrangement with Mason: "they thought only of the thirty thousand pounds, and joined in the plot against me" (333). The settlement from Bertha's dowry, along with his inheritance of the estate following the deaths of his father and brother, made Rochester quite a rich man.

38. Armstrong's suggestion that madness such as Bertha's is a "form of resistance" is particularly intriguing, considering Bertha's periods of lucidity (*Desire and Domestic Fiction,* 58). Armstrong argues that both madness and prostitution are forms of resistance; in the context of this discussion, both represent comparatively externalized forms of women's responses to oppression.

39. Showalter, *Female Malady,* 24.

moral decline." Of the many archetypes Brontë employs in this novel, one of the most striking is the link between the imagery of bloodred moons, reproductive cycles, and Bertha's most aggressive psychotic episodes. As my textual examples (fiction and nonfiction) repeatedly demonstrate, maternity was, to use Shuttleworth's term, "sacred." But maternity also has the potential for "anarchic disruption"; left unregulated, "Motherhood, and all processes leading up to it" can have murderous connotations, evidenced by such phenomena as puerperal fever, lactational insanity, and infanticide. Showalter agrees, adding that female insanity was linked to all the "biological crises of the female life-cycle" from puberty to menopause, "during which the mind would be weakened and the symptoms of insanity might emerge." But according to the period's "doctrine of crisis," failure to bear children complicates the issue even further.[40] No less than childbearing women, childless women like Bertha signify reproductive biology gone berserk, since untapped maternal energy was believed to transform into negative, sometimes murderous, energy. This line of theorizing also applies to Jane's hysteria in the red room, an emotive expression of what would have coincided with the onset of puberty.

Extending the analogy, the notorious case of a midcentury woman who killed and ate her husband (in the interest of domestic economy, she pickled the leftovers) exemplifies a projection of such cyclical rage onto the adult most directly implicated in her sexual processes.[41] By association, the childless Bertha unleashes her cannibalistic tendencies on her brother ("She sucked the blood: she said she'd drain my heart" [242]) and on Rochester (she bites his face, [321]); Brontë's narrative presents no examples of such physical violence against women.[42] Even Bertha's nocturnal visit to Jane's room, though threatening, contributes to Jane's realizing her compromising situation, an insight comparable to the dream vision of her mother urging her to flee the temptation Rochester represents. The image of female cannibalism effectively "highlights the ideological anxieties underlying the projections of female angelic subservience. . . . women represented to the

---

40. Shuttleworth, "Demonic Mothers," 36–37; Showalter, *Female Malady*, 104, 55; Poovey, *Uneven Developments*, 36.

41. Discussed in Shuttleworth, "Demonic Mothers," 33; "Woman in Her Psychological Relations"; and Henry Maudsley, *The Physiology and Pathology of the Mind*.

42. Carol Adams discusses the link between British colonialism and cultures that eat little or no meat. The English "Beefeaters" were associated with a culturally superior civilizing force, while Hindus, the Chinese, the Irish, and women were associated with cultural inferiority and vegetarianism. This "theory of meat-eating" is consistent with social Darwinism's "scientific" justification of cultural hierarchies.

bourgeois male imagination an ever-present threat to their dominance, a threat, moreover, that was enshrined within the sanctuary of their own home."[43] This presents a compelling image of the marriage between angelic domesticity in the parlor and the domestication of insanity in the attic, ideological extremes contained in the shared space of the middle-class home, that haven from the world's polluting influence. Mrs. Kay's anorexia and Bertha's characteristically externalized behaviors compare interestingly in this context; both are expressions of rage medically regarded as sexual aberrations, and both result in death for the woman.

Bertha's rage manifests itself through other animalistic behaviors as well. The bestial Bertha scurries back and forth in the shadows of her windowless attic prison—"it grovelled, . . . it snatched and growled like some strange wild animal; . . . a quantity of dark, grizzled hair, wild as a mane, hid its head and face" (321)—while Grace Poole (whose character belies both her names) hovers witchlike over a "boiling mess" on the fire. Bertha's "purple face—those bloated features" (321) and corpulent bulk compare unfavorably with Jane's white-faced, diminutive sexual purity, while Rochester's mere presence antagonizes Bertha, who promptly attacks him and bites his cheek. He pins her arms and ties her with ropes to a chair, demanding that the horrified onlookers "judge whether or not I had a right to break the compact" (320); clearly, the "rights" of neither Bertha nor Jane are for him a consideration.

Rochester's penchant for surrounding himself with women—at one point, Bertha is in the attic, Adèle is in the nursery, Jane and Blanche Ingram are in the parlor, while Rochester himself ludicrously masquerades as a gypsy woman—suggests Thornfield Hall is a sort of seraglio-on-the-moors: one wonders if he does this to antagonize Bertha during her moments of lucidity. Clarissa Estes's analysis of "Bluebeard," to which the concept of "the predator" is central, is relevant to all *Jane Eyre*'s women characters, "regardless of whether they are very young and just learning about the predator, or whether they have been hounded and harassed by it for decades and are at last readying for a final and decisive battle with it." Estes's configuration, which assumes that the predator is an internal as well as an external opponent, incorporates both Jane's romanticized naïveté and Bertha's experienced dementia. As expressions or versions of each other, these women are vicariously aligned in a struggle centered less on Rochester than on Victorian sexual ideology. As Bertha prepares herself

43. Shuttleworth, "Demonic Mothers," 33.

for "a final and decisive battle" with her demons, Jane struggles with her prescient dreams and her propensity to lose consciousness when confronted by her eroticized fear of insanity. According to Estes, successful completion of one's quest requires "the ability to stand what one sees," something that neither the unconscious Jane nor the irrational Bertha seems capable of sustaining.[44]

However, even when deliberately displaced or avoided, the truth manifests itself through the unconscious: "When a woman is attempting to avoid the facts of her own devastations, her night dreams will shout warnings to her, warnings and exhortations to wake up! or get help! or flee! or go for the kill!" Jane's dreams, superimposed as they are with Bertha's nocturnal wanderings, lead with deadly accuracy toward confrontation with the predatory force that would bind them both. According to Estes, resolution comes not from running away from the predator, as Jane does, but from dismantling or dismembering it, as Bertha does.[45] In the novel's apocalyptic event, Bertha destroys her external predator: sexual and political ascendancy represented by Rochester and Thornfield Hall, both of which are dismantled. In the process, she also destroys her internal predator—what the "medical men" call insanity—in her suicidal "fall" from the heights of Thornfield mansion. But most significant to the immensely powerful madonna-harlot archetype, Bertha performs Jane's work for her, in effect providing Jane with a suitably chastened Rochester, after which she removes herself from the site of contention.

Is redemption for Bertha's idiosyncratic "fallenness" conceivable, or is she even more irretrievably lost than the most hardened Victorian prostitute? In order to answer this question, at least by Victorian standards, we would need to resolve the enigma posed by insanity: specifically, if insanity is a condition beyond the scope of one's conscious will to control, then Bertha—insofar as we accept the diagnosis of the "medical men" and Rochester—cannot be held accountable for her behavior, no matter how "intemperate" or "unchaste." This lack of agency also accounts for the fact that Bertha's deviance remains unredeemed by repentance, motherhood, philanthropy, transportation, or illness, as are other characters' falls, although death has redemptive qualities, in a perverse sort of way. Bertha's death does conveniently remove all obstacles to Rochester and Jane's love match, which, as a motive for marriage, is presented by Brontë as superior to class or

44. Estes, *Women Who Run*, 47, 53.
45. Ibid., 54, 64.

economic interests. The narrative's powerful invitation to accept that "they all lived happily ever after" fails to account for the issues raised by Bertha Mason Rochester that are not resolved by her physical death. Recalling Clarissa Estes's emphasis on confrontation, such a "figure of rage" as Bertha represents "must be acknowledged . . . by the angelic protagonist to whom s/he is opposed," yet Bertha is as unvindicated in death as she was in life.[46] Instead of recognizing her alignment with this worthy opponent, Jane seems smug in the knowledge that chastity and restraint is rewarded by unimpeded union with her true love, an equation from which Bertha is strikingly absent. Although she dissociates herself from Bertha and what she represents, Jane is herself a "figure of rage." Only once does she express empathy toward Bertha, and then only in response to Rochester's excessive vehemence ("you are inexorable. . . . she cannot help being mad"), yet it is Bertha's sacrificial death that makes possible Jane's domesticated respectability. Jane's spatial separation from Bertha in Thornfield Hall emphasizes the disparity between their fates: yet, like the horse-chestnut tree so prophetically split by lightning (285), both women remain rooted in the same ideological foundation. To interpret *Jane Eyre* as a Victorian fairy tale in which the deserving heroine ultimately triumphs over the Bluebeardian predators and redundant women obstructing her progress is to remain blind to the specter of imprisonment underpinning Victorian sexual ideology.

With the exception of some contemporary feminist scholarship, critical analyses generally collude with the text's elision of Bertha's perspective.[47] But Bertha is more than the narrative's evil foil against which to measure Jane's worth; her madness resonates with the character Jane, and she is both Jane's most worthy opponent and her ally. While it is not my purpose to analyze Bertha's psychiatric state, she can at least be seen as sharing the same gender, class, and cultural constructs that shaped the lives of other fallen women.[48] Her existence is necessary to middle-class angelic ideology, yet her elimination is just as integral to its perpetuation. In the sense that all women were assumed to be "always already" fallen, *Jane Eyre* is less about women who rise or fall than it is about modes of survival on a continuum

---

46. Gilbert and Gubar, *Madwoman in the Attic,* 78.

47. For contemporary scholarship, see ibid. and Showalter's *Female Malady.* Auerbach's work with *Jane Eyre* focuses primarily on Jane's character, although she does note that Bertha "is in her mad confinement the spirit of home," making this character a potent manifestation of angelic ideology (*Woman and the Demon,* 43).

48. Late-Victorian writer Charlotte Perkins Gilman compellingly illustrates this in "The Yellow Wallpaper."

of oppression in which Jane and Bertha occupy extreme positions by only a random twist of fate. It is not enough to celebrate Jane Eyre or Aurora Leigh as early feminists who "had it all" unless we acknowledge Bertha Mason Rochester and Marian Erle as integral to a process in which one woman's liberation often results from another woman's oppression.

Florence Nightingale's fragmentary *Cassandra,* written in 1852, employs the rhetoric of mental illness to implicate Victorian domestic ideology in the very dynamic it purports to prevent: women's fallenness. For Nightingale, Martineau, and others, failure to develop one's capacities fully *is* a form of fallenness. Women's categorical relegation to domesticity "dooms some minds to incurable infancy, others to silent misery," while the prioritization of bodies over minds and souls promotes the sexualization of women's issues and lies at the root of the "psychic split" between parlor and attic, madonna and harlot, conformity and rebellion. Nightingale presents this gendered demoralization through the metaphors of hunger and starvation, from which all the women in this study suffer in one form or another:

> To have no food for our heads, no food for our hearts, no food for our activity, is that nothing? If we have no food for the body, how do we cry out, how all the world hears of it, how all the newspapers talk of it . . . DEATH FROM STARVATION! But suppose one were to put a paragraph in the "Times," *Death of thought from starvation,* or *Death of moral activity from starvation,* how people would stare, how they would laugh and wonder![49]

Anorexia, as Victorian women of all classes knew, was not solely a condition of the body but also of the mind and spirit.

Cassandra concludes with the melodramatic dying words of an archetypal female whose potential was limited by her sex: "My people were like children playing on the shore of the eighteenth century. I was their hobbyhorse, their plaything . . . till I, who had grown to woman's estate and to the ideas of the nineteenth century, lay down exhausted, my mind closed to hope, my heart to strength." Nightingale regarded individual development as necessary to a healthy world community, and believed civilization's progress retarded "by the death of every one who has to sacrifice the development of his or her peculiar gifts . . . to conventionality."[50] As this

49. Nightingale, *Cassandra,* 37, 41–42.
50. Ibid., 55, 42.

discussion proves, the language of starvation, madness, addiction, and defeat employed by such female anomalies as Martineau, Eliot, Brontë, and Nightingale demonstrates their recognition of its power to speak for those female experiences generally relegated to the attic.

6

Harem Life, West and East

There can be but one true method in the treatment of each
human being of either sex, of any color, and under any outward
circumstances—to ascertain what are the powers of that being,
to cultivate them to the utmost, and then to see what action they
will find for themselves. This has probably never been done for
men. . . . It has certainly never been done for women.

—Harriet Martineau, letter to
1851 women's rights convention

He told me there was no career for free negroes, no rights, no
public position. All he said might have been said about any
woman anywhere.

—Barbara Bodichon, *An American Diary, 1857–1858*

NATIONALISM AND xenophobia, sexual deviance and insanity formed
a specifically gendered nexus peculiar to the Victorian period.
"Women and 'savages,'" notes Helen Small, were assumed to be "vulnerable
to . . . derangement since in both the will was held to be notoriously weak."
Bertha Mason Rochester's foreign character presents a disturbing combination of tainted blood, insanity, alcoholism, and promiscuity. Emphasizing
that race (in terms of "breeding anxiety" about racial purity) is the primary
factor underscoring all such deviant tendencies, Linda Shires observes
that "gender and madness are used in the service of nationalism—the
maenadic woman is alien to English propriety . . . her sexual life is not
'normal.' She may be licentious, or she may be a prostitute, or she may bear

159

guilt by association."[1] Resistance to assimilating foreigners into Victorian culture resonates with transportation schemes, which were also designed to eliminate any factor "alien" to British ideology.

The authenticity of her story remaining questionable, Bertha bears "guilt by association" to an "infamous mother," an insane, alcoholic Creole. Charlotte Brontë's narrative invites readers to regard Bertha's blackened, empurpled, reddened "visage" as marks of her insanity; yet her foreignness arouses xenophobic anxieties as well. Deirdre David notes that the definition of "Creole" specifies Negro heritage but, oddly, does not necessarily connote color, an interesting indeterminacy effectively employed in *Jane Eyre*. David agrees that, although Brontë never presents Bertha's heritage as black, readers are encouraged to "associate her with Victorian fantasies of African Negro behavior . . . which makes her thus doubly horrible (and fascinating) to the Victorian sexual imagination."[2] Rochester, whose ambivalent account of his tempestuous marriage to Bertha reflects this revulsion-in-compulsion, projects his participation in such behaviors entirely onto Bertha by displacing her to the realm of madness and locked garrets.

My discussion to this point has focused on sexual fallenness as a gender and class issue, with characters chosen exclusively from the cultural milieu that constructed, and was constructed by, the period's domestic ideology. But as the potent example of Bertha Mason Rochester suggests, the place of foreign and especially nonwhite women in this construct is well worth investigating. Such scholars as Lynda Nead and Judith Walkowitz and, more recent, Deirdre David and Helen Small note the imperialist underpinnings of Victorian sexual mores, an analogy in which women are colonized (domesticated if middle class; sexually exploited if working class) by the dominant male culture. As the literary examples in the following discussion demonstrate, the regulation of women's sexuality at home transforms into the exploitation of slave's sexuality in the colonies. This chapter explores slave women's sexuality as a type of fallenness that was generally inaccessible in mainstream Victorian literature.[3] Viewed through the lenses of Martineau's fiction and travel journals and Elizabeth Barrett Browning's

1. Small, *Love's Madness*, 164; Shires, "Of Maenads, Mothers, and Feminized Males: Victorian Readings of the French Revolution," in *Rewriting the Victorians: Theory, History, and the Politics of Gender*, ed. Shires, 156.

2. Brontë, *Jane Eyre*, 334; David, *Rule Britannia: Women, Empire, and Victorian Writing*, 108–9.

3. Although to Middle Easterners harem women are wives, not slaves, Martineau regards these women as enslaved by harems' systematized concubinage no less than are the actual slave women who serve them. The material differences between harem

poetry, this issue poses some interesting dilemmas to the culture-specific ideology by which these women were assessed.[4]

As a prelude to discussing literary treatments of slavery by white English-women, some consideration of abolitionist rhetorical conventions provides a useful basis for comparison. Perhaps nowhere in literary history is the cultural silencing of women more clearly exemplified than in the dearth of black slave women's narratives. While recent scholarship in American literary studies aims to fill in those silences by recuperating such texts as Harriet Jacobs's *Incidents in the Life of a Slave Girl* and Harriet E. Wilson's *Our Nig,* and the series *The Schomburg Library of Black Women Writers,* edited by Henry Louis Gates, the existence of similar extant texts remains unlikely. The fact that educating slaves was illegal in pre–Civil War America largely accounts for the absence of black nineteenth-century writing, representing the silencing of an entire race not rectified simply by revoking such laws. Slave-period literature continues to be associated with such works as Harriet Beecher Stowe's *Uncle Tom's Cabin* and Mark Twain's narratives, although, by modern standards, Twain seems racist, while Stowe's sentimental Evangelicalism obscures slavery's more subtle— or, for many Victorians, indelicate—issues.

True also of English literary history, the search for black writing during this period yields little. This is explained in part by the fact that slavery was abolished in England earlier in the century and because, in contrast to the American experience, slavery was not a highly visible element on English soil but was displaced to the West Indies. One exception is *The History of Mary Prince, a West Indian Slave, Related by Herself,* published in London in 1831. This brief autobiography has the important distinction of being the first West Indian slave narrative written by a woman, although its credibility is somewhat qualified by the censorial attitudes that dictated the book's composition and publication. Born into slavery, Mary spent the first thirty-five years of her life working for a variety of owners. Driven and abused mercilessly, Mary nevertheless strove to earn money to buy her freedom. This was repeatedly refused her, until a journey to England with her owners resulted in her seeking asylum with the Anti-Slavery Society.

---

wives and slaves do not, for Martineau, obscure the powerlessness they share. The same is true of slave women on American plantations and their materially privileged counterparts, quadroons.

4. See Anita Levy's 1995 *Other Women* (Princeton: Princeton University Press, 1991), which is based on the premise that racism is a direct result of a class-based society.

With a view toward promoting the cause of abolition, particularly among those classes capable of contributing monetarily, the society's members encouraged Mary to record her experiences as a slave, prompting her to become the "first black British spokeswoman for general emancipation" and the first to write "a polemic against slavery." Aptly reflecting the moral standards of the period, Mary achieved credibility among her sponsors by promoting religious and ethical values and by sanitizing some of the more graphic scenes of physical violence and, especially, sexual encounters with her masters. The character Mary's narrative conveys obliquely casts her as a "sinner" prior to her religious conversion, after which she strives to live a decent or chaste life despite unchanged circumstances. Viewed in this context, Mary Prince may be seen as performing important work on behalf of her fellow slaves, albeit to some degree at the expense of black females, the primary victims of sexual exploitation. Although Mary does make clear that many of the cruelties she suffered were inflicted by jealous mistresses whose husbands freely used women slaves sexually, her mentors refused to sanction more explicit accounts of such encounters. In his appendix to Mary's narrative, editor Thomas Pringle explains a prominent elision as an account of circumstances "too indecent to appear in a publication likely to be perused by females."[5] As the following discussion illustrates, although white women writers on black women's issues were similarly constrained by hegemonic propriety, they, like Mary, succeeded in conveying at least some of what was unsayable about slave women's lives. Unlike Pringle, Martineau and Barrett Browning chose to confront the ideological fallacy that sanctioned racial sexual slavery as a safeguard for whites' domestic purity.

While acknowledging the importance of modern scholarship's interest in British colonialism in terms of race and gender and especially concerning any dominant ideology's appropriation of minority voices—an idea central to this book's organization—my discussion continues to focus on what Victorian women writers had to say about the subject of sexual fallenness in its various forms. That these women writers are all white, educated (informally), and situated somewhere above the working classes speaks volumes about their social privilege in relation to those of whom they write. Nevertheless, while I do not claim that these women *speak for* minority experiences or in any way *replace* minority voices, I do argue that what these

5. Moira Ferguson, introduction to *The History of Mary Prince, a West Indian Slave, Related by Herself,* 22–23; ibid., appendix, 91.

writers had to say about the exploitation of women of color is fundamental to our comprehension of literary and social history. That the women writers I discuss throughout this book chose to employ their (often international) literary fame to expose social injustice is itself worth exploring. As the period's criticism—always a reflection of reigning ideology—reveals, rarely were these women applauded for their efforts to speak on others' behalf.

According to Harriet Martineau, the extent to which a country is civilized can be measured by the status of its women, that is, women of any and all classes, races and ethnicities, and socioeconomic milieus. Martineau's observation that "The degree of the degradation of woman is as good a test as the moralist can adapt for ascertaining the state of domestic morals in any country" defines the parameters for her writing on women's issues.[6] As a self-styled sociologist, an indefatigable traveler, and a prolific writer of travel journals, the intrepid Martineau studied the women of America, Europe, the British Isles, and the Middle East and wrote compellingly about what she regarded as the culturally transcendent subordination of women.

Martineau refines this theory by noting that, despite the cultural truism that casts women as the preservers and embodiment of morality, the state of a country's morals actually reflects less on its women than on its men. Since it is men who grant or deny women social status, then men are ultimately accountable for a society's moral climate, an analogy that includes nonwhites of either gender. In "Morals of Slavery," Martineau assures readers that "This title is not written down in a spirit of mockery; though there appears to be a mockery somewhere, when we contrast slavery with the principles and the rule which are the test of all American institutions: . . . slavery exists; and what we have to see is what the morals are of the society which is subject to it."[7] Living in the age of British imperialism, Martineau saw a clear link between men's subordination of women and whites' oppression of blacks. Her discussions of the situations of women and the institution of slavery in America, the West Indies, and the Middle East reflect her singular approach to the topic of fallenness. Although branded an infidel and an amalgamationist, Martineau in her clarity on these issues

6. Harriet Martineau, *How to Observe Morals and Manners*, 167. This remarkable book, penned during her voyage to America, establishes the criteria Martineau thought necessary to understanding a foreign culture. Modern scholars consider this work a pioneering contribution to the then infant discipline of sociology.

7. Martineau, *Society in America*, 219–20. Future quotations will be designated *SA* and cited parenthetically in the text.

anticipates modern theories on the mutability of social oppression and on the fallacy that the sexuality of nonwhite women is "always already" fallen.

Although Martineau wrote extensively on slavery and its related issues, "Demerara," part of her influential and popular *Illustrations of Political Economy,* is her only fictional treatment.[8] Written prior to her empirical observation of slavery in America, "Demerara" presents a compelling tale about British exploitation of blacks in Guiana and slavery's inevitable dehumanization of both races. This excerpt from Martineau's preface, which refutes critics' charges that women's writing is inferior because grounded in emotion rather than (masculine) reason, demonstrates her commitment to these issues: "If I had believed, as many do, that strong feeling impairs the soundness of reasoning, I should assuredly have avoided the subject of the following tale, since SLAVERY is a topic which cannot be approached without emotion."[9] The plot of "Demerara" contains both emotional and rational appeal; it dramatizes atrocities committed by whites against blacks and by blacks against each other, and it records lengthy expository conversations concerning the ethics and economics of colonialism.

A case in point is chapter 5, "No Haste to the Wedding in Demerara," which features a discussion of marriage as an institution central to whites' sexual and economic ideology. In what would be the first black marriage at Demerara in more than ten years, Nell wants to marry her lover, but her brother, Willy, objects, pointing out that slave marriages have no civil rights. He argues that, should the husband become freed, his wife could not go with him, and if she is sold, he cannot go with her; if they have children, "They cannot do their children any good. They cannot make them free, nor save them from labour, nor help them to get justice." As for conjugal "rights," "a black must first be a slave and then a man . . . but a slave's wife must obey her master before her husband." If the master chooses to brand her, flog her, place her in the stocks, or use her sexually, her husband "cannot save her."[10] Because the family cohesion promised by marriage does not extend

---

8. Aside from addressing slavery issues in her travel journals, Martineau wrote articles about slavery and related topics, including American Civil War politics, Lincoln, Reconstruction, the ethics and economics of the cotton market, boycotting versus using West Indian products like sugar and coffee, the slave trade, and more. See particularly *London Daily News,* 1852–1866; and Elisabeth Sanders Arbuckle, *Harriet Martineau in the "London Daily News."* Martineau also wrote a biography (published in 1840) of Haiti's black radical political leader, Toussaint L'Ouverture.

9. Martineau, "Demerara," 60.

10. Ibid., 61. Slavery's disruption of familial integrity is demonstrated by Mary Prince's early, and permanent, separation from her mother. As her master beats her,

here to nonwhites, Willy denounces the convention as a meaningless ritual. As critical outrage on both sides of the Atlantic demonstrates, "Demerara" deconstructs whites' domestic ideology through exposing its racist, classist, and—Martineau's unique contribution—sexist underpinnings.

The stereotype of female fragility, chastity, and moral superiority loses its a priori status when presented, as in "Demerara," as a power differential grounded not in nature but in politics. This enables Martineau to pose some disturbing questions about her culture's domestic ideology: If marriage is civilization's natural state, then why do white masters use black slaves sexually? Why are slave women not protected by the standards protecting white women? And why are they judged as fallen by those same standards? Martineau's appeal to domestic values strikes at the heart of Victorian moral ideology, earning her a reputation for abolitionist sympathies that preceded her visit to America. "Demerara" generated controversy by humanizing slaves—they spoke for themselves—and by presenting them as inherently moral and intelligent, devices employed also in Mary Prince's narrative. As a result, despite her intention to remain nonpolitical while a guest in America—her policy was "never to evade the great question of colour; never to provoke it; but always to meet it plainly"—the author of the infamous "Demerara" found herself swept into America's raging slavery debate, an issue so intense as to allow no neutrality, even in foreigners.[11] "Having thus declared on the safe side of the Atlantic," she later observed, "I was bound to act up to my declaration on the unsafe side" (*RWT,* 1:163).

The seriousness of the dangers courted by Martineau's abolitionist politics in "Demerara" should not be underestimated. In 1830s America, possession of "papers for the purpose of exciting to insurrection, conspiracy or resistance" slaves against masters was punishable by death—true for whites no less than for blacks.[12] Given the degree of emotionalism slavery debates were capable of arousing, "Demerara" (though a fictional tale) was considered insurrectionist propaganda. Martineau notes that even the "vaguest suspicion" resulted in fines, flogging, and/or imprisonment. As a result, having already received several death threats during her American tour, Martineau was forced to arrange for the safety of her papers and

---

Mary Prince longs to "run away to my mother; but mothers could only weep and mourn over their children, they could not save them from cruel masters" (Ferguson, introduction to *The History of Mary Prince*, 60).

11. Martineau, *Retrospect of Western Travel*, 1:229. Future quotations will be designated *RWT* and cited parenthetically in the text.

12. Jane Louise Mesick, *The English Traveller in America, 1785–1835*, 127.

journals and to alter her itinerary when she learned of plans to tar, feather, and hang her.

Martineau's American travel journals record an incident in a Washington boardinghouse illustrating her enduring concern for female slaves. A little black girl "attached" herself to Martineau, holding onto her skirts, following her about, sitting at her feet playing with her laces while she read. Although charmed by this "bright-eyed, merry-hearted child, —confiding, like other children, and dreading no evil," Martineau's mood is overshadowed by the realization that this girl is "hopelessly doomed to ignorance, privation, and moral degradation. . . . the dooming to blight a being so helpless, so confiding and so full of promise . . . sickened my very soul" (*RWT*, 1:233). Her phrase "moral degradation" demonstrates her understanding of the probability of this girl's sexual exploitation.

Because opportunities for uncensored observation were limited during this tour (since the Americans were anxious to favorably impress this unofficial ambassador from England, it is unlikely she would have been granted access to the more sordid side of plantation life just for the asking), Martineau focused on the racist attitudes she encountered in Americans' middle-class drawing rooms. As is true of the other writers I discuss, she made culpability for sexual falls a primary consideration: for Martineau, it is the adults, not the children; the men, not the women (with some exceptions); the whites, not the blacks; and the victimizers, not the victims, who must be held accountable for the sort of systematized sexual exploitation practiced in America. *Society in America* addresses this subject by aggressively questioning the "purity of manners" of Southern white men. Writing more than a decade before her Eastern tour, she here draws a striking analogy between sexual exploitation, East and West: any plantation owner "may have his harem, and has every inducement of custom, and of pecuniary gain, to tempt him to the common practice."[13] She clarifies "pecuniary gain" by explaining the "practice of planters selling and bequeathing their own children." Elsewhere, Martineau critiques the institution of marriage "as it exists among us at this time" (*SA*, 223) and condemns the open practice of polygamy in the Middle East; but the white masters' overt monogamy and

---

13. Echoing Martineau's analogy between plantations and harems, Friedrich Engels, in *The Condition of the Working Classes in England* (New York: Macmillan, 1958), discusses industrialization's disruption of family life. Factory owners are configured as harem masters, their factories as harems, and women employees as harem wives and slaves. The resulting emasculation of working-class men (and of black slave men) casts them as eunuchs. See also Nord, *Walking the Victorian Streets*, 141–42.

covert polygamy to her represents a mockery of America's self-proclaimed commitment to individual freedom and dignity.

The analogy between plantations in the American South and Middle Eastern harems enables Martineau to broach the topic of female slaves' sexuality, which most of her contemporaries avoided. Such institutionalized immorality must be met on its own brutal terms; simply put, the "boundless licentiousness" practiced on plantations is intended to breed more slaves, "as many as possible, like stock, for the southern market" (*SA,* 226), a cruel parody of the maternal paradigm and a barbaric display of capitalist greed. No delicate euphemisms here: the planter's wife is rendered "the chief slave of the harem," while it was generally "understood that the female slaves were to become mothers at fifteen" (*SA,* 226). Martineau condemns associating such ideas as "purity of manners" and "domestic fidelity" with "pecuniary gain," a practice with tragic repercussions for the "morals and manners" of America.

Martineau directly links "savage violences" against Southern black men —lynching, burning alive, cutting out their hearts—with the "very general connexion" (*SA,* 226) (a euphemism for interracial sexual relations) that makes black women the sexual property of their masters. Routinely, "The negro is exasperated by being deprived of his wife, —by being sent out of the way that his master may take possession of his home"; if the black man protests or attempts to retaliate, "much that is dreadful ensues" (*SA,* 227), often including death.[14] Martineau collapses the stereotype of black women's promiscuity by shifting this epithet onto white men: "I am confident that the licentiousness of the masters is the proximate cause of society in the south . . . being in such a state" (*SA,* 227). It is through thus exposing white men's actions and white women's complicity that Martineau dismantles unexamined assumptions about the sexuality of nonwhite races.

Martineau objects to the hard labor that slave women endure (even when they are pregnant with the master's child) as a disturbing visual metaphor for an unwholesome moral climate. The filthy rags that serve as the slave woman's clothing, the "perspiration streaming down her dull face, the heavy tread of the splay foot, the slovenly air with which she guides her plough" (*RWT,* 2:53) present "hideous" affronts to Martineau's utilitarian vision of a healthy, laboring social body. Contrasting with such

14. Martineau employs the terms *husbands* and *wives* with an awareness (demonstrated in "Demerara") that slaves' actual status in this regard was probably "common-law."

images are the complaints of leisured white women, who argue that blacks' "immorality and foolishness" justify their enslavement. Examples of such self-aggrandizing attitudes abound in both *Society in America* and *Retrospect of Western Travel,* illustrating the active complicity of many Southern women in a system that in fact oppressed them as well. Dramatizing some of the more visible effects of that system is Martineau's discussion of a Southern orphanage where "none but whites are admitted, . . . for the licentiousness of the South takes the women of colour for its victims" (*RWT,* 2:82). The inescapable evidence of the "general connexions" between black women slaves, white masters, and their mulatto children is more fully discussed in her chapter "New Orleans."

But it is Martineau's account of Charleston's slave market that most compellingly challenges maternal values, which in practice do not apply to slave women. A mulatto woman, "neatly dressed, with a clean apron," stood on the auction block with her two children, "one at the breast, and another holding by her apron. . . . She hung her head low, lower, and still lower on her breast. . . . I should have thought that her agony of shame and dread would have silenced the tongue of every spectator: but it was not so" (*RWT,* 2:84–85). The woman's "shame" may be explained by Jane Mesick's observation that a slave auction "differs in nothing from that of selling a horse. The poor object of traffic is mounted on a table, intending purchasers examine his points. . . . When a woman is sold," the auctioneer "puts his audience in good humor by a few indecent jokes." But the woman's "dread" probably concerns the likelihood that she will be permanently separated from her children as a result of the auction.[15] Maternal ideology, as Martineau recognized, is a powerful medium for redeeming (or, in some instances, for incriminating) unconventional sexualities and for inspiring compassion for (or condemnation of) the oppressed.

Perfectly illustrating what is for Martineau the lack of comprehension typical of an unhealthy moral climate, a white female spectator "complacently" announced that since "one race must be subservient to the other . . . if the blacks should ever have the upper hand, I should not mind standing on that table, and being sold with two of my children" (*RWT,* 2:85). Martineau heartily wishes that were the case, so that those on the block could go free

15. Mesick, *English Traveller,* 139–40. Mary Prince's account of her own sale verifies these points. Along with her mother and sisters, Mary was "examined and handled" as if she were livestock; each family member was sold to a separate owner that day, never to be reunited. See also Ferguson, introduction to *The History of Mary Prince,* 52–53.

and those responsible could be punished. It is episodes like this that must be told, Martineau contends, lest America's image as a symbol for freedom be mistaken for the corruption paving its very streets.

As in "Demerara," Martineau's American travel journals consider the price black women pay to maintain white domestic ideology. Distinct from the literal sexual fallenness of slave women (fallen because not legitimated by marriage), slavery degrades white women as well, although this does not "imply any doubt of the purity of their manners, . . . [since] there is ever present an unfortunate servile class of their own sex to serve the purposes of licentiousness" (*SA*, 231). What it does imply is that women whose respectability depends on the rape of black slave women are themselves fallen by their silent complicity in systematized exploitation. This observation echoes the theory that prostitution (an institution comparable to racial slavery) is necessary to the preservation of white middle-class sexual ideology.

The most poignant metaphor for Martineau's writing on slave women's sexuality is Ailsie, an eight-year-old mulatto girl from New Orleans. Ailsie, the only nonwhite female in Martineau's travel accounts to have a name, a story, and an identity, functions to remove the masses of nameless "dusky" faces from obscurity and make their oppression more than a collection of sociological data. Ailsie is "perfectly beautiful, and one of the most promising children I ever saw. . . . quick, obedient, and affectionate" (*RWT*, 2:146). The product of a white master and his black cook, the child was subjected to the hatred and abuse of her mother's black husband, for whom her presence was a constant reminder of his powerlessness. Emphasizing the even greater powerlessness of her mother, Ailsie's white father places the child in another establishment with a mistress whose subsequent death left the child prey to the sexual exploitation that had no regard for childhood. Martineau is "in despair" over the "future lot" of this "forlorn little creature," since "None but a virtuous mistress can fully protect a female slave,—and that too seldom" (*RWT*, 2:147). She attempts to adopt Ailsie to raise her in England, but Ailsie's former master/father reclaims her, and Martineau hears no more of her fate.

Martineau's sojourn in New Orleans validated her concerns about the exploitation of nonwhite women's sexuality in other ways. The large mulatto population, another confirmation of the "positive licentiousness of the south," helped perpetuate a moral climate specifically damaging to "domestic purity and peace" (*SA*, 225) for blacks and whites. If the sexual fates of black slave women proved difficult to verify empirically, the institution of "quadroon connexions" was more easily observed. The term *quadroon* refers to those whose genetic makeup is one-quarter black and three-quarters white; lest the numerical factor be questionable, "quadroon" is more loosely defined as the product of white and mulatto parentage.

The lives of female quadroons differed significantly from other nonwhite women in that they were "brought up by their mothers to be what they have been; the mistresses of white gentlemen" (*SA*, 225). But no condemnation of mothers' complicity in this system is forthcoming from Martineau. Instead, consistent with her exculpation of black sexuality, Martineau's attitude toward quadroon "connexions" charges white men with full moral responsibility. Considering that this institution may be defined as a highly organized form of prostitution—with their own mothers acting as procurers, quadroons are materially provided for in exchange for sexual intimacy, without benefit of a legally binding marriage contract—Martineau's presentation of "the graceful Quadroon women . . . taking their evening airing on the Levee" (*RWT*, 2:134) is uncharacteristically sympathetic. As her Eastern travel journals reveal, this sympathy does not extend to harem wives, whose lifestyle is remarkably similar.

Martineau describes quadroon girls as "highly educated, externally, and . . . as beautiful and accomplished a set of women as can be found" (*SA*, 225), striking contrasts to black slave women who dressed in rags and were overworked, underfed, uneducated, and inarticulate. This situates quadroons in a position more analogous to that of white women in that they are well schooled in those feminine graces designed to create the sort of "accomplished" women desired by men. Yet, sexual purity is central to this ideology, which directly links womanly accomplishments with marriageability, the only social legitimation for women. In outward form, then, or as Martineau says, "externally," quadroons are elegant ladies living materially privileged lives; in practice, they are by definition unmarriageable because sexually fallen and racially "impure."

Therefore, despite the comparative luxury and material opportunity available to quadroons, they remain as subject to sexual slavery as black slave women on Southern plantations and as wives and slave girls in Middle Eastern harems. Like girls exploited by parents and panderers in child-prostitution rings, these women are bred for the purpose of sexually serving a man (like plantation wives, in a one-sided monogamy) who "early selects one, and establishes her in one of those pretty and peculiar houses, whole rows of which may be seen in the Remparts" (*SA*, 225). Martineau notes that such "connexions" may last a lifetime or be of short duration; either way, "when the time comes," as it inevitably does, "for the gentleman to take a white wife" (*SA*, 225), the degraded status of the quadroon reflects in the callousness with which she is subsequently treated. Some quadroons learned of their altered status by letter or gossip or by reading of their lover's engagement in the newspaper; seldom were they dignified by a direct confrontation. Some men never broke the "connexion," but continued it after marriage, effectually keeping both wife and mistress in concubinage.

Martineau observes that, distinct from the presumably jaded emotions of hardened prostitutes, these women are emotionally invested in their lovers and their relationships, as well as in the children produced by such "connexions": "Quadroon ladies are rarely or never known to form a second connexion. Many commit suicide: more die broken-hearted" (*SA*, 225). Sentimentalism aside, most striking about this passage is that, although lacking the legitimation of marriage, these women are committed to long-term monogamous unions, which for both the social scientist and the moralist in Martineau signifies their moral superiority to their lovers. The powerful ideological appeal accomplished by this presentation recalls the slave woman on the auction block, modestly breast-feeding the infant from whom she is about to be permanently separated: compelling and unforgettable images posing authentic against perverted domestic values.

According to Martineau's estimate, situated as they are between the accoutrements (conspicuous display) valued by white women and the assumed sexual availability and promiscuity of nonwhite women, quadroons merit compassion for the sexual fallenness that has shaped their lives since birth. Martineau questions to which wife, which children, and which home Southern men are morally responsible, the prior "connexion" or the legally binding one: "Every Quadroon woman believes that her partner will prove an exception to the rule of desertion. Every white lady believes that her husband has been an exception to the rule of seduction" (*SA*, 225). As Martineau's sociological observations repeatedly prove, the romanticized powerlessness and sexual deception of women recognizes no cultural, class, racial, or economic boundaries.

One final example illustrates the "positive licentiousness" exhibited by so-called cultivated white women and strengthens the analogy drawn by Martineau between American slavery and Middle Eastern harems. One such woman related the story of a "very pretty mulatto girl" in her "possession" of whom "she declared herself fond." When a young white man expressed sexual interest in the girl, she appealed to her mistress for protection, "which

I gave her." But the man persisted, and the mistress "pitied" him: "so I sold the girl to him for 1,500 dollars" (*SA*, 229–30). Clearly, this woman's interest in "pecuniary gain" outweighs her allegiance to the daily companion of whom she was so "very fond"; it is also clear, amazingly, that she does not consider herself either racist or a procurer. Whether in the American South or the Middle East, women's oppression of other women signified for Martineau the most insidious collusion of all.

Martineau concludes her account of the status of American women by admitting she earlier had dreaded visiting the Southern states because of their reputed "licentiousness." As an admittedly impassioned social observer, Martineau recorded the effects of slavery and of sexual exploitation on whites, blacks, and "duskys" alike. Though there is much to be learned in the American South, Martineau concludes, "it is the last place . . . where one who prizes . . . Humanity would wish to live" (*RWT*, 2:160).

Martineau's 1846–1847 tour of Egypt and Palestine revealed types of female exploitation remarkably similar to what she observed in America. The travel journals published as *Eastern Life, Present and Past* provide valuable insights into nineteenth-century Middle Eastern culture, considered fallen, by Western standards, because polygamous. Although Martineau's sociological objectivity at times conflicts with her moral and utilitarian ideologies, her critique of harem women's fallenness is ultimately tempered by compassion for the sexual subjection that defines their lives.[16] Complicating her role as social observer is a "disgust" that "arises from the link of femaleness that binds the observer to women whose lives appear to be defined by unlicensed sexuality . . . it is this bond that makes objectivity or relativism unthinkable," although this is true only initially.[17] Her conviction that woman's duty is, first, to cultivate her individual autonomy and, second, to live a productive life demonstrates Martineau's refusal to participate in the assessment of women on sexual standards alone.

Early in the Eastern tour, a visit to a monastery that refused to admit "any woman within their gates, under any stress of weather or other accident"

16. Continuing work begun during the American tour, *Eastern Life, Present and Past* provides important insights into Martineau's radical attitudes toward British imperialism and nonconformist theology. As John Barrell notes, the book "is remarkable for the liberal position it takes up in relation to the politics of Egyptology. Martineau held what to many in the mid-nineteenth century had become incompatible beliefs: that the Ancient Egyptians were black, and that they had created one of the great civilizations of the world" ("Death on the Nile: Fantasy and the Literature of Tourism, 1840–1860," 98).

17. Nord, *Walking the Victorian Streets*, 123.

aptly characterizes the gender issues of interest to Martineau both at home and abroad.[18] Camping with the other women outside the monastery walls and thus exposed to bandits and the elements, Martineau notes caustically that women there were regarded as dangerous enemies by "monks too holy to be hospitable, except to gentlemen who need it least" (*EL*, 129). The deeply ingrained misogyny this episode conveyed to Martineau proved to be a consistent theme throughout the tour.

Martineau opens her chapter "The Hareem" with the same sort of disclaimer with which she concludes "New Orleans" in *Retrospect of Western Travel*. Of harems she observes, "it would be wrong to pass them over in an account of my travels; though the subject is as little agreeable as any I can have to treat" (*EL*, 147). The transparency of Martineau's "objectivity" is seen in her assertion that the poorest slum in London is preferable to harems' opulence: "There are there at least the elements of a rational life, however perverted; while here humanity is wholly and hopelessly baulked."[19] Despite her sociological aims, her desire to visit "hareems" in Cairo and Damascus seems daring and radical for a woman circumscribed by Victorian fastidiousness about sexuality. From a cultural perspective in which the monogamous nuclear family was regarded as sacrosanct (although not a lifestyle Martineau personally endorsed), polygamy ranks with prostitution and all the other deviancies examined in this study as yet another form of sexual fallenness. Martineau's struggle to remain the objective social scientist is clearly at odds with her moral values, as her comments on polygamy demonstrate: "I declare that if we are to look for a hell on earth, it is where polygamy exists: and that as polygamy runs riot in Egypt, Egypt is the lowest depth of this hell. . . . These two hellish practices, slavery and polygamy, which . . . can never be separated, are here avowedly connected. . . ." (*EL*, 148, 159).

Martineau regards harem life as legitimated sexual slavery unmitigated by either material productivity, intellectual study, or spiritual aspiration. Put another way, to paraphrase Jeremy Bentham, the sexual needs of the one outweigh the individual development of the many. The system thus perverted the utilitarian ideology Martineau endorsed, another factor accounting for her unusual definition of Eastern women's fallenness. Distinct from more modern standards of sociological measurements, Martineau's

18. Martineau, *Eastern Life, Present and Past*, 128. Future quotations will be designated *EL* and cited parenthetically in the text.

19. Martineau quoted in Gayle Graham Yates, ed., *Harriet Martineau on Women*, 178.

contributions to this discipline—like those of her contemporaries—conflate such ideas as morality, ethics, and cultural practices. It is important to approach Martineau's work, particularly the Eastern notebooks, with an awareness that her empirical observations are viewed through the lens of utilitarianism and colored by her complex relationship with her culture's moral code.

Thus, Martineau's attitude toward harem women's sexuality is difficult to distinguish from her critique of their unproductive lives. As her writing on American slaves reveals, Martineau could certainly comprehend women's sexual victimization by a system beyond their control; what she could not accept was the material luxury and sensory overindulgence that marked harem women's lives and that clearly served as compensation for their sexual enslavement. Like American quadroons, harem wives' ornamental existence aimed exclusively at "conspicuous display," as did, interestingly, the lifestyle of middle-class Englishwomen. Martineau was as critical of her own countrywomen as she was of harem women on this point, but quadroons merited only her sympathy. Harem wives participate in what I have called a hierarchy of deviances, which includes black slave women, whose meager subsistence was regarded as compensation for both field and sexual labor; quadroons, whose role as mistresses was a racist parody of whites' monogamous marriage; and prostitutes, whose exchange of sex for money was, if more overt, at least less hypocritical. Linking all these categories is an economics of sexuality of the sort noted fifteen years earlier in "Demerara."

In this sense, there is little distinguishing middle-class Western women from harem women, with the important exception of marital practices (monogamy or polygamy). Martineau recounts an exchange between the harem wives and their Western visitors that marked what in modern parlance would be called a "paradigm shift." When Martineau's companion retained her bonnet and veil inside the wives' living quarters (as Western propriety dictated), the wives protested and insisted she remove them. In a culture known for its strict veiling practices, remaining veiled while indoors and in the company of women was not "respectable." This is one of several pivotal moments in an interview strained by linguistic and cultural constraints, constraints the harem wives seemed more determined to overcome than did the social observer, Martineau. Deborah Nord argues that it is shared gender concerns that inhibit Martineau, preventing her from engaging honestly with these women; yet, as "The Hareem" later reveals, the Englishwoman and her attitude are profoundly altered as these episodes progress.[20]

Martineau's conflicted objectivity is further tested by harems' maternal standards. When presented to the harem's "chief" wife, whose face wears the "strong expression of waywardness and peevishness" (*EL*, 150–51) that one might expect of dissolute sexuality, Martineau is surprised to learn the woman is in fact mourning the death of another wife's child, "a curious illustration of the feelings and manners of the place!" (*EL*, 151). She notes that those "houses at home which morally most resemble these hareems"—brothels, which, interestingly, she never visited: prostitution is one of the rare exceptions to Martineau's prolific commentary on virtually every subject of interest to Victorians—are similarly marked by the intensity of the women's emotions toward their own and each others' children: "when the rare event of the birth of a child happens, a passionate joy extends over the wretched household." Like most Victorians, Martineau is reluctant to associate such emotions with prostitutes or harem wives or anyone else whose unconventional sexuality seems inconsistent with maternalism—with the exception, inexplicably, of quadroons.

But not all harem births are welcomed; some end in infanticide, a result of the intense jealousy generated when childbirth raises a woman's status above that of the other wives: "what happens then?—why, the strangling the innocent in its sleep,—or the letting it slip from the window into the river below,—or the mixing poison with its food;—the mother and the murderess, always rivals . . . shut up together for life" (*EL*, 152). Yet, Martineau's question "If the child lives, what then?" implies death is preferable, since harem girls experience only the "nothingness of external life, and the chaos of interior existence," while boys witness scenes between harem women and eunuchs that "brutalize" them "for life." Both Martineau's Middle Eastern and her American memoirs reflect her theory that children are the primary sufferers of cultural dysfunction, and that they also provide the greatest potential for change. But she refuses to "dwell on these hopeless miseries" further, although she does address them at length in her later series of articles on infanticide in the *London Daily News*.

The harem wives are perplexed by Martineau's single status, and pity her "for not being taken care of—that is, watched": they regard the unchaperoned Westerners as "strangely neglected in being left so free, and

20. Nord, *Walking the Victorian Streets*, 123–24.

boast of their spy system and imprisonment as tokens of the value in which they are held" (*EL*, 154). The unhappy alternative to harems' protection, as Martineau knows, was suggested by her experience at the monastery. She attempts to explain her career as a professional writer, "but the information was thrown away, because they did not know what a book was" (*EL*, 166). And when told that Martineau had built her own home, an achievement of which she was particularly proud, the Eastern women "could make nothing of it": "There is nothing about which the inmates of hareems seem to be so utterly stupid as about women having anything to do. That time should be valuable to a woman, and that she should have any business on her hands, and any engagements to observe, are things quite beyond their comprehension" (*EL*, 166).

Martineau is (to borrow Deborah Nord's term) *disgusted* by these "dull, soulless, brutish" women: "There cannot be a woman of them all who is not dwarfed and withered in mind and soul by being kept wholly engrossed with that one interest" (*EL*, 155), sexual slavery. Martineau's conflation of sexual issues with productivity implies that harem women's immorality could be somewhat mitigated by their finding something useful to do. Clearly, she is challenged by the systematic victimization of women whose "grossness is revolting" (*EL*, 155), and by harem women's participation in this process; she is disturbed by their pitying her, and by their apparent satisfaction with this lifestyle. Martineau's observations of harem life further verify her theory that women throughout the world are degraded; excepting black American female slaves, harems presented the most debased form of female subordination she had encountered in all her travels. For Martineau, the comparative material comforts of harem life not only failed to diminish its barbaric dehumanization of women, but also rendered the institution the more reprehensible for this hypocrisy.

Prior to these harem visits, Martineau admired the physical strength, beauty, and agility of Egyptian young people, and noted that stiff, reserved English children would do well to imitate their naturalness and spontaneity. But, echoing her earlier concerns about American slave children, she now regards these children as tragic in that so many are destined to be sold as eunuchs and slave girls to establishments "whose mere presence is a perpetual insult and shame to humanity" (*EL*, 157) instead of marrying each other and establishing monogamous households. She is appalled by eunuchs' reputed physical familiarity with the wives, whom they often held emotional hostage by their complicity with the master. Despite their sexual unmanning, eunuchs exercised great power within the harem system: they acted both as spies for the master and as the women's primary source of communication with the outside world. Although "closer attachments" ("connexions") between the wives and eunuchs were not uncommon, this did not concern the master "so long as he knows that the cage is secure" (*EL*, 158).

When not "wholly engrossed with that one interest" (*EL*, 155), harem wives were preoccupied with eating, drinking, and smoking "intemperately," and, worst of all, dancing. Introduced to an expectant harem wife, Martineau thought her handsome and graceful until she began to dance, and "the charm was destroyed for ever" (*EL*, 165). Martineau's views are typical of a culture that dictated a strict separation between motherhood and sexuality, neither of which should be openly celebrated by suggestive dancing. Accordingly, when a young, nonpregnant girl performed a similar dance, "but with downcast eyes and an air of modesty," she was not regarded as "utterly disgusting" (*EL*, 165), although the Cairo street dancers are "a horrid sight, which we were glad to turn away from. So hideous a creature as the one who was dancing I never saw. . . . it appeared to us . . . a disagreeable and foolish wriggle, without activity of limb, or grace of attitude" (*EL*, 129). The public nature of this display no doubt precludes the "air of modesty" that for Martineau somewhat vindicated the sensuality of Middle Eastern dancing.

Martineau questions the integrity of those empowered by the harem system, like the owner of the Cairo harem: a "sensible looking man, with gay, easy and graceful manners. . . . He is a liberal-minded man," a description at odds with the lingering "impression of discontent and uneasiness which I shall be glad to sleep off" (*EL*, 156). Not one to criticize without offering alternative solutions, Martineau observes that it is up to parents to end this practice by refusing "to become restless when their daughter reaches eleven years old, and afraid of disgrace if she remains unmarried long after that" (*EL*, 160). This complex system of sexual exchange in which the protectors of innocent children are also the catalysts of or mediums for their exploitation is demonstrated by the mother who, at the arrival of the Western women, hugs her seven-year-old daughter closely, as if afraid "we should carry her off to London," assuring them she "would not sell her for much money" (*EL*, 164). The woman assumes that her only option is to delay the inevitable as long as possible, and that her lack of material greed somehow ameliorates selling her child into sexual slavery. These points recall issues raised during the American tour and, most notably, Martineau's failure to comment on quadroon mothers' role in exploiting their own daughters.

Leila Ahmed contends that, although the system "permits males sexual access to more than one female," it also provides women with a source of empowerment and solidarity: "the female relatives of a man—wives, sisters, mother, aunts, daughters—share much of their time and their living space, . . . which enables women to have frequent and easy access to other women in their community." However, if, as Ahmed claims, objection to a sexual system so clearly beneficial to men but not to women reflects Western ethnocentrism, then some insight into the cultural philosophy behind this practice is in order—which Ahmed does not provide. Ahmed avoids analyzing the basic conflict between gender separatism as a source of "women's strength and perhaps mobilization" and gender separatism as the wholesale disempowerment of females.[21] Female community at the price of personal autonomy is a bad bargain at best, whatever the cultural orientation.

Islam, a primary Middle Eastern religion, also dictates strict gendered separatism in terms of space, sexual practices, public appearance, and so on, indicating that there is some overlap of the cultural and religious roots of gender separatism in the Middle East. But followers of Islam regard polygamy, harems, and belly dancers as immoral and inconsistent with their religious beliefs. What Ahmed calls "Western ethnocentrism"—especially feminist critiques of institutionalized sexual slavery—is an attitude shared by devout Muslims. Clearly, these issues are far more complex than Ahmed implies.

Martineau's critique of the institutions of polygamy and harems in *Eastern Life, Present and Past* alters in tone by its conclusion. Her description of a Cairo harem in which three of the wives are sisters—"what a tragedy lies under this; what the horrors of jealousy must be among sisters thus connected for life"—marks a distinct shift in attitude from disgust to compassion. Despite her opulent surroundings, one of the wives, a new bride aged twelve, "looked so grave, and sad and timid. . . . she never smiled, but looked on listlessly" (*EL*, 162). This girl, like Ailsie and the Washington girl before her, seems instinctively drawn to Martineau, whose persistent efforts to make her smile are at length rewarded: "but there was far less of the gaiety of a child about her than in the elderly widows" (*EL*, 163). Struck by the tragedy of this child-woman, as she has been in other contexts, Martineau regrets the lost youth and wasted potential in one powerless over the events of her life.

21. Ahmed, "Western Ethnocentrism and Perceptions of the Harem," 524, 527.

Conceivably, such scenes revealed how deeply entrenched are these cultural practices, suggesting that even education—Martineau's usual prescription for correcting social inequity—is of limited value at this point in Middle Eastern women's history. Therefore, ever the proponent of physical activity and the well-being it fosters, Martineau (with probably unintentional humor) suggests that "skipping ropes" (*EL*, 167) be given to these women in order to improve their abused digestive systems through exercise (she does not, clearly, regard belly dancing as a suitable exercise). An admittedly ludicrous image, it nevertheless indicates a shift in her attitude toward harem women's fallenness: "Poor things! . . . human beings, such as those of whom Christ made friends!" (*EL*, 167), emphasizing Martineau's renewed focus on women's shared subordination, and on the complex associations linking magdalens with madonnas.

What accounts for this change in attitude? On Martineau's leaving the harem, the "chief lady" earlier described as petulant and spoiled presents her with roses as a parting gift. Surprised and touched, Martineau notes: "I kept those roses, however. I shall need no reminding of the most injured human beings I have ever seen,—the most studiously depressed and corrupted women whose condition I have witnessed; but I could not throw away the flowers which so found their way into my hand as to bespeak for the wrongs of the giver the mournful remembrance of my heart" (*EL*, 167). This suggests that Martineau has been, in a sense, shamed into compassion by a spontaneous, childlike gesture of friendship from one whose face she phrenologically "interprets" as peevish with depravity. In this gesture, Martineau perhaps also reads vestiges of the naturalness and grace of uncorrupted youth she earlier mourned, which struck a chord with her awareness of the wasted human potential of slaves East and West, none of whom have "discovered their powers" much less "cultivated them to the utmost." Through this simple gesture, the woman presents Martineau with clear evidence of the otherwise invisible fates of the Ailsies and child brides of the world, proof that enables her to regard these women as victims rather than harlots. In modern phraseology, Martineau stops blaming the victims and becomes instead their champion.

A highly popular genre of the period, travel journals like Martineau's record sometimes perplexing cultural differences, descriptions of which are often complicated by moral and religious biases. Martineau's accounts, like those of Mary Prince, are constrained by censorious attitudes in the publishing field and reading audience. Yet, as I have shown, Martineau found other ways to question the period's concerns about the preservation of women's sexual purity and about the legitimacy of paternal issue. This approach, like Stowe's religious emphasis, may not have propelled women's interests into radical change, yet it challenged firmly entrenched ideas and stereotypes that succeeded in naturalizing the image of fallenness among certain groups of women. Although somewhat muted, these pioneering texts performed important work for both the abolitionist and the feminist causes. Nearly two decades after Mary Prince's censored narrative, a more graphic articulation of the sorts of sexual exploitation these women endured was provided by one unafraid to "rush in" where others "fear to tread."

A more confrontational writer than Martineau or Stowe, Elizabeth Barrett Browning observed that white women's silence on the issue of slavery amounted to tacit approval of a system disturbingly reminiscent of the period's domestic ideology: "She had better subside into slavery and concubinage herself." "The Runaway Slave at Pilgrim's Point," written for the 1848 Boston National Anti-Slavery Bazaar and first published in its journal, *The Liberty Bell,* breaks women's silences as well as gender, class, and cultural boundaries with a violence "too ferocious, perhaps, for the Americans."[22] With a rhetorical power undiminished in the century and a half since its composition, this poem provides a graphic depiction and vindication of infanticide, a topic with an unparalleled capacity to arouse class anxieties about fallen sexuality, particularly when complicated, as in this poem, by racial issues. Although its author is removed racially, geographically, and economically from the Runaway Slave's experience, this dramatic monologue compellingly captures the spirit of rage engendered by the triple dehumanization of one race, one class, and one sex by another.

The term *engendered* is appropriate in other ways as well: the narrator's rage is crystallized by the image of her child's "too white" face, providing a clear focus both for the degradation marking every aspect of her life and for the expiation of that rage and degradation. Like Stowe and Martineau, Barrett Browning demands that concepts of human dignity be extended to incorporate blacks; but unlike those writers, she resists qualifying her presentation with euphemistic subtleties designed to make unsavory topics more palatable. "Runaway Slave" is an uncompromising poem about slavery, lynching, murder, rape, and infanticide, unseemly topics for a woman writer and, she argues, unconscionable experiences for any living being to

---

22. Elizabeth Barrett Browning, letter to Mrs. Jameson, April 12, 1853, quoted in Frederic Kenyon, ed., *The Letters of Elizabeth Barrett Browning,* 2:111; Barrett Browning, letter to H. S. Boyd, December 21, 1846, quoted in ibid., 1:315.

endure. The poet's treatment of these issues is untempered by her concern that the poem might be "too ferocious" for some readers.

From the poem's authoritative opening words, "I stand," Barrett Browning's first-person narrator asserts a tone of immediacy, urgency, and energy fueled by the agitation of having been "on the run" and now arrived at her final destination: Pilgrim's Point.[23] The Runaway Slave invokes the dead "pilgrim-souls" (8) to inform them of the atrocities being committed "in your names" (14), thus setting the stage for the tragedy soon to be enacted on this historic site. The images of land, sea, and sky are early introduced as ideas central to the narrator's extreme position: she is literally at land's end, in contrast to those for whom Pilgrim's Point represents freedom and the beginning of a vast domain. Although land generally connotes stability and rootedness in the earth, for her land's end signifies life's end. Similarly, the sea can connote escape to freedom, as it did for the pilgrims; for this woman it represents the final insurmountable obstacle in her flight from slavery.

The sky serves a distinctly different function and has special significance throughout the poem as "That great smooth Hand of God stretched out / On all His children fatherly" (44–45). But even this protective, nurturing image assumes menacing qualities as the poem progresses. Her questions and appeals remain unacknowledged and unanswered, and when she cries out to God "nothing didst Thou say!":

> Coldly Thou sat'st behind the sun:
> And now I cry who am but one,
> Thou wilt not speak to-day.
> (88–91)

Later passages demonstrate a similar ambivalence in the images of stars ("every star, / Did point and mock at what was done" [181–82]) and of trees ("The forest's arms did round us shut" [171]), yet "silence through the trees did run: / They asked no question" (172–73), nor did they respond to her plight despite the animating quality suggested in these lines. Barrett Browning's variation on the silenced woman paradoxically invests the speaker with a clear, distinct voice that makes logical observations and asks reasonable questions, all of which meet with silence and indifference

23. Elizabeth Barrett Browning, "The Runaway Slave at Pilgrim's Point," l. 1. Future quotations will be cited by line numbers parenthetically in the text.

from the white culture from which she runs, the nature to which she flees, and the God to whom she prays.

Strikingly, this poem employs the term *black* instead of the nineteenth century's conventional "Negro" or "dusky." The speaker lifts her black face and black hand "to curse this land" (20), proclaiming "I am black, I am black" (22) as an insistent refrain throughout the poem. Yet, she also rejects race as a qualification of her humanness: she experiences life "as if" she were not black, and experiences love "as if unsold, unbought" (65). The introduction of her black lover alters "I" to "We," but this relationship almost immediately shifts to past tense: "We were black, we were black, / We had no claim to love and bliss" (92–93). The narrator's lover is so termed not to suggest illicit behavior—she sings his name while still a "maid," or virgin—but to emphasize that the lack of human rights being enacted here makes impossible the legitimacy of blacks' claims to ordinary marriage and family. Marriage between slaves was extremely rare and, as a legal event, impossible without the master's consent. Those who did manage to marry anyway, perhaps through a folk, religious, or community ceremony, found this bond no guarantee of keeping their family intact. All members of the black family were property of the master, and anyone could be sold off at any time regardless of such ties. The idea that black sexuality was animalistic and depraved was used to excuse masters' rape of black women, who were in turn regarded as breeders of children who were also likely to be sold. What this social structure says about the domestic ideology employed to defend it has significant parallels in the prostitution discourse I have discussed throughout this study. Barrett Browning's slave woman defies this powerful stereotype; like Martineau's Ailsie she is poised at the apex of unrealized potential and extreme sexual vulnerability. But with the lynching of her lover, "They dragged him—where? I crawled to touch / His blood's mark in the dust" (96–97), the idea of humans as property assumes sexual meaning. More emphatically than Martineau's "Demerara," this narrative makes clear that the woman's function as a breeder of more slaves for the master does not accommodate such ideas as love, marriage, and family.

It is at this point that Barrett Browning departs from the religious rhetoric of Stowe and the domestic rhetoric of Martineau, and enters a new realm of discourse on the topic unmatched, in my opinion, until Toni Morrison's 1987 *Beloved*. Wishing only to grieve her lover's death, the narrator is instead raped, "the white men brought the shame ere long / To strangle the sob of my agony" (101–2), the plural "men" suggesting gang rape. Wanting to die, she instead gives birth to a child "far too white, too white for me" (116). Barrett

Browning inserts an appeal (more typical of Gaskell) to both Christian and "womanly" compassion, here perverted by the white churchwomen who condemn the slave for bearing a bastard. What such attitudes suggest about some women's "mission to women" is a theme the poet also addresses later in *Aurora Leigh*.

The narrative's tempo shifts from one of agitated intensity to a methodical, deliberate pace, a rhetorical manipulation that enslaves readers to this woman's nightmarish perspective. The slave woman describes in relentless detail her infanticide of the child on whose face she "could not bear / To look" (120–21). She covers its head, then ties it up tightly until he "moaned and struggled" (124). "He moaned and beat with his head and feet" (127), striking at her breast and heart as if searching for a nurturance long dead. She thinks of her lover buried "between the roots of the mango . . . where?" (137), and then of the child's resemblance to his father, which prompts her to twist the head "round in my shawl":

> And he moaned and trembled from foot to head,
> He shivered from head to foot;
> Till after a time, he lay instead
> Too suddenly still and mute.
>
> (147–51)

The idea that the silenced woman has the power to silence the white man's son permanently is so radical as to strain against the boundaries of sane behavior, which is ironic, considering she is systematically excluded from normal social categories. The woman's diabolical "ha, ha!" is a litany repeated throughout the poem, inviting us to speculate on her sanity and on whether the only palatable infanticide, even under such circumstances as murder and rape, is that committed by a madwoman. An early manuscript of this poem listed the title as "Black and Mad at Pilgrim's Point."[24] The change to "The Runaway Slave at Pilgrim's Point" shifts Barrett Browning's emphasis from madness, which obscures the broader political issues being enacted here, to a phrase that highlights the conflicts between freedom and captivity, appropriation and autonomy. The idea of agency is crucial to

24. I am indebted to Professor Beverly Taylor at the University of North Carolina at Chapel Hill for calling this point to my attention. See Philip Kelley and Betty A. Coley, *The Browning Collections: A Reconstruction with Other Memorabilia* (Winfield, Kans.: Armstrong Browning Library, Browning Institute, Mansell Pub. and Wedgestone Pr., 1984), 324, #D800.

the poet's social criticism: deliberate infanticide by a sane woman has far different connotations from the unaccountability of a random act prompted by insanity. Further, by aggressively rejecting the period's ready association between madness and foreignness, the poem remains focused on the issues of race, sexuality, and maternity as they coalesce in the slave's character. As the slave pointedly reminds us, "I am not mad: I am black" (218); accordingly, her admission that she carried the dead infant's body for a month before burying it must be seen as something other than evidence of insanity. It must be seen as an act of spiritual regard and reverence for life, if not between mother and child, then between human beings. Although she considers his death necessary, she does grieve its loss, which "lay on my heart like a stone" (166)—the image used also by Hetty Sorrel.

A key device linking the poem's events and the slave's responses to them is the idea of song. Earlier, her invocation to the pilgrim-souls invites them to "hum / In undertone to the ocean's roar" (17–18) during the recital of her story. Like other "dark things" such as singing birds and chanting frogs, she intones her lover's name as a song. In a narrative otherwise laced with curses, the Runaway Slave sings her lover's name out of love, "I sang his name instead of a song, / Over and over I sang his name" (78–79), and later out of grief as she comes to terms with the infanticide and buries the child at last. As a result, there ensued

> Some comfort, and my heart grew young;
> I sate down smiling there and sung
> The song I learnt in my maidenhood.
> And thus we two were reconciled.
> (187–90)

The sense of appeasement conveyed in these lines suggests some alignment between her grief both for her murdered lover and for her murdered infant. Reconciliation occurs through her vindication of her lover's death and through her singing his name over the child's grave.

Whatever her feeling for the child, it is far too complex for her to allow for the possibility that he will grow up to assume his "master-right," like his father. The appropriateness of her behavior gains credence from the infant's ghostly response:

> . . . as I Sang it soft and wild,
> The same song . . .
> Rose from the grave . . .

It was the dead child singing that,
To join the souls of both of us.
                    (192–96)

Whether "us" indicates the slave and her lover or the child and his mother is unclear, although, in the poem's final stanza, the slave envisions reunion with the child who is "waiting for me," but she does not envision a similar reunion with her lover. That this woman commits infanticide and then buries the evidence only after she has made peace with herself and her victim demonstrates her rejection of the code that brands her an outlaw. Why does she delay the burial—or bury the body at all—if not to exercise her "mother-right"? The threat this woman poses involves her race, her rape, her infanticide, and her rebellious rage, yet her actions—in effect, she is her own judge, jury, and executioner—clearly participate in issues larger than maternity and sexuality alone.

This poem's extremism is best evidenced by the poet's expectation that readers will accept the slave's infanticide as necessary and justified. As Martineau and Barrett Browning both recognize, slave women are categorically relegated to the "harlot" category; they are expected to bear children for the master who in turn sells them as a commodity; in effect, these women are doubly prostituted without remuneration. Barrett Browning's presentation implies that such a perversion of maternal ideology is most appropriately met with a retaliatory act like infanticide. Ultimately, what outweigh this crime are the crimes committed against the slave woman, both before and after the child's death, crimes that remain unpunished and unvindicated, crimes that only begin to hint at the atrocities committed against untold numbers of silenced victims in the name of freedom.

Given the circumstances, readers are compelled to consider carefully whether her act is criminal or justified, her behavior civilized or barbaric, her mind coherent or insane. Deirdre David argues that "the genuine horror of the poem lies in the mother's hatred of her infant," which aligns the slave with the sort of mindless disregard for life the whites demonstrate toward her. But she buries the child with a ritualized ceremony, an act traditionally regarded as a sacred privilege denoting respect for the dead, as opposed to the sort of hate-inspired disregard that would have left the body as carrion or tossed it into the sea to destroy its evidence. Alternatively, Helen Cooper claims the author "identifies our sympathy with the despised outsider and our judgment with the privileged law-abiding citizen. She thereby makes the 'unnatural' act of infanticide . . . seem natural in a culture that violently distorts the bond between mother and child."[25] More potently, in some respects, than the class-inscribed example of Hetty Sorrel's child, this child symbolizes the basic contradiction in the madonna-harlot dichotomy: that maternal ideology, far from immutable, is manipulable according to changing political needs. Therefore, the reasoning that permits "bad" women's redemption through "good" mothering must also permit the slave's wrongs to be redeemed through her eliminating so obvious a flaw in the system as this child represents. The slave woman's child cannot be allowed to live; its death signifies her rejection of the "master-right" to appropriate her body, her vindication of her lover's death, her empathy for the child's violation, her grief over a social structure that engenders such pointless tragedies, and her example of humane behavior in an inhumane culture.

As the thoughtful idyll of the infanticide concludes, the pilgrim-ghosts give way to the white lynchers who have tracked her down at last, and the narrative pace intensifies to its tragic conclusion. There is a quality of the absurd in this final scene, as five white men circle one black woman, stoning her, yet "shrinking back" from her raging curses: "I wish you . . . Each . . . A little corpse as safe at rest / As mine" (stanza 31). They tie her up and flog her until "I hung, as a gourd hangs in the sun" (226), but unlike Christ, slaves who bleed for nothing "are too heavy for our cross, / And fall and crush you and your seed" (244–45), as she has already done. The slave's defiance continues undiminished by physical torture, "lift your hands, / O slaves, and end what I begun!" (230–31), and her shrieks arise not from pain but rage. Until the poem's final line, the voice once raised in song ends life in curses.

The poem's last stanza incorporates the potent images of sky, sea, and land with those of child and lover. The Runaway Slave dies appealing to the sky/God, "I fall, I swoon! I look at the sky" (246), but it remains silent. She is "floated along, as if I should die / Of liberty's exquisite pain" (248–49), but it is unclear whether she escapes to the sea, is thrown there by her tormentors, or floats in some less material realm. Finally, the Runaway Slave invokes the spirit of the child buried in the "death-dark" of earth as she joins him through the ultimate leveler, death, where all may "kiss and agree." The poem never clarifies whether she is killed because she is a runaway slave or because she murdered the white man's bastard or both; like rape,

---

25. David, *Intellectual Woman and Victorian Patriarchy: Harriet Martineau, Elizabeth Barrett Browning, George Eliot*, 139; Cooper, *Elizabeth Barrett Browning*, 114.

slave murder is simply another master-right. But this woman demonstrates her corresponding "mother-right" one last time before dying. The heart that once belonged to her lover now broken, and her body crushed and mangled, her final word, "disdain!" (253), signifies a spirit unbroken by physical torture and degradation, by a silent, indifferent God, by the loss of love, or by the death of her child.

Far from Martineau's image of the neat slave woman in her clean apron, head modestly bowed, holding her children as she passively waits to be sold on the block, Barrett Browning's slave woman is positively titanic in her relentless, all-consuming rage. Whereas Martineau appeals to images of tame domesticity at its most pitiable, Barrett Browning voices an outraged appeal to a primal level of violated human dignity that demands respect regardless of race, class, age, or gender. True, this is violation "at its most pitiable" but, more to the point, at its most disturbing; readers are not permitted to turn from the slave woman's relentless agony until the speaker herself releases us. Like spectators surrounding the auction block, readers look away from Martineau's demure slave woman, embarrassed for her plight, yet trusting vaguely in her "innate purity" to survive her circumstances. Barrett Browning's slave woman is not bowed but defiant; she is not contrite but unrepentant. She does not wait passively but tempts her fate, hurling curses at her tormentors until her last breath. The Runaway Slave's Byronic qualities, which enable her to defy humanity, nature, God, and death, have broader implications than the self-indulgent posturing typical of the stereotype. Barrett Browning's embellishment of Byronism resides in the "fatal flaw" being located outside the protagonist, a character whose integrity remains intact despite a corrupt system. Also distinct from other characters of the type, this Byronic hero has found something worth dying for.

The Runaway Slave's position as cultural outsider, whether she passively accepts her fate as the white man's concubine or aggressively meets his violence with her own special violence, must by definition place her beyond that culture's moral and legal standards. Ostracizing the rape victim as the seducer of white men or condemning the infanticidal mother as criminally insane collapses in the absence of any protection provided her by social and legal paradigms. The Runaway Slave is "made so marginal by the white man's system that she cannot be judged by its laws. What from their white perspective seems a crazed black woman strangling her child . . . is a brutalized woman's totally coherent act."[26] In the absence of black voices

---

26. Cooper, *Elizabeth Barrett Browning,* 119.

speaking for themselves, Barrett Browning demonstrates that slave owners' "white perspective" can be and is met with an alternative white perspective, one that charges that what is worse than infanticide is the system that engenders it.

7

"The Problem to Be Solved, the Evil and Anomaly to Be Cured"

[Deborah Jenkyns] altogether had the appearance of a strong-minded woman; although she would have despised the modern idea of women being equal to men. Equal, indeed! she knew they were superior.

—Elizabeth Gaskell, *Cranford*

She is perfectly innocent, and I am indeed thankful to think that at eighteen she knows nothing of the world and its wickedness, and is therefore eminently qualified to make somebody an excellent wife.

—Sarah Grand, *The Heavenly Twins*

$\mathcal{M}$ ODERN SCHOLARSHIP on Victorian literary history reveals broader insights into the status of women then and now than fallen-woman literature alone suggests. The creative growth of the woman writer in *Aurora Leigh*, for example, the acute intelligence of Eliot's Dorothea Brooke in *Middlemarch*, the triumph of the plain heroine in *Jane Eyre* and *Villette:* such characters represent "Woman Question" issues essential to a comprehensive understanding of Victorian women. My complementary perspective, which aims to "unpack" the madonna-harlot polarity by focusing on the figure that was reviled even as it evoked surreptitious fascination, is in some ways even more crucial to our understanding than depictions of triumphant Victorian heroines. Because her active role, followed by her absence or elimination, is necessary to the period's "plot" of respectability, the compelling image of the deviant woman is the richest and most conflicted site of nineteenth-century social ideology. Indeed, women's quest for independence and autonomy beyond the domestic circle itself became a version of fallenness.

Throughout, this study has examined issues of female sexuality, particularly maternal ideology, and considered shifts in social attitudes toward both as the century evolved. The literature reveals that, despite the general tendency to categorize all women's social unconventionalities as "fallen," an isolated fall such as Ruth's or Marian's gradually assumed different connotations from those of professional prostitutes (Esther) or infanticidal mothers (Hetty). Similarly, alcoholism might be prompted by motivations other than illicit sexuality, whether one is childless (Janet Dempster) or a mother several times over (Mrs. Kay), while enslavement—whether of one's mind (Bertha) or body (Ailsie, the Runaway Slave)—was often a political or legal issue rather than a moral or medical one.

Redundancy is another factor linked with fallenness, evidenced by widows like Eleanor Gwynn in "The Well of Pen-Morfa," Anne Leigh in "Lizzie Leigh," and Janet Dempster's mother, Mrs. Raynor, in "Janet's Repentance," characters who clearly have not outlived their usefulness despite their cultural invisibility. Hellerstein reminds us that even older women were not exempt from the power of maternalism: "Most prescriptive literature focused heavily on women's maternal duties under the assumption that a natural metamorphosis would transform mothers into grandmothers."[1] This "second" motherhood was promoted as a "cure" for such maladies as loneliness and communal indifference suffered by spinsters and widows alike. It also argued against the disruptive idea that, once women had performed their expected social roles, they should be permitted to work outside the home for remuneration. Women's economic dependence—in modern parlance, the feminization of poverty—was aggressively promoted as essential to the nation's "moral" economy.

Marked by a fluidity that defies the fallen stereotype's static characterization, these examples demonstrate the cultural scapegoating endemic to angels and harlots alike. By the late Victorian period, the "Woman Question" acquired yet another aspect as debates raged over New Women's desires to exercise control over their sexuality and reproduction. Mid-Victorian sexual standards purported to protect women's chastity; yet, as later Victorians learned, the contagion of syphilis—no less than the earlier "moral" contamination of prostitution and infanticide—proved no respecter of class or gender boundaries. This chapter explores both New Women's

1. Hellerstein, Hume, and Offen, *Victorian Women,* 457.

pursuit of greater sexual autonomy—which includes making choices to protect themselves from venereal disease—and the medical establishment's retaliatory hystericization of these aberrant "girls of the period."

For many Victorian social critics, Eliza Lynn Linton's "girl of the period" was synonymous with the term *New Woman*. Linton's controversial essay on the topic bemoans the passing of the type of English girl whose "innate purity and dignity of . . . nature" produced "a tender mother, an industrious housekeeper, a judicious mistress." In contrast, Linton charges, "The Girl of the Period is a creature who dyes her hair and paints her face"; she is "too fast and flourishing" to be checked by moral considerations and lives only to "please herself." As a result, "though men laugh with her, they do not respect her, though they flirt with her they do not marry her."[2] Chronologically, Linton's infamous girl anticipates the scandalous typewriting, bicycle-riding New Woman by about twenty years. But as Grand's heroines demonstrate, nonconformity is not always reducible to moral values, though it does highlight ideological flaws.

What predates the New Woman icon is the pathologizing of single women earlier in the century, a precedent no less disturbing in its implications. "Proving that the rule is the exception," argues Jane Flanders, "is the spinster who, although not 'fallen,' is also held up to criticism or mockery because of [her] anomalous sexual role"; in Auerbach's phrase, "she evaded family definition."[3] Testifying to its wide-ranging tenacity, the madonna-harlot ideology lends itself to even so disparate a combination of factors as celibacy and venereal disease. The cultural fears aroused by unaccountable or redundant women find a compelling parallel in those attached to celibate married women. Earlier beliefs that the chaotic tendencies of female sexuality required constant management and monitoring quite literally returned to haunt those institutions whose existence depended on such notions. This "haunting" assumed two primary forms: first, "good" women who were "chaste" wives and mothers found that conformity offered no protection against venereal infection; and second, the medical establishment's pathologizing of women's sexual processes exposes the fallacy of the moral and ethical roles in which those processes were cast. The resulting nature/culture opposition raises the question, if female sexuality is in fact

2. Linton, "The Girl of the Period," quoted in Helsinger, *The Woman Question,* 1:108–12.

3. Flanders, "Fallen Woman in Fiction," 102; Nina Auerbach, foreword to *Old Maids to Radical Spinsters: Unmarried Women in the Twentieth-Century Novel,* ix.

medically controllable, then why should women not manage their sexuality themselves? Why, indeed.

Consideration of nineteenth-century attitudes toward celibacy, most often exemplified by spinsters or "old maids" and widows, illuminates the intersections of venereal disease and marital celibacy enacted in *The Heavenly Twins*. The most visible "problem" posed by spinsters concerned economics and employment. Anna Jameson notes that, according to the 1851 census, women outnumbered men by "more than half a million" in Great Britain, yet considerations of gentility, which prevented them from working for remuneration, kept many in a state of penury. In 1862, Frances Power Cobbe wrote that 30 percent of English women never marry, yet the double standard extends even to the celibate: "writers on this subject constantly concern themselves with the question of *female* celibacy, deplore it, abuse it, propose amazing remedies for it, but take little or no notice . . . of batchelors [*sic*]. . . . Their moral condition seems to excite no alarm, their lonely old age no foreboding compassion, their action on the community no reprobation."[4]

W. R. Greg's novel casting of redundant women as symptomatic of an unhealthy (social) disease, as an "anomaly" to be "cured," invites the analogy by prescribing permanent removal (transportation) of the offending organism. Greg's fantastic scheme, peopled by virginal old maids, women criminals (infanticidal mothers, for example), and diseased prostitutes dramatizes the collapsing of boundaries separating the other "in-between" behaviors I have traced throughout this study of fallen sexuality. Interestingly, Greg's proposal foregrounds the classist underpinnings of the term *spinster*. Distinct from women criminals, working-class women whose only crime was singleness or redundancy "were expected to fend for themselves, merging unobtrusively into the general body of the female labour force" and were therefore not candidates for transportation.[5] The period's discourse on old-maidism was addressed to middle-class spinsters who lacked familial support and "genteel" or respectable employment options, women whose presence mocked a socioeconomic ideology based on a class-specific binary gender system. This is true of all the "redundant" women in the following discussion.

4. Jameson, *Sisters of Charity, Catholic and Protestant, and the Communion of Labor* (Westport, Conn.: Hyperion Press, 1976); Cobbe, "What Shall We Do with Our Old Maids?" 594.

5. Greg, "Why Are Women Redundant?" 434–60; Thompson, *Rise of Respectable Society*, 91.

Responding to W. R. Greg's query "Why Are Women Redundant?" Frances Power Cobbe notes that marriage, presented as "the only true vocation for women [is] promoted at any cost, even by the most enormous schemes for the deportation of 440,000 females." The presence of so many superfluous females visibly challenged the culturewide pressure to domesticate women through marriage and motherhood. Aside from the paradox of linking celibate spinsters with promiscuous women, the more disturbing connotations of ethnic cleansing are revealed by the rhetoric used to justify such "schemes." Emigration proponent Charles Dickens notes that, with the "object that they may be restored to society," repentant women will be sent "abroad, where in a distant country they may become the faithful wives of honest men, and live and die in peace."[6] Dickens's stirring rhetoric does little to disguise the fact that Englishwomen who live and die in a foreign country are obviously *not* "restored to society." As the denouements of fallen-woman literature repeatedly demonstrate, the social integration of women, whether they are disfranchised through sexual impropriety or social redundancy, occurs somewhere other than in England, if at all.

Contrary to the stereotype, there are examples of women who did not suffer pain or humiliation from singleness but instead regarded spinsterhood as an appealing, even preferable, state. Harriet Martineau's account of the anxiety caused by her engagement, "my own special trial," is punctuated by an almost audible sigh of relief when she reveals that her fiancé's death prevented the marriage.[7] Years later she wrote, "I am probably the happiest single woman in England," having had the freedom to pursue "my business in life." She makes clear that this blighted engagement served as her realization of society's expectations that she marry, from which she was now and forever exempt. At the age of twenty-four, she declared herself a spinster and a professional writer, and (excepting a few minor skirmishes or "annoyances") was accordingly left alone: Martineau was not a woman to be trifled with in this matter.

Similarly, some fictional spinsters, such as those in Elizabeth Gaskell's *Cranford*, which was published in 1853, are also content to be single and are even mystified that women should desire to live otherwise. The embodiment of anachronism, Cranford's "elegant economy" defines the lives of "our

6. Cobbe, "What Shall We Do," 594–610; Dickens, "An Appeal to Fallen Women," in *Letters from Charles Dickens to Angela Burdett Coutts, 1841–1865,* ed. Edgar Johnson, 98–100.
7. Martineau, *Autobiography,* 1:130–33.

society," which is, in Auerbach's words, "the last well-bred gasp in the face of vulgarity, men, and machinery."[8] Unlike the world traveler Martineau, who enjoyed being "lionized" by the period's literary set, Cranford's widows and spinsters preferred their own insular society, seldom venturing beyond the confines of their quaint, exclusively female, circle. Should a man present himself as a potential member of this elite society, the impossibility of his integration is illustrated by his being promptly "killed" out of the narrative. As was true of Captain Brown—his being hit by a train while reading Dickens (Gaskell's response to the literary colleague who remarked that, if she were his wife, he would beat her) emphasizes Cranford's rejection of modern technology and contemporary literature as well as men—and of Miss Matty's ancient suitor, Mr. Holbrook, "somehow the gentleman disappears."[9] Here, it is the men who are redundant—men are "*so* in the way"—whereas "the ladies of Cranford are quite sufficient" (10).

The Jenkyns sisters are at the forefront of Cranford society, their greatest claim to gentility being that their father (though dead for decades) was a rector. The two spinsters construct a nuclear family of sorts, with the stern, inimitable Miss Deborah Jenkyns representing the patriarchal regime vacated by her father, and the weak, fluttering, soft-spoken Miss Matty in the complementary maternal role. But even a surrogate male figure like Deborah, though revered by "our society," is early removed from the narrative, centering the remaining plot on the feminine trials of Miss Matty. On her own for the first time in her life (she is well past middle age) and left penniless by Deborah's ill-chosen investments, Matty reveals an identity long obscured by patriarchal authoritativeness. She sells the heavy, oppressive, old parsonage furniture, burns her parents' love letters, and pronounces somewhat tremulously that "Mathilda" is the preferred form of her name, not the diminutive "Matty."

Matty's "mysterious dread of men and matrimony" (49) surfaces through her relationships with Mr. Holbrook and her servant, Martha. A suitor from her girlhood who reappears after Deborah's death (it was Deborah who had forbidden their union), the bachelor Mr. Holbrook reveals his interest is undiminished after all these years, an interest Matty clearly shares. But Cranford's unspoken prohibition against men outweighs even unrequited love, and he dies soon after. Deprived of both Deborah's iron rule and the economic shelter promised by marriage to Mr. Holbrook, Matty is forced

8. Auerbach, *Communities of Women,* 82.
9. Gaskell, *Cranford,* 9. Future quotations will be cited parenthetically in the text.

to prove her capacity for independence, which she does by selling tea and comfits out of her house.

Left without resources for the first time in her approximately sixty years, the problem of what she can do to earn a living poses a dilemma. Not only are the few talents Matty possesses unlikely to prove lucrative, but class considerations are another impediment. Gentility prevents her acquiring useful or marketable skills and prohibits certain types of employment: "I thought of all the things by which a woman past middle age, and with the education common to ladies fifty years ago, could earn or add to a living without materially losing caste; but at length I put even this last clause on one side, and wondered what in the world Miss Matty could do" (230). Matty reluctantly agrees to sell tea because it is "neither greasy nor sticky" (qualities denigrated for their associations with tradespeople) and because she can operate out of the privacy of her house where "No shop-window" exposing her to public view "would be required" (234).

Matty tests her mettle in other ways as well, for instance by allowing her maid, Martha, to accept an "admirer"—behavior strictly forbidden under Deborah's regime. Musing on her own missed opportunity, Matty's sanctioning Martha's marriage to Jem ultimately yields benefits that see her through old age: Martha remains a loyal companion, her husband obligingly makes himself scarce, and their sharing expenses allows Matty to keep her house. This extended family also provides Matty with an outlet for expressing her latent maternalism. Matty's recurring dreams about babies— often experiencing "the clasp of . . . dear little arms round my neck" (190)— find expression through Martha's children, casting Matty in the role of surrogate mother or grandmother. The unexpectedly fruitful alliance between mistress and maid promotes a vicarious regeneration for this woman whose spinsterhood stigmatizes her as barren and loveless. Ultimately, the class intersections between the sexually productive, working-class Martha and the chaste, genteel Miss Matty anticipate other unconventional relations threatening Cranford's outmoded insularity.

But although these events suggest that the Jenkyns household is at this point somewhat democratic, class differences continue to be observed. Matty is lady of the manor to Martha's maid-of-all-work; Matty plays with the children but performs none of the chores related to child rearing. As her baby dreams imply, Matty has regrets, but they are gentle regrets, and she makes amends for lost opportunities by promoting others' domestic happiness. The narrative's appeal to Matty's thwarted maternalism does not, however, obscure its implication that the unproductive Matty represents a dying "race" or breed that must ultimately give way to the stalwart Jems and self-sufficient Marthas of the world. While it is true that Matty defies the stereotype of dry, embittered, loveless, nonmaternal old maids, it is also true that her only scope for action is in living through others, not in developing her capacities "to the utmost."

But *Cranford*'s quaintly amusing depiction of Amazonian spinsters is an anomaly among literary presentations of the type. Elizabeth Gaskell's Misses Brownings, in her 1866 *Wives and Daughters,* who are regarded as meddling and gossipy from having no interests (like children) of their own, hint at the difficulties of social integration more compellingly realized by Charlotte Brontë in *Shirley,* published in 1849. Caroline Helstone's fear of impending spinsterhood—her marital prospects dim, she has "nothing to do" and is forbidden employment for remuneration—manifests itself through spinsters Miss Ainley and Miss Mann. Brontë reflects communal attitudes toward this "very unhappy race" of spinsters through a variety of characters.[10] Caroline's maid, Fanny, for instance, pronounces: "They are all selfish" but admits that since "gentlemen think only of ladies' looks" (192), such women are probably rejected on this basis alone. Initially prompted by fear of her own impending spinsterhood rather than compassion for others, Caroline decides to explore reasons for spinsters' "unamiability." What she learns is that the philanthropic Miss Ainley is the most self*less* woman she knows, and that Miss Mann's hard, soured demeanor stems not from an "unnatural" celibacy but from the disease and death that define her existence. Brontë shows that "unamiability" is not endemic to these women but rather a projection of those who fear the cultural instability they represent.

The misogynistic Robert Moore is a viciously outspoken opponent of spinsters. Moore targets even his own sister, Hortense (who is also his devoted housekeeper), no less than Miss Mann, and is determined "not to be dependent on the femininity in the cottage yonder" (58). Malone applauds this rejection of "petticoat-government" and boasts, "you and I will have no grey mares in our stables when we marry" (59), demonstrating as inauspicious an attitude toward dependent female relatives as toward any potential Mrs. Malone. Women like Hortense and Miss Mann, whose thwarted sexuality manifests in "the vinegar discourse of a cankered old maid," are "repulsive," made by nature out of "briars and thorns" (193). Moore claims that, since he was struck by Miss Mann's medusan gaze, his "flesh . . . [is]

10. Brontë, *Shirley,* 192. Future quotations will be cited parenthetically in the text.

stony in texture" (194). Leaving the "remedy" for Moore's sophomoric attitudes to the capable Nurse Horsfall, Brontë replaces ridicule with compassion: "Reader! when you behold an aspect for whose constant gloom and frown you cannot account, whose unvarying cloud exasperates you by its apparent causelessness, be sure that there is canker somewhere, and a canker not the less deeply corroding because concealed" (195). By thus reminding readers that the "disease" of spinsterhood is symptomatic of her culture's disrespect for women in other regards, Brontë offers a novel variation on the still radical claim that not all women's issues are reducible to sexuality.

Shirley's other spinster, Miss Ainley, is poor, plain, and "*very* ugly" (196). Proving Fanny's earlier comments, women respect Miss Ainley for her devotion to charitable causes, whereas "lively young gentlemen, and inconsiderate old ones . . . declared her hideous" (197). Contrasting with Moore, the Reverend Mr. Hall venerates his housekeeper/spinster sister, Margaret, an attitude he extends to Miss Ainley. Of the sexual issues confronting Shirley and Caroline, he counsels: "Young ladies, when your mirror or men's tongues flatter you, remember that, in the sight of her Maker, Mary Anne Ainley—a woman whom neither glass nor lips have ever panegyrized—is fairer and better than either of you. She is indeed . . . she is, indeed" (284–85). And, whereas Moore's shunning of Caroline threatens to render her a spinster, the Reverend Mr. Hall invites her to live with him and his sister, "If ever you want a home": "Should the old maid and bachelor be still living, they will make you tenderly welcome" (283). The compelling issues Caroline is being asked to evaluate—having been presented with the story of her mother's brutal marriage, with the determined endurance of Miss Mann and Miss Ainley, with the experiences of Hortense Moore and Miss Hall, and with her own vexed relationship with Robert Moore—are undercut by a wedding denouement that is not marked by any conceptual epiphany in Moore's attitude toward women.

Several distinct types emerge from the category of "spinster." Deborah Jenkyns devotes those years typically spent in preparing for courtship and marriage to assisting her father in his work. By the time her role as personal assistant ceases at his death, she is no longer considered marriageable; in effect, Deborah has been masculinized by intellectual pursuits. Matty represents the type forbidden to marry for "love" in favor of more pragmatic considerations like preserving class boundaries. Even for a poor rector's daughter, spinsterhood is preferable to marriage to a "self-made" man whose wealth was earned rather than inherited. Miss Ainley's saintliness does not compensate for her unattractiveness, perhaps the stereotype's most popular reason for spinsterhood. Finally, Miss Mann's youth was spent nursing her ill and dying parents, after which her own ruined health consumed what energy and time remained to her. Others, like Martineau, receive offers, but marriage is prevented, perhaps through untimely death; her response to this turn of events demonstrates her reluctance either to rebel against or to conform with this social expectation. Rare women like Florence Nightingale, whose refusal of marriage offers stemmed solely from her desire to do something more productive with her life and abilities, faced formidable social and familial opposition as a single woman by choice rather than circumstance.

These very different depictions of spinsters' plights and communal responses to them reveal the range of considerations contributing to their alienation. While portraying spinsters as gentle and harmless, not monstrous or aberrant, *Cranford* nevertheless demonstrates that the interdependence between these women is necessary to their survival, within the Cranford community no less than in the world community. The loyalties displayed by "our society" during Matty's economic trials demonstrate more than social solidarity: although Matty vaguely believes her tea shop makes her self-supporting, she is in fact secretly subsidized by friends' contributions. For these middle-class women, independence and autonomy— economic or otherwise—cannot coexist with respectability, which is the central paradox of this novel. Everyone, even her maid, Martha, participates in the lie that enables Matty to maintain the illusion of gentility, however hollow and unsupported that status is. Only in imaginary Cranford is the fiction of middle-class leisured gentility for single women possible: in the real world, people were neither so supportive nor so eager to protect one's delusions.

More realistically, what little communal respect Brontë's spinsters earn emanates from those able to assess these women on other than sexual terms. Such people see not Miss Ainley's ugliness but her devotion to charitable works; they understand that illness and death account for Miss Mann's "vinegared" countenance. Contrasting with "our society" in *Cranford*, notes Nina Auerbach, *Shirley*'s old maids participate in a broader social realm—their nursing and charity work marking them clearly as selfless, not self-absorbed—yet they "seem never to approach each other."[11] Here, community even among similar types proves impossible, suggesting that social alienation is necessary to this punitive stereotype.

11. Auerbach, *Communities of Women*, 85.

The cordoning off of *Cranford*'s community of old maids and widows and of *Shirley*'s spinsters dramatizes the lack of social integration accorded these women. Why should this group be marginalized? What is the source of the fear they inspire? What threats do they pose to social cohesion that could possibly justify the period's transportation schemes? In an ideology relying heavily on "nature" for its justification, spinsters in their involuntary challenge to the marriage-and-motherhood mystique are social pariahs. Like more explicitly fallen literary examples, they are too potentially subversive to be presented in a positive light. As a result, notes Kathleen Hickok, two primary conventions emerge in the period's treatment of spinster characters: ridicule (as seen in *Shirley*) and pathos (as in *Cranford*).[12] Although I have argued that old-maidism stems from factors other than sexuality, their cultural presence highlights the fallacies of an economy based on sexual roles.

But perhaps the relation between celibacy and promiscuity is not so indirect: Greg's proposal that eliminating the superfluous would not only bring about gender balance (statistically speaking) but also, amazingly, eliminate the need for prostitution is revelatory in its lumping together of prostitutes and spinsters while ignoring the glaring differences in their sexualities. "If Greg viewed competing for work with men as the 'evil' that 'redundant women' inflicted on England's economy," argues Poovey, "then the 'evil' with which they threatened the moral order posed just as serious a problem. This evil . . . was epitomized in prostitution"—and finds an unlikely counterpart in spinsterhood. Victorian society depends on women keeping to their proper place and upon "naturalizing monogamous marriage"; thus, there is no place for the unmarried woman.[13] In real life there were no Cranfords to contain whole communities of redundant women, other than convents or asylums. The dormant sexuality of women who are neither madonnas nor harlots defies the viability of the dichotomy and by analogy possesses the potential to erupt as a "crisis" in the form of insanity, alcoholism, murder, hysteria, or, what was to some even more anarchic, in the form of a single woman leading a productive, autonomous, dignified life.

The problems posed by spinsterhood include these women's lack of place in the social structure, their exposure of the elaborate middle-class lie

12. Hickok, "The Spinster in Victoria's England: Changing Attitudes in Popular Poetry by Women."
13. Poovey, *Uneven Developments*, 4–5; Nead, *Myths of Sexuality*, 95.

underlying the "naturalness" of the separate-spheres ideology, the pressure their existence places on the imperative that genteel women must not work for remuneration, and the subversiveness of the idea that women might increasingly regard singleness and economic independence as preferable to a life in servitude to others. The argument that, instead of transportation, such women should be trained for employment that would enable them to be self-supporting was deemed radical rather than sensible. Nevertheless, women were beginning to regard education and a career "not [as] a fail-safe but an alternative, one which might give them the option of choosing not to marry even where they might do so if they wished."[14]

Typical of the period's amorphous discourse boundaries, the threat posed by the possibility that spinsterhood might be a conscious choice rather than an anomaly of "nature" is configured in terms of racial survival: "on those women who became wives and mothers depends the future of the race; . . . if either class must be sacrificed to the other, it is the spinsters whose type perishes with them who should be sacrificed to the matrons." Resistance to education that would lead to employment and economic independence signifies that, to some, women's having the option of choosing not to marry is a contagious idea threatening to infect what Catherine Gallagher calls the "social body." "The freedom from family and home enjoyed by the old maids does give them a potentially subversive autonomy," notes Constance Harsh, but this is a potential unrealized by the literary examples I have discussed.[15]

The perennial infantilization implied by the epithet "old maid" serves as a reminder that spinsters were constantly belittled for both their "arrested development" (unrealized sexuality) and their thwarted maternalism. Childlessness is, as the characters Bertha Mason Rochester and Janet Dempster illustrate, a sign of potential, if not already realized, errant behavior. Although employing various tactics for the management of female physiology was an accepted practice of the time, ideological aims were confused and challenged by cases in which women failed to progress, as it were, to the next stage: childbearing.

Reigning theory dictated that the nonconceiving body represented an accumulation of untapped maternal energies, "natural" energies made unnatural and therefore threatening in their potential to erupt in dangerous ways.

14. Terry Lovell, *Consuming Fiction*, 98.

15. Grant Allen, *Fortnightly Review* (October 1889), quoted in ibid., 98; Constance D. Harsh, *Subversive Heroines: Feminist Resolutions of Social Crisis in the Condition-of-England Novel*, 125.

The medical term for this condition—the "doctrine of crisis"—depicts an antagonism between the unnatural female and her body not unlike the confrontational stance pitting the medical establishment against the female biology it pathologized. Mary Poovey outlines Victorian medicine's agenda as one seeking to legitimate its policy of sexual management and intervention through presenting "natural" female functions as disorders. As a result, if menstrual cycles and pregnancy were, by definition, disorders requiring constant monitoring, then childless women were serious aberrations. But, as Poovey notes, the construction in which "natural" is pathologized as continually "unnatural" collapses through women's having "always already exceeded the control that medicine could exercise."[16] The aberrance of childlessness attributed to the vinegared medusan countenances of Miss Mann and Miss Ainley, to Matty's recurring baby dreams, as well as to Janet's alcoholism, Bertha's madness, and Evadne Frayling's hysteria demonstrates the ultimate uncontrollability of the "natural" and reminds us that even middle-class women—including spinsters—are "always already" fallen.

Proving a suggestive link between disparate types, the midcentury spinster "was replaced in prominence in the popular imagination" by the "New Woman" of the 1890s. A relatively short-lived literary genre, the New Woman novel reflects "end-of-the-century controversies over 'rational' dress, contraception and venereal disease, occupations and votes for women." Demonstrating the period's fears that women's autonomy threatens the separate-spheres ideology, opponents like Mrs. Oliphant characterized the writers of New Woman fiction as an "anti-marriage league." But although the literature is marked by fin-de-siècle angst concerning the limitations marriage imposes on women, it is more emphatically marked by "sympathetic characters who will not or cannot find happiness, despite their possession of both strong minds and womanly virtues."[17] Limited as they are by social constrictions, these heroines embody sexual fallenness in the Victorian sense of the term, not by inappropriate or promiscuous behaviors but by virtue of their resistance to traditional roles. Earlier cast as a strictly moral issue, this avatar of fallenness is now pathologized as mental illness and, thus, a scientific issue. The political agenda so transparent in midcentury prostitution discourse, no less than in that period's transportation schemes for redundant women, assumed a more sinister

16. Poovey, *Uneven Developments*, 37–38.
17. Hickok, "The Spinster," 120; John Sutherland, *The Stanford Companion to Victorian Fiction*, 460; Helsinger, *The Woman Question*, 3:110.

aspect as Freudianism entered the cultural mainstream. Clearly, the fin-de-siècle hystericization of women proves that psychoanalytic discourse—far from being innovative—merely rehearses a tradition in which all aberrant behaviors are reducible to transgressions of prevailing sexual and maternal values.[18]

Sarah Grand's "New Woman" novel *The Heavenly Twins,* published in 1893, features three distinctive heroines: Angelica, one of the twins of the title; the bishop's daughter, Edith Beale; and Evadne Frayling. Unlike the other protagonists I have discussed, these characters are upper middle class, chosen to demonstrate how pervasive is the idea of fallenness and to reconsider the claim that protecting the purity of this class of women justifies both the sexual double standard and the exploitation of lower-class women. None of these characters are victimized by poverty, seduction, or other class issues, or by such destructive internalizations of cultural violence as alcohol or laudanum, rape or physical brutality. Angelica, Edith, and Evadne are all prototypes of the angelic ideal: they are sexually pure before marriage and chaste (monogamous) after; they are not nonsexual; nor are they too responsive for reigning tastes. How, then, are these women fallen?

Like the other authors in this study, Grand implicates the social context as primarily culpable for her characters' fates. A particularly daring feature of this novel is Grand's focus on the middle- and upper-class clients of prostitutes and the effects of men's dual sexual identity on the domestic sphere. But Grand also suggests that her characters' falls result from their failure to resist cultural pressures to act against their best interests—in Helsinger's phrase, they "will not or cannot find happiness"—and that the fate of each is proportionate to her "crime": the acquisition of, and subsequent avoidance of, knowledge. The call for reforms in women's education was a radical idea when promoted decades earlier by Harriet Martineau, Florence Nightingale, and others. Grand's novel suggests that this aspect of women's development may still be ahead of its time, not because of women's intellectual limitations but because of persistent cultural resistance. The emergence of the New Woman provides fresh ground on which to continue the ancient battle between the sexes, as the Freudianism that defines twentieth-century gender

18. Examples of New Woman fiction repeatedly attest to this idea: see Grant Allen's *The Woman Who Did* (the heroine's advocacy of free love results in an illegitimate daughter who betrays her mother, as does Ada McGrath's daughter in *The Piano*); Thomas Hardy's *Jude the Obscure* (Sue Bridehead's love children are murdered by their legitimate sibling); and George Gissing's *The Odd Women* (their "oddness" resides in their spinsterish redundancy).

ideology attests. The idea of fallen womanhood, as contemporary feminists know, is hardly anachronistic.

Sarah Grand casts these issues in various highly suggestive ways. From birth, Angelica customarily plays the role of instigator in relation to her twin brother, Diavolo: her mind is brilliant, and her physical reflexes are unerring, as her battle-scarred brother well knows. The twins are perpetually involved in scrapes of Angelica's imaginative devising. An early indication of her fascination with gender roles occurs when the twins arrive at Evadne's wedding wearing each others' clothes. Shocked wedding guests interpret this mockery of separate-spheres ideology and the sanctity of marriage as an inauspicious omen for Evadne's married life, which it proves to be that same day. Although the weddings of Evadne and Edith influence Angelica to lengthen her skirts and put up her hair, she is permanently scarred after witnessing the results of Edith's ill-advised union with a syphilitic aristocrat, particularly Edith's gruesome death and the unforgettable visage of her infected child, the hideous "speckled toad." Revolted by all the broken promises made to "good" women signified by such images (even as his wife lies dying in the next room, Moseley suggestively leers at Angelica), Angelica appropriately pitches a Bible at Edith's husband, breaking his nose.

This episode considerably delays Angelica's progress toward conforming with her culture's expectations of feminine womanhood, further evidenced by her attempt to control her destiny by proposing to Mr. Kilroy: "Marry me, *and let me do as I like.*"[19] This is radical New Woman behavior, to be sure, as is this unconventional marriage in which both go their separate ways. During this period, Angelica's cross-dressing escapades continue with "the Tenor." Her motivation for concealing her sex from him involves a desire to experience "the delight of associating with a man intimately who did not know I was a woman" and to engage with a "masculine mind undiluted by . . . masculine prejudices and proclivities with regard to my sex" (458). But the friendship ends in her unmasking and his death, for which the Tenor holds her unwomanly behavior responsible. Angelica's precocious search for knowledge and insight into the male psyche is fueled initially by the twins' androgynous relationship, then by an enforced separation into their respective spheres—Diavolo directed to books, horses, and opportunities, Angelica consigned to long skirts, needlepoint, and limitations—and finally

19. Grand, *The Heavenly Twins*, 321. Future quotations will be cited parenthetically in the text.

by her inability to accept the idea that girlhood freedom was but a cruelly deceptive prelude to the constrictions of adult womanhood.

Angelica's retribution for exceeding her gender's knowledge boundaries in part includes the Tenor's shaming her—"Poor misguided girl! . . . may God in heaven forgive you, and help you" (462)—his death, and her subsequent depression. Her impulse toward knowledge irreparably broken, a chastened Angelica pleads with her husband, "Don't let me go again, Daddy, keep me close. I am—I am grateful for the blessing of a good man's love" (551). Although Kilroy blames himself for marrying Angelica while she was still a child, then neglecting her "as if the mere making a wife of her must make her a mature and sensible woman" (550), he still seems less inclined to assume the role of husband than of father. Aside from presenting the issues, Grand declines to comment on Angelica's fall into dependency: Is she fallen because of her reluctance to move into womanhood, in effect, as the Tenor charges, betraying her sex? Or is it because of her acquiescence to infantilized wifehood, instead betraying herself? Either way, Angelica's transformation into a child wife who calls her husband "Daddy" aligns with the definition of the New Woman as one who is strong-minded and virtuous, but cannot find happiness. For women like Angelica, caught between her culture's need for and resistance to social change, such unhappiness represents a poor compromise between equally disempowering alternatives.

The least developed of the three principal women characters but the most poignant, Edith Beale is characterized as the antithesis of Angelica. From her shrinelike bedroom, unadorned except for paintings of the holy family, to her nunlike draperies of white and gold, Edith is purity incarnate. Her life is thoroughly encased in domestic ideology, particularly with regard to ignorance of sexual matters, and her vulnerability is further complicated by her religious faith, which promotes unquestioning compliance with everyone outside herself, from her husband and parents to God. No image could be further removed from Edith Beale than that of syphilis, that "index of cultural deprivation [whose] prevalence mirrored existing levels of filth, poverty, malnutrition, and overcrowding" in evidence not far from her father's door.[20] Like Evadne, Edith trusts her parents' choice of a husband; unlike Evadne, Edith never doubts her ability to reform and domesticate even the most depraved man. As a result, Edith trips blithely into marriage. A year later, as the mother of a grotesque-looking infant and the wife of a

---

20. Englestein, "Morality and the Wooden Spoon," 170.

man still consorting with prostitutes, she is spiritually broken, physically diseased, and afflicted by episodes of murderous insanity.

Edith goes home to die, summoning to her deathbed all those "who represent the arrangement of society which has made it possible for me and my child to be sacrificed in this way" (300): her parents, representing domestic ideology and religious conformity in its most rigid patriarchal sense; Dr. Galbraith, representing the jealously guarded secrets of the male medical establishment; and her husband, Moseley, representing the perversion of the nuclear-family modality. To this symbolic assemblage she declares: "I have nothing more to say to any of you—except," turning to Moseley, "Don't let me ever see that dreadful man again!" (300). Edith's first self-actualizing articulation—which lacks the rhetorical force required by such a dramatic moment—is also her last, although her mutated son survives as a powerful reminder of his father's sexual fallenness. The heir to Sir Moseley Menteith's estate provides eloquent proof that Edith's issue is purely and wholly that of the legitimate father. Although Grand does not detail the child's fate, the notoriety of the issue ensures readers will understand the significance of congenital syphilis. This "syphilis of the innocents," says Elaine Showalter, is "more devastating than the acquired form . . . because it has already entered the second phase and begun to attack the nervous system." The infant mortality rate for congenital syphilis was dramatic: 60 to 90 percent died in their first year.[21]

Prior to her marriage, Edith and her mother encounter a tramp woman and her infant lying by the roadside. Unwilling to expose herself or her daughter to the vice they represent, Mrs. Beale sends the coachman, who suggests they turn the matter over to the workhouse. The footman reports, " 'She's French, and was a dressmaker. . . . There were two of them, sisters, doing a very good business, but they got to know some of the gentry—' Mrs. Beale stopped him. She would not have heard the story for the world" (160). Significantly, the footman expresses compassion for the woman's plight; the bishop's wife and daughter are repelled, as if the very existence of such women insulted, rather than protected, their purity. Satisfied, they drive off without its occurring "to either of the two ladies, gentle, tender, and good as they were, to take the poor dusty disgraced

21. Showalter, *Sexual Anarchy: Gender and Culture at the Fin de Siècle*, 197. Chesney reports that, of a total of 468 recorded deaths in Great Britain from syphilis in 1855, 269 were infants (one year and under), and 343 were children under fifteen (*The Anti-Society*, 355).

tramp into their carriage, and restore her to 'life and use and name and fame' as they might have done" (160). Instead, the bishop's wife and daughter hurry home to tea in the drawing room in order to erase the "painful impression" as quickly as possible. The episode, rich in class and gender symbolism, of course anticipates Edith's tragic fate. Haunted by that "painful impression," Edith later learns this woman was another of Moseley's victims. Although Mrs. Beale "very gladly dismissed the whole matter from her mind" (170), her daughter's subsequent fate prevents her from doing so for long.

Edith is the consummate victim in this narrative; unquestioning and compliant in every way, she falls as a result of the gender system into which she was born, a system that fails to deliver the protection that it promises. Edith conforms perfectly with the angel-in-the-house idea and, because she is too good to live, endures the same fate suffered by absent angels in earlier Victorian literature. Edith can be held culpable in one sense, however, for she ignores Evadne's explicit warnings against this marriage. Prompted by her medical studies, Evadne suspects Moseley is syphilitic. When Edith refuses to listen, she appeals to Mrs. Beale, who questions how Evadne, brought up as she was among "the most long suffering *womanly* women I ever knew" (233), could even conceive such a shocking notion. Evadne pleads with Edith to reconsider, pointedly offering Colonel Colquhoun's support of her contention (as a military man with a lively sexual history, he is an expert on the topic), but Edith is dazzled by romanticism: "If he is *bad,* I will make him good; if he is lost, I will save him!" (234). Evadne's warnings go unheeded, and Edith falls through refusing to accept the truth when it is offered to her, paying for her conformity and her intellectual blindness with her life.

The fates of Edith and her child reflect the period's concerns about the spread of venereal disease, a more insidious manifestation of the double standard than prostitution and illegitimacy. W. R. Greg's recognition that men introduce syphilis "into the bosom of families; and the most virtuous women, and . . . innocent children . . . become the victims" reflects an aspect of the Contagious Diseases debates too often elided. The almost exclusive focus on prostitutes' culpability for the spread of venereal disease demonstrates Victorians' limited vision in matters of class, morality, and contagion. Providing a significant variation on this narrow perspective, V. M. Tarnovskii argues that prostitutes and the men who used them were "equally depraved": brothel visitors are "morally insensitive, with an innately intensified sexual drive. . . . Just as the prostitutes infect the healthy population, so they are in turn . . . infected by these moral cripples, the true refuse of contemporary society."[22] Unlike many of his contemporaries, Tarnovskii distinguishes clearly between biological and moral contagion, situating the latter—by far the more ideologically weighted term—with male clients.

Illustrating both Greg's and Tarnovskii's observations, Grand's novel demonstrates the extremes to which both types of contagion can reach, influences capable of infiltrating the best families and the purest women, despite the rarified atmosphere in which they exist. Ultimately, the Contagious Diseases Acts were rescinded because the regulation of prostitution could not by itself eradicate the spread of either moral or infectious diseases in society's upper echelons. The idea that such eradication would also require *men's* voluntary regulation of their sexuality was not yet regarded as a viable option.

In the meantime, by refusing altogether to participate in the period's sexual and maternal debates, Evadne Frayling's example of celibacy offers a controversial but dramatically effective alternative to managing the problem. Distinct from her more typical counterparts in celibacy (that is, spinsters), Evadne is marriageable in every respect: she is young, attractive, accomplished, and well dowered. Her unconsummated marriage thus mocks the period's most revered institution while exposing the fallacy of double-standard, separate-spheres ideology, as the cross-dressing antics of the twins so aptly parodied. Although the Frayling manor house is well stocked with books, the young Evadne's intellectuality finds little encouragement because she is a girl. Self-tutored, Evadne reads avidly and keeps a diary called her "Commonplace Book." Her interests range from literature and history to science, medicine, and advanced mathematics: "She found herself forced to put prejudice aside in order to see beneath it, deep down into the sacred heart of things, where the truth is, and the bewildering clash of human precept with human practice ceases to vex. . . . It was a need of her nature to know" (3).

Most dramatically illustrated by legislation forbidding slaves' literacy, nineteenth-century education was a privilege of class and gender; by regulating access to education, the economy that benefits so few at the expense of so many is preserved and perpetuated. Similarly, Victorian women of all classes met with resistance to their "need to know" as demonstrated by the

---

22. Greg, "Prostitution," 492; V. M. Tarnovskii, quoted in Englestein, "Morality and the Wooden Spoon," 195.

inaccessibility of male sources of knowledge. Self-taught Maggie Tulliver, in *The Mill on the Floss,* whose impulse to learn is consistently thwarted, tutors her comparatively dull brother in mathematics. Outwardly, Barrett Browning's Aurora Leigh conforms with her aunt's stilted ideas of proper education for girls, then hides out in the garret, secretly teaching herself the classics from her father's books. Although at first Evadne's parents insist on monitoring her reading material, she pesters them for permission so often they inadvertently sanction her reading medical books. Of such treatises Jill Matus notes, "they draw attention to [man's] authority as a doctor and his license to speak about matters of sex, as well as to the specialised nature of scientific discussion, usually conducted among professionals in . . . appropriately inaccessible text books."[23] Evadne's medical knowledge proves to be relevant to her experience not the less because it was surreptitiously acquired.

Evadne's intellectual precocity in the medical field first appears when Diavolo severs an artery. She understands the hemorrhaging must be stopped and instinctively applies the pressure that saves his life. Impressed, the doctor agrees to teach her about tourniquets, bandaging, and nursing "generally," although her father maintains that, like all women, she can imitate like a parrot but has no intellectual depth or substance. Although Evadne is "quite unharmed" by her studies—her femininity is not compromised by unseemly ambitions to attend medical school—it is not true that "she made no personal application of her knowledge" (23), as the examples of Diavolo and her diagnosis of Moseley Menteith demonstrate. Lady Adeline warns Mrs. Frayling that Evadne's "beautiful innocence" is actually "*dangerous ignorance,* . . . not a safe state in which to begin the battle of life" (41)— meaning marriage; but arrangements for the union between Evadne and Colonel Colquhoun proceed nevertheless. With a complacency matched only by Mrs. Beale's, and a blindness to apparent truths matched only by Edith's, Mrs. Frayling responds: "He was rather wild as a young man, I am sorry to say, but he has been quite frank about all that to Mr. Frayling, and there is nothing now that we can object to" (55). To the Fraylings, Colquhoun's *moral* reformation, despite the recentness of its inception, offers sufficient proof against the potential for the *physical* contamination of their daughter and future grandchildren. Thus, her parents, whom Evadne trusts completely, deliberately compromise their daughter as surely as Marian Erle's did her.

23. Matus, *Unstable Bodies,* 25.

Immediately following her wedding ceremony, Evadne learns of Colquhoun's sexually active past, not from her parents or her husband, but from an anonymous letter from the voice that will not be silenced: that of the fallen woman. In the wake of Evadne's rebellion—she seeks verification of the letter's charges, and refuses to live with her husband, much less to consummate the marriage—Frayling disinherits her for creating a scandal and forbids any further contact with the family. Such damaging attitudes are deplorable enough when used against an outcast like Elizabeth Gaskell's Esther, whose efforts to act ethically result in imprisonment. But Evadne Frayling, who lacks Esther's street-savvy, is forced either to return to her wayward husband or walk the streets herself.

E. W. Thomas's reconstruction of prostitutes' social ostracism bears a striking resemblance to Evadne's rejection by family and community for the "crime" of celibate marriage: "In the old familiar home they never mention her name; even the edge of parental affection is blunted; her sisters are taught to forget her; her brothers proscribe her memory. She is abhorred of her acquaintance. Friends pass by on the other side. Her own sex shrink from her instinctively. Men dread to risk their reputation by recognising her."[24] The precariousness of Evadne's social position, tinged as it is by the hint of scandal on *her* part, demonstrates how deeply entrenched are social attitudes toward fallenness, real or imagined.

Evadne's medical studies serve her well following this turn of events. Even now, she is not physically repulsed by Colquhoun, to whom she is quite frankly sexually attracted, so much as intellectually repulsed: "Marrying a man like that, allowing him an assured position in society, is countenancing vice, and . . . *helping to spread it!* . . . There is no past in the matter of vice. The consequences become hereditary, and continue from generation to generation" (79–80). Her warnings to Edith clarify that she understands the potential for venereal infection and its hereditary transmission; but, as her parents' attitude demonstrates, the implications of such warnings are so far removed from the sexual ideology of this class as to be unthinkable, a clear example of "the bewildering clash of human precept with human practice."

Grand does not explicitly claim that Colquhoun has venereal disease; Evadne never learns the truth empirically because, based on her medical reading and her anonymous "tip," she avoids consummation of the marriage, thus also evading (a possible source for her unusual name?)

24. Thomas, "Great Social Evil," in *The Magdalen's Friend*, 158.

contagion.[25] Although many regarded this management of her sexuality and assumption of control over her reproductivity as strident New Woman behavior, to others Evadne manifests sexual and maternal ideology in the purest sense of the term. "Taking to heart Darwinian arguments about women's self-sacrifice for the good of the species," contends Showalter, "[some] women envisaged themselves as chaste yet maternal heralds of a higher race, who protect mankind by saying no to syphilitic men."[26] Realizing too late the import of Evadne's insights, the dying Edith observes, "the same thing may happen to any mother—to any daughter—and will happen so long as we refuse to know and resist" (304); as my discussion demonstrates, knowledge for Grand is pointless unless accompanied by active resistance.

Evadne and Colquhoun ultimately develop an amicable, but strictly celibate, relationship; this "unnatural" state, aggravated by Evadne's rejection by her family and by Edith's tragedies, results in a dispiritedness diagnosed by Dr. Galbraith as "hysteria" (627). Whereas her father blames Evadne's nonconformity on her intellectual pursuits (there is some truth in this), some experts blame those parents who "leave their daughters altogether unadvised upon the important subject of marriage, thus exposing them to the force of such temptations as render them an easy prey to the tempter." Sally Mitchell notes the medical profession's complicity in this issue: "A doctor's advice about what to tell girls approaching matrimony is reported by C. Willett Cunnington: 'Tell her nothing, my dear madam, for if they knew they would not marry.' "[27] As shown by the cases of Edith and Evadne, what E. W. Thomas calls "the tempter" can take the form of one's husband, which, by the post–Contagious Diseases Acts era, was no longer a contradiction in terms.

One of the many contradictions revealed in sexologists' discourse concerns the celibacy argument, which, like alcoholism, was erroneously thought to be relevant only to men. Although E. W. Thomas condemns

25. Worth considering by association is the Contagious Diseases debates' intense focus on the health of Britain's military men, who were not initially implicated in the spread of venereal disease. Sole blame for this was reserved for prostitutes. Colonel Colquhoun's military associations clearly link him with this milieu. See also Englestein, who notes that among Russian military men of the same period, venereal disease was three times more common among officers than among enlisted men for various social and economic reasons ("Morality and the Wooden Spoon," 185).

26. Showalter, *Sexual Anarchy*, 198–99.

27. Thomas, "Great Social Evil," in *The Magdalen's Friend*, 199–200; Mitchell, *Fallen Angel*, xii.

men's use of prostitutes prior to marriage, he also argues that "compulsory celibacy" preceding marriage is "wrong in itself, and contributes largely to the support of the vice." Prostitution arises "from the enforcement of celibacy on the men—a practice which must be denounced as a contra-vention of God's arrangements, an injustice to humanity, and a source of ruin to thousands, who are thus deprived of those virtuous safeguards which a wise and gracious Providence has deemed necessary." Of married celibacy, William Acton charges that wives who practice celibacy to avoid conception (as distinct from Evadne, who seeks to avoid contagion) are directly responsible for damaging their husband's health. Alternatively, in "Celibacy v. Marriage," Frances Power Cobbe argues that voluntary celibacy is a healthy practice for both men and women.[28] The pattern in which men employ medical and religious rhetoric to denounce celibacy while women promote abstention as health preserving is worth considering more fully in terms of gendered arguments in this and other arenas.

One of the curiosities of *The Heavenly Twins* is Grand's shift from omniscient narrator to Galbraith's narrative voice in the last book of the novel. This final section functions as the doctor's case history of Evadne's progressive hysteria, effectively displacing her own account of intellectual growth as recorded earlier in the "Commonplace Book." At one point, Evadne rallies long enough to renew old interests by nursing during a smallpox epidemic; but, although the physician in charge praises her work, Galbraith disapproves and expresses satisfaction when she takes to her bed from exhaustion. This episode accords with organized medicine's tradition of denigrating women healers, who were outlawed by the legitimation of the male medical establishment: women belonged at home, unless, of course, they were sexually fallen, a conflation of economics and morality linking all my examples. Interestingly, Evadne's impulse toward the medical profession could be construed as evidencing women's "natural" caregiving tendency (an idea exploited by Nightingale and others), yet she meets with resistance from every quarter. Although no doubt intellectually qualified to be a physician herself given more amenable circumstances, Evadne seems content to practice nursing. But what Galbraith offers her is not a career in nursing, much less as a physician, but a position as a volunteer flower arranger in his hospital.

28. Thomas, "Great Social Evil," in *The Magdalen's Friend*, 200–201; Acton, *The Functions and Disorders of the Reproductive System* (London: John Churchill, 1857); Cobbe, "Celibacy v. Marriage," *Fraser's Magazine* 65 (February 1862): 89.

Galbraith compares Evadne to the Lady of Shalott, who is condemned to a sexless existence weaving tapestries—here, not in a medieval tower, but in a Victorian drawing room. He clearly aligns himself with Lancelot, the knight who will rescue her through sexual awakening, an odd, though prophetic, analogy, considering that Tennyson's lady dies seeking to gratify her sexual curiosity. Colquhoun's sudden death conveniently allows Galbraith to shift his role from Evadne's physician to her husband. But despite the normalcy implied by her sexually consummated marriage and motherhood, Evadne's "hysteria" does not respond to the elimination of intellectualism and celibacy as Galbraith had anticipated. Instead, depressive episodes punctuate the remainder of her life, while her earlier capacity to confront even medical emergencies with equanimity gives way to a morbid revulsion against life's most commonplace aspects. Evadne's "doctrine of crisis" thus results not from childlessness but from acquiescence to the maternal mystique.

When Galbraith forbids her to read his medical texts, Evadne asks: "Why are we never taught as you are? We are the people to be informed" (662), "we" meaning childbearing women: no doubt Evadne is still haunted by the specters of Edith and her "speckled toad." Galbraith aggressively deprives Evadne of knowledge, demonstrating—like Ada McGrath's husband—an imperiousness that presumes to know what women need, which generally differs from what they want. Separating Evadne from her impulse to acquire knowledge is like separating Ada from her piano. Horrified by her "sin" of attempted suicide during pregnancy (recalling Hetty Sorrel, such unnatural behavior at the height of woman's most "natural" state can mean only insanity), Galbraith finds his original diagnosis confirmed by the "divine example" Evadne offers as explanation for her behavior: "Christ committed suicide to all intents and purposes by deliberately putting himself into the hands of his executioners; but his motive makes *them* responsible for the crime; and my motive would place society in a similar position" (671). Evadne's counter-"diagnosis"—that women who turn all their power over to men, as daughters, wives, sisters, or mothers, deliberately put themselves into the hands of their executioners—implies that the only act of will left to women is taking their own lives, yet even this option is shrouded in moral judgment. Grand's implicating society (not the individual deviant) as criminally liable more clearly articulates an idea suggested by earlier women writers: that social resistance to the evolution of women's cultural status is the real source of "race suicide."

Evadne's first marriage, for all its irregularities, is marked by Colquhoun's complete support of her intellectual interests: he retrieves her books from the manor, and ensures her more time and privacy to pursue those interests than she had as an unmarried woman. Are we to believe that it is this marriage that broke Evadne's spirit? Apparently not, since her second marriage, conventionally domesticated in every way, produces a completely transformed Evadne: sexuality results in depressive episodes, and maternity in attempted suicide. Countering popular associations between the New Woman's increased intellectual pursuits and the corresponding rise in female reproductive and nervous diseases, Grand presents marriage as a metonym for all that is hazardous to women's health in the period's domestic ideology. Victorian physicians pathologized childlessness by predicting that untapped maternal energy would most likely find expression through unwomanly, even perverted, behaviors, a theory demonstrated by Janet Dempster's alcoholism and Bertha Mason's madness, and now by Evadne's "hysteria." Yet, like Hetty Sorrel's, Evadne's "accumulated force" erupts *through* motherhood, producing an intellectual collapse that reduces her to a childlike state comparable to Angelica's. Recalling her earlier observation that the consequences of vice are hereditary, Evadne here casts intellectual oppression and the rage it engenders in a similar light:

> No, don't ask me to think! . . . All my endeavour is not to think. Let me live on the surface of life, as most women do. I will do nothing but attend to my house-hold duties and the social duties of my position. I will read nothing that is not first weeded by you of every painful thought. . . . Let me live while you live, and die when you die. But do not ask me to think. I can be the most docile, the most obedient, the most loving of women as long as I forget my knowledge of life; but the moment I remember I become a raging fury. . . . I could preside with an awful joy at the execution of those who are making the misery now for succeeding generations. (672)

Bertha Mason Rochester's imprisonment in the attic and her final silencing through death demonstrate the price women pay for expressing that "raging fury," as does Barrett Browning's murdered Runaway Slave; in contrast, Evadne suppresses her rage and, like Edith and Angelica, ends in a neurotic whimper.

Always referring to her in diminutive terms, Galbraith "pets" and "distracts" Evadne "as one does with a child" (677), and further infantilizes her by asserting he has three children: two babies and a wife. Whereas he is earlier aligned with Lancelot and sexual virility, he is now, like Mr. Kilroy, "Daddy." Galbraith and his colleague, psychiatrist Sir Shadwell Rock, analyze Evadne's every move so that her home, rather than a safe haven from worldly influences, becomes an asylum in which she is an object for voyeuristic medical scrutiny. Characteristic of hysterical women is their desire for privacy, hardly surprising in view of the demand for women's perpetual availability to satisfy others' needs. The desire for privacy was pathologized as "unnatural," "unsocial," and "insane"; resistance to woman's "natural" state was called "morbid self-contemplation."[29] Grand's dismal conclusion, which casts Evadne as completely broken and Galbraith heroically vowing to "make her life endurable" (679), aligns disturbingly with Brontë's *Jane Eyre* and Gilman's "The Yellow Wallpaper," texts whose deviant women characters are labeled "mad" for their unconventionalities and relegated to the attic by "the medical men."

The Female Malady, Elaine Showalter's study of Victorian madwomen, psychiatric Darwinism, and Freudian hysteria, offers important insights into why the image of Dr. Galbraith—wise, all-knowing, patriarchal, and authoritative—is compromised by his triple role as Evadne's physician, father, and husband. Showalter calls the period between 1870 and World War I the "golden age" of hysteria, a condition that "assumed a peculiarly central role in psychiatric discourse, and in definitions of femininity and female sexuality. By the end of the century, 'hysterical' had become almost interchangeable with 'feminine' in literature, where it stood for all extremes of emotionality."[30] Galbraith's diagnosis associates Evadne with women who fail to perform their domestic, social, and especially conjugal duties, by the same discourse community termed, interestingly, both "willfulness" and "paralysis of will." Since "respectable" sexual ideology is marked by such outward and visible signs as prolific childbearing, the New Woman's quest for personal autonomy and professional opportunities were met with the medical establishment's dire warnings that such pursuits would result in race suicide. The unhappy fates of Grand's heroines imply that in order for the New Woman to prevail, she must embody the moral standards of an Edith, the intellectual vigor of an Evadne, and the fiery spirit and gender insights of an Angelica. None of these characters is sufficient to stand alone as a New Woman in a man's world.

29. Showalter, *Female Malady,* 134.
30. Ibid., 129.

The progressive idea that the cause of female hysteria was not only organic but also linked with one's social environment was prevalent in the psychiatric debates of the 1890s. Recalling midcentury fallen-woman discourse, hysteria was believed to result from perverted acts of will and equated with "moral perversion," "moral insanity," and defective breeding stock: all lower-class stereotypes. But such diagnoses are inadequate to account for the social milieu of Grand's novel without implicating upper-class social mores. The author does so by suggesting that perversions and defects also result from the social attitudes and prejudices of the *upper classes.* The paradox is seen clearly in Edith's rejecting information that conflicts with her ideology, Evadne's suppressing all aspects of her personality that differentiate her from her husband, and Angelica's reverting to the childlike state she believes will afford her the freedom lacking in adult womanhood. Demonstrating the period's persistent reduction of women's issues to sexual terms, Showalter notes, "It was much simpler to blame sexual frustration . . . than to investigate women's intellectual frustration, lack of mobility, or needs for autonomy and control"—no less than women's chronic economic disadvantages.[31]

As the examples in this study demonstrate, literary history reveals that women's silences are most often culturally imposed, rarely self-imposed. Ada McGrath is one exception, Evadne and Angelica are two more, if only in the sense that, once they realize their opponents' power to silence them, each colludes—or, perhaps, asserts herself one last time—by silencing herself. Medical science found itself faced with empirical proof that the extreme degree of suppression domestic ideology required of women posed threats to their physical and mental health. In a period marked by efforts to establish scientific "proofs" justifying the separate-spheres social structure, it is certainly ironic that, once discovered, those proofs threatened to dismantle the system. Patriarchy's response to the threat posed by the New Woman was to pathologize her demands as hysteria, neuroses, and insanity. Caught in the cross fire between two powerful ideologies—domestic and scientific—Grand's progressive protagonists were fated to be silenced in this "contest for mastery."

And silenced they are when Grand's narrative voice shifts into the male perspective. Galbraith's medical authoritativeness, pompous patronizing, and expansive collaboration with other medical men concerning Evadne align him with this study's other self-aggrandizing male characters, each

31. Ibid., 133, 132.

of whom demands female conformity as his right. Does Grand imply that her heroines' fates reflect the degree to which women failed to progress during the Victorian period? Is she suggesting that girls who begin as "New Women" will only "fall" all the harder into midcentury angelic domesticity? Finally, does she invite readers to equate her collusion in male usurpation of narrative voice with the continued silencing of women despite class or circumstance?

Perhaps answers to such questions may be found by challenging the notion that rebellion is pathological and considering instead the likelihood that deviant behavior not only highlights ideological gaps but also presents opportunities for progressive social change. When, in 1838, Harriet Martineau claimed that a culture's degree of civilization is measured by the status of its women, she referred not to demure angels ensconced in middle-class parlors but to the realities of oppressed women's lives and to future generations of educated women who would be economically self-sufficient, participating in the public realm with their capacities fully developed. But W. Tyler Smith's 1847 measure of women's status indicates a very different set of criteria: "The excellence of obstetric medicine is one of the most emphatic expressions of that high regard and estimation in which women are always held by civilized races. . . . obstetric science must flourish most in countries where the marriage tie is most respected."[32] Judging by this survey of Victorian literature, Smith's sexualized interpretation of civilized society precludes Martineau's and indeed continues to do so today.

It is the extreme tension between nature and culture, and morality and science, that fuels the intense energy surrounding the "border cases," the "in-between" cultural anomalies, and the "gaps" in ideological theory and practice that motivated this book. As my examples have shown, female rebellion and its management are symptomatic of a deeply entrenched, thoroughly gendered, unabashedly biased ideology. For this reason, whether social change results from nonconformist behavior or is granted by the ruling class is a matter of special significance. Echoing John Stuart Mill and Elizabeth Cady Stanton, Showalter argues: "Until women break them for themselves, the chains that make madness a female malady, like Blake's 'mind-forg'd manacles,' will simply forge themselves anew."[33] The women writers discussed in this study have most emphatically broken the chains of silence, although their words often fall on deaf ears. Sarah Grand's final

32. W. Tyler Smith, quoted in Poovey, *Uneven Developments*, 43.
33. Showalter, *Female Malady*, 250.

image of the fatherly physician/husband vowing to protect his hysterical child wife provides a suggestive bridge linking the midcentury "fallen woman" with the pathologizing of the New Woman's intellectual pursuits, and with what contemporary social theorists term *feminist backlash*. As feminist scholarship repeatedly concludes, the rhetoric may change with the times, but the issues remain the same.

BIBLIOGRAPHY

Abbott, Mary. *Family Ties: English Families, 1540–1920.* London and New York: Routledge, 1993.

Acton, William. *Prostitution Considered in Its Moral, Social, and Sanitary Aspects in London and Other Large Cities; with Proposals for the Mitigation and Prevention of Its Attendant Evils.* London, 1857.

Adams, Carol J. *The Sexual Politics of Meat: A Feminist-Vegetarian Critical Theory.* New York: Continuum Publishing, 1992.

Ahmed, Leila. "Western Ethnocentrism and Perceptions of the Harem." *Feminist Studies* 8 (1982): 521–34.

Amussen, Susan Dwyer. *An Ordered Society: Gender and Class in Early Modern England.* London: Basil Blackwell, 1988.

Arbuckle, Elisabeth Sanders. *Harriet Martineau in the "London Daily News."* New York and London: Garland Publishing, 1994.

Armstrong, Nancy. *Desire and Domestic Fiction: A Political History of the Novel.* New York and Oxford: Oxford University Press, 1987.

Auerbach, Nina. *Communities of Women: An Idea in Fiction.* Cambridge: Harvard University Press, 1978.

———. Foreword to *Old Maids to Radical Spinsters: Unmarried Women in the Twentieth-Century Novel.* Ed. Laura L. Doan. Urbana and Chicago: University of Illinois Press, 1991.

———. *Romantic Imprisonment: Women and Other Glorified Outcasts.* New York: Columbia University Press, 1986.

———. *Woman and the Demon: The Life of a Victorian Myth.* Cambridge: Harvard University Press, 1982.

[Aytoun, W. E.]. "Poetic Aberrations." *Blackwood's* 87 (1860): 494.

Barrell, John. "Death on the Nile: Fantasy and the Literature of Tourism, 1840–1860." *Essays in Criticism* 41 (1991): 97–127.

Barret-Ducrocq, Françoise. *Love in the Time of Victoria: Sexuality and Desire among Working-Class Men and Women in Nineteenth-Century London.* Trans. John Howe. New York: Penguin Books, 1991.

Barrett, Dorothea. *Vocation and Desire: George Eliot's Heroines.* London and New York: Routledge, 1989.

Barrett Browning, Elizabeth. *Aurora Leigh.* Ed. Kerry McSweeney. Oxford and New York: Oxford University Press, 1993.

———. "The Runaway Slave at Pilgrim's Point." In her *Poems 1850.* London, 1850.

Basch, Françoise. *Relative Creatures: Victorian Women in Society and the Novel.* New York: Schocken Books, 1974.

Bell, Loren C. "A Kind of Madness: Hetty Sorrel's Infanticide." *The Platte Valley Review* 11 (1983): 82–87.

Bick, Suzann. "'Take Her Up Tenderly': Elizabeth Gaskell's Treatment of the Fallen Woman." *Essays in Arts and Sciences* 18 (1989): 17–27.

Bodichon, Barbara Leigh Smith. *An American Diary, 1857–1858.* London: Routledge and Kegan Paul, 1972.

———. *A Brief Summary of the Most Important Laws Concerning Women.* London, 1854.

Bonaparte, Felicia. *Will and Destiny: Morality and Tragedy in George Eliot's Novels.* New York: New York University Press, 1975.

Bonnell, Marilyn. "The Legacy of Sarah Grand's *The Heavenly Twins:* A Review Essay." *English Literary History* 36 (1993): 467–78.

Brontë, Charlotte. *Jane Eyre.* New York and London: Penguin Books, 1966.

———. *Shirley.* New York and Middlesex, England: Penguin Books, 1974.

Carroll, David, ed. *George Eliot: The Critical Heritage.* London: Routledge and Kegan Paul, 1971.

Chesney, Kellow. *The Anti-Society: An Account of the Victorian Underworld.* Boston: Gambit, 1970.

Cobbe, Francis Power. "What Shall We Do with Our Old Maids?" *Fraser's Magazine* (November 1862): 594.

Cooper, Helen. *Elizabeth Barrett Browning, Woman and Artist.* Chapel Hill: University of North Carolina Press, 1988.

Cosslett, Tess. *Woman to Woman: Female Friendship in Victorian Fiction.* Atlantic Highlands, N.J.: Humanities Press International, 1988.

Craik, Dinah Mulock. *A Woman's Thoughts about Women.* New York: New York University Press, 1993.

Cross, J. W., ed. *George Eliot's Life as Related in Her Letters and Journals.* Edinburgh: W. Blackwood, 1885.

David, Deirdre. *Intellectual Women and Victorian Patriarchy: Harriet Martineau, Elizabeth Barrett Browning, George Eliot.* Ithaca: Cornell University Press, 1987.

———. *Rule Britannia: Women, Empire, and Victorian Writing.* Ithaca: Cornell University Press, 1995.

Donzelot, Jacques. *The Policing of Families: Welfare versus the State.* Trans. Robert Hurley. New York: Pantheon Books, 1979.

Eagleton, Terry. *Ideology: An Introduction.* London and New York: Verso, 1991.

Easson, Angus, ed. *Elizabeth Gaskell: The Critical Heritage.* London and New York: Routledge, 1991.

Eliot, George. *Adam Bede.* New York: Penguin Books, 1980.

———. "Janet's Repentance." In her *Scenes of Clerical Life,* ed. David Lodge, 245–412. Middlesex, England: Penguin Books, 1973.

Englestein, Laura. "Morality and the Wooden Spoon: Russian Doctors View Syphilis, Social Class, and Sexual Behavior, 1890–1905." In *The Making of the Modern Body: Sexuality and Society in the Nineteenth Century,* ed. Catherine Gallagher and Thomas Laqueur, 169–208. Berkeley and Los Angeles: University of California Press, 1987.

Estes, Clarissa P. *Women Who Run with the Wolves.* New York: Ballantine Books, 1992.

Faulk, Barry. "Spies and Experts: Laura Ormiston Chant and Victorian Professionals." *Victorians Institute Journal* 23 (1995): 51–83.

Ferguson, Moira. Introduction to *The History of Mary Prince, a West Indian Slave, Related by Herself.* London: Pandora, 1987.

Finnegan, Frances. *Poverty and Prostitution: A Study of Victorian Prostitutes in York.* Cambridge: Cambridge University Press, 1979.

Flanders, Jane. "The Fallen Woman in Fiction." In *Feminist Visions: Toward a Transformation of the Liberal Arts Curriculum,* ed. Diane L. Fowlkes and Charlotte S. McClure, 97–109. University, Ala.: University of Alabama Press, 1984.

Foucault, Michel. *The History of Sexuality, Volume One.* Trans. Robert Hurley. New York: Vintage Books, 1990.

Fryckstedt, Monica Correa. *Elizabeth Gaskell's "Mary Barton" and "Ruth": A Challenge to Christian England.* Sweden: Uppsala, 1982.

Gallagher, Catherine. *The Industrial Reformation of English Fiction: Social Discourse and Narrative Form, 1832–1867.* Chicago: University of Chicago Press, 1985.

Gallagher, Catherine, and Thomas Laqueur, eds. *The Making of the Modern Body: Sexuality and Society in the Nineteenth Century.* Berkeley and Los Angeles: University of California Press, 1987.

Garrigan, Kristine Ottesen, ed. *Victorian Scandals: Representations of Gender and Class.* Athens: Ohio University Press, 1992.

Gaskell, Elizabeth. *Cranford.* New York: Penguin Books, 1976.

———. "Lizzie Leigh." In her *Works of Mrs. Gaskell: "Cranford" and Other Tales,* 206–41. London: John Murray, 1920.

———. *Mary Barton: A Tale of Manchester Life.* New York and Oxford: Penguin Books, 1970.

———. *Ruth.* New York and Oxford: Oxford University Press, 1985.

———. "The Well of Pen-Morfa." In her *Works of Mrs. Gaskell: "Cranford" and Other Tales,* 242–66. London: John Murray, 1920.

———. *Works of Mrs. Gaskell: "Cranford" and Other Tales.* London: John Murray, 1920.

Gay, Peter. *The Cultivation of Hatred.* New York: W. W. Norton, 1993.

Gerin, Winifred. *Elizabeth Gaskell: A Biography.* Oxford: Clarendon Press, 1976.

Gilbert, Sandra. "From Patria to Matria: Elizabeth Barrett Browning's *Risorgimento.*" *PMLA* 99 (1984): 194–211.

Gilbert, Sandra M., and Susan Gubar. *The Madwoman in the Attic: The Woman Writer and the Nineteenth-Century Literary Imagination.* New Haven: Yale University Press, 1979.

Gorham, Deborah. "The 'Maiden Tribute of Modern Babylon' Re-examined: Child Prostitution and the Idea of Childhood in Late-Victorian England." *Victorian Studies* 21 (1978): 353–79.

Grand, Sarah. *The Heavenly Twins.* Ann Arbor: University of Michigan Press, 1992.

The Greatest of Our Social Evils: Prostitution. London: H. Bailliere, 1857.

Greg, W. R. "Prostitution." *Westminster Review* 53 (1850): 448–506.

———. Review of *Ruth,* by Elizabeth Gaskell. *National Review* 8 (January 1859).

———. "Why Are Women Redundant?" *National Review* 14 (1862): 434–60.

Haight, Gordon S. *George Eliot: A Biography.* New York: Penguin, 1985.

———, ed. *Selections from George Eliot's Letters.* New Haven: Yale University Press, 1985.

Hapke, Laura. "Reflections on the Victorian Seduction Novel." *The Nassau Review* 5 (1988): 35–43.

Harris, Mason. "Infanticide and Respectability: Hetty Sorrel as Abandoned Child in *Adam Bede.*" *English Studies in Canada* 9 (1983): 177–96.

Harrison, Brian. *Drink and the Victorians.* London: Faber and Faber, 1971.

Harsh, Constance D. *Subversive Heroines: Feminist Resolutions of Social Crisis in the Condition-of-England Novel.* Ann Arbor: University of Michigan Press, 1994.

Hellerstein, Erna Olafson, Leslie Parker Hume, and Karen M. Offen, eds. *Victorian Women: A Documentary Account of Women's Lives in Nineteenth-Century England, France, and the United States.* Stanford: Stanford University Press, 1981.

Helsinger, Elizabeth K., Robin Lauterbach Sheets, and William Veeder, eds. *The Woman Question: Society and Literature in Britain and America, 1837–1883.* 3 vols. Chicago: University of Chicago Press, 1983.

Hickok, Kathleen. "The Spinster in Victoria's England: Changing Attitudes in Popular Poetry by Women." *Journal of Popular Culture* 15 (winter 1981): 119–31.

Higginbotham, Ann R. " 'Sin of the Age': Infanticide and Illegitimacy in Victorian London." In *Victorian Scandals: Representations of Gender and Class,* ed. Kristine Ottesen Garrigan, 257–88. Athens: Ohio University Press, 1992.

The History of Mary Prince, a West Indian Slave, Related by Herself. London: Pandora, 1987.

Holmstrom, John, and Laurence Lerner. *George Eliot and Her Readers: A Selection of Contemporary Reviews.* Totowa, N.J.: Barnes and Noble, 1966.

Honig, Edith. *Breaking the Angelic Image: Women and Power in Victorian Children's Fantasy.* New York: Greenwood Press, 1988.

Hood, Thomas. *The Complete Poetical Works of Thomas Hood.* Ed. Walter Jerrold. London: Oxford University Press, 1920.

"Hospital Nurses as They Are and as They Ought to Be." *Fraser's Magazine* 37 (May 1848): 540.

Jaffe, Audrey. "Under Cover of Sympathy: *Ressentiment* in Gaskell's *Ruth.*" In *Victorian Literature and Culture,* ed. John Maynard et al., 51–65. New York: AMS, 1993.

Johnson, Edgar, ed. *Letters from Charles Dickens to Angela Burdett Coutts, 1841–1865.* London: Cape Publishing, 1953.

Johnson, Wendell. *Living in Sin: The Victorian Sexual Revolution.* Chicago: Nelson Hall, 1979.

————. *Sex and Marriage in Victorian Poetry.* Ithaca: Cornell University Press, 1975.

Kalikoff, Beth. "The Falling Woman in Three Victorian Novels." *Studies in the Novel* 19 (1987): 357–67.

————. "Victorian Sexual Confessions." *Victorians Institute Journal* 18 (1990): 99–112.

Kaplan, Cora. Introduction to *Elizabeth Barrett Browning: "Aurora Leigh" and Other Poems.* London: Women's Press, 1978.

Kasl, Charlotte Davis. *Women, Sex, and Addiction.* New York: Harper and Row, 1989.

Kenyon, Frederic, ed. *The Letters of Elizabeth Barrett Browning.* 2 vols. London: Smith and Elder, 1897.

Kurata, Marilyn J. "Wrongful Confinement: The Betrayal of Women by Men, Medicine, and Law." In *Victorian Scandals: Representations of Gender and Class,* ed. Kristine Ottesen Garrigan, 43–68. Athens: Ohio University Press, 1992.

Lansbury, Coral. *Elizabeth Gaskell: The Novel of Social Crisis.* New York: Barnes and Noble, 1975.

Leighton, Angela. " 'Because men made the laws': The Fallen Woman and the Woman Poet." *Victorian Poetry* 27 (1989): 109–27.

Logan, William. *The Great Social Evil: Its Causes, Extent, Results, and Remedies.* London, 1871.

Lovell, Terry. *Consuming Fiction.* New York and London: Verso, 1987.

MacPike, Loralee. "The Fallen Woman's Sexuality: Childbirth and Censure." In *Sexuality and Victorian Literature,* ed. Don Richard Cox, 54–71. Knoxville: University of Tennessee Press, 1984.

The Magdalen's Friend and Female Home's Intelligencer. Vol. 3. London: Wertheim, Macintosh, and Hunt, 1862.

Mahood, Linda. *The Magdalenes: Prostitution in the Nineteenth Century.* London and New York: Routledge, 1990.

Martineau, Harriet. "Criticism on Women." *London and Westminster Review* 32 (1838–1839): 454–75.

————. *Dawn Island: A Tale.* Manchester: J. Gadsby, 1845.

————. "Demerara." In her *Illustrations of Political Economy.* London: Fox, 1832–1834.

————. *Eastern Life, Present and Past.* Vol. 2. London: Edward Moxon, 1848.

————. *Harriet Martineau's Autobiography: With Memorials by Maria Weston Chapman.* 3 vols. Boston: J. R. Osgood, 1877.

————. *How to Observe Morals and Manners.* London: Knight, 1838.

————. *Illustrations of Political Economy.* London: Fox, 1832–1834.

————. *Retrospect of Western Travel.* 3 vols. London: Saunders and Otley, 1838.

————. *Society in America.* Gloucester, Mass.: Peter Smith, 1968.

————. "Sowers not Reapers." In her *Illustrations of Political Economy.* London: Fox, 1832–1834.

Matus, Jill. *Unstable Bodies: Victorian Representations of Sexuality and Maternity.* Manchester and New York: Manchester University Press, 1995.

Maudsley, Henry. *The Physiology and Pathology of the Mind.* London: Macmillan, 1867.

Mayhew, Henry. *London Labour and the London Poor.* 4 vols. London, 1851–1862.

McHugh, Paul. *Prostitution and Victorian Social Reform.* London: Croom Helm, 1980.

Mesick, Jane Louise. *The English Traveller in America, 1785–1835.* New York: Columbia University Press, 1922.

Mill, John Stuart. *Subjection of Women.* Arlington Heights, Ill.: Harlan Davidson, 1980.

Milton, John. *Paradise Lost.* In *Complete Poems and Major Prose,* by John Milton, ed. Merritt Y. Hughes. Indianapolis: Bobbs-Merrill, 1957.

Mitchell, Sally. *The Fallen Angel: Chastity, Class, and Women's Reading, 1835–1880.* Bowling Green, Ohio: Bowling Green University Popular Press, 1981.

Morgan, Susan. "Gaskell's Heroines and the Power of Time." *Pacific Coast Philology* 18–19 (1983–1984): 43–51.

Murray, Janet Horowitz. *Strong-Minded Women and Other Lost Voices from Nineteenth-Century England.* New York: Pantheon Books, 1982.

Nead, Lynda. *Myths of Sexuality: Representations of Women in Victorian Britain.* Oxford and New York: Basil Blackwell, 1988.

Nightingale, Florence. *Cassandra.* New York: Feminist Press at CUNY, 1979.

Nord, Deborah Epstein. *Walking the Victorian Streets: Women, Representation, and the City.* Ithaca: Cornell University Press, 1995.

Pearson, Michael. *The Age of Consent: Victorian Prostitution and Its Enemies.* Newton Abbot, England: David and Charles, 1972.

Perkin, J. Russell. *A Reception-History of George Eliot's Fiction.* Ann Arbor and London: UMI Research Press, 1990.

The Piano. Directed by Jane Campion. Hollywood: Miramax, 1993.

Poovey, Mary. *Uneven Developments: The Ideological Work of Gender in Mid-Victorian England.* Chicago: University of Chicago Press, 1988.

Prochaska, F. K. *Women and Philanthropy in Nineteenth-Century England.* Oxford: Clarendon Press, 1980.

Review of *Jane Eyre,* by Charlotte Brontë. *Quarterly Review* 84 (December 1848): 173–74.

Review of *Mary Barton,* by Elizabeth Gaskell. *British Quarterly Review* (February 1849).

Review of *Ruth,* by Elizabeth Gaskell. *British Quarterly Review* (April 1, 1867).

Review of *Ruth,* by Elizabeth Gaskell. *Eliza Cook's Journal* (March 1853).

Review of *Ruth,* by Elizabeth Gaskell. *Literary Gazette and Journal* 79 (1858): 79–80.

Review of *Ruth,* by Elizabeth Gaskell. *North British Review* 19 (1853): 154–55.

Review of *Ruth,* by Elizabeth Gaskell. *Sharpe's London Magazine* (January 15, 1853): 125–26.

Rich, Adrienne. *Of Woman Born: Motherhood as Experience and Institution.* New York: W. W. Norton, 1986.

Rubenius, Aina. *The Woman Question in Mrs. Gaskell's Life and Works.* Cambridge: Harvard University Press, 1950.

Sapiro, Virginia. *Women in American Society.* Mountain View, Calif.: Mayfield Publishing, 1990.

Sheffield, Carole J. "Sexual Terrorism." In *Women: A Feminist Perspective,* ed. Jo Freeman, 3–19. Mountain View, Calif.: Mayfield Publishing, 1989.

Shires, Linda M., ed. *Rewriting the Victorians: Theory, History, and the Politics of Gender.* New York and London: Routledge, 1992.

Showalter, Elaine. *The Female Malady: Women, Madness, and English Culture, 1830–1980.* New York: Penguin Books, 1985.

———. *Sexual Anarchy: Gender and Culture at the Fin de Siècle.* New York: Viking, 1990.

Shuttleworth, Sally. "Demonic Mothers: Ideologies of Bourgeois Motherhood in the Mid-Victorian Era." In *Rewriting the Victorians: Theory, History, and the Politics of Gender,* ed. Linda M. Shires, 31–51. New York and London: Routledge, 1992.

Small, Helen. *Love's Madness: Medicine, the Novel, and Female Insanity, 1800–1865.* Oxford: Clarendon Press, 1996.

Smith, Sheila M. *The Other Nation: The Poor in English Novels of the 1840s and 1850s.* Oxford: Clarendon Press, 1980.

Stallybrass, Peter, and Allon White. *The Politics and Poetics of Transgression.* Ithaca: Cornell University Press, 1986.

Stoneman, Patsy. *Elizabeth Gaskell.* Bloomington and Indianapolis: Indiana University Press, 1987.

Sutherland, John. *The Stanford Companion to Victorian Fiction.* Stanford: Stanford University Press, 1989.

Tait, William. *Magdalenism: An Inquiry into the Extent, Causes, and Consequences, of Prostitution in Edinburgh.* Edinburgh: P. Rickard, 1842.

Thompson, F. M. L. *The Rise of Respectable Society: A Social History of Victorian Britain, 1830–1900.* Cambridge: Harvard University Press, 1988.

Trevelyan, G. M. *English Social History: A Survey of Six Centuries, Chaucer to Queen Victoria.* London: Longmans, Green, 1842.

Valverde, Mariana. "The Love of Finery: Fashion and the Fallen Woman in Nineteenth-Century Social Discourse." *Victorian Studies* 32 (1989): 169–88.

Walkowitz, Judith. *Prostitution and Victorian Society: Women, Class, and the State.* Cambridge: Cambridge University Press, 1980.

Wiesenfarth, Joseph. *George Eliot: A Writer's Notebook, 1854–1879, and Uncollected Writings.* Charlottesville: University Press of Virginia, 1981.

Wise, Thomas J., and J. A. Symington, eds. *The Brontës: Their Lives, Friendships, and Correspondence.* 4 vols. Oxford: Basil Blackwell, 1932.

Wolf, Naomi. *The Beauty Myth: How Images of Beauty Are Used against Women.* New York: Doubleday, 1991.

"Woman in Her Psychological Relations." *Journal of Psychological Medicine and Mental Pathology* 4 (1851): 18–50.

Yates, Gayle Graham, ed. *Harriet Martineau on Women.* New Brunswick, N.J.: Rutgers University Press, 1985.

INDEX

Abortion, 116, 120; and class, 117

Abuse. *See* Battered Women; Children

Adam Bede (Eliot), 92–125; madonna-harlot dichotomy in, 7; as agrarian novel, 105–6; Romanticism and Victorianism in, 120

Ada McGrath *(The Piano)*, 1–5; and silence and articulation, 1, 5, 26, 212, 215; as fallen woman, 4; and social assimilation, 10; and transportation, 15; and Bertha Mason Rochester, 23; and the Beekeeper, 71

Agency, female: celibacy as, 57, 209–11; and prostitution and economics, 66; absence of, 68; and suicide and anorexia, 133, 133–34*n11*; infanticide as, 183–84. *See also* Articulation; Sexual Management

Ailsie *(Retrospect of Western Travel)*: sexual exploitation of slave girls, 169

Alcohol: and food and poverty, 84, 131, 133–34; cultural uses and social functions of, 132; medicinal uses of, 132–33, 141; and suicide, 134

Alcoholism, 126–58; and deviance, 22; and prostitution in *Mary Barton*, 83–89 *passim*, 129–30; as "moral" disease, 126, 136; and nurses, 127–30; and

working-class economics and anorexia in "Sowers not Reapers," 130–37; female, 131, 131*n8*; in "Janet's Repentance," 137–45; in *Jane Eyre*, 146–56 *passim*; and sobriety, 141

Angelica *(The Heavenly Twins)*, 203–4; as New Woman, 203; as cross-dresser, 203, 207; infantilized through marriage, 204

Angel in the house, 5; as cultural anomaly, 6; and necrophilism, 6; and madonna-harlot dichotomy, 20. *See also* Ideology

Anorexia, 135–36, 157; as sexual management, 36*n18*, 136–37*n16*, 137; and sexual trauma, 110*n25*; and alcohol and poverty in "Sowers not Reapers," 130–37; as political protest, 136*n16*; and sexual ideology, 136, 137*n17*

Archetypes: silenced woman, 2, 4, 26; fallen woman, 2, 7, 26, 47, 71, 74, 141; "Silver Hands," 4; Bluebeard, 4, 23, 147–48, 154; Eve, 6; Virgin Mary, 55–56; Mary Magdalen, 56, 67, 80; madonnas and harlots, 71; Medusa, 111*n27*, 196; female, in "Cassandra," 157

Articulation, and Elizabeth Barrett Browning, 1, 16, 180; women's, 2; music

229

Needleworkers, 28; as white slavery, 20, 30, 33; apprenticeships, 32–35, 39, 51, 84; and prostitution, 33; and seduction, 34; and unwed motherhood, 34

Nest Gwynn ("The Well of Pen-Morfa"), 71–75

New Women: and fallenness, 10; Victorian sexual ideology, 10; venereal disease, 25; sexual management, 190–92; as "girls of the period," 191; spinsters as fallen, 201; "anti-marriage league," 201; medical establishment's hystericization of, 201, 213; as literary genre, 202*n18*

Nightingale, Florence, 127, 157, 198

"Once fallen, always fallen," 17, 28, 31, 70; and William Acton, 9

Phrenology: in *Aurora Leigh,* 49, 52, 58; in "Lizzie Leigh," 80; in *Jane Eyre,* 150; in *Eastern Life, Present and Past,* 179

Philanthropy: in *Ruth,* 46–48; in *Aurora Leigh,* 58; in "The Well of Pen-Morfa," 75; in "Lizzie Leigh," 81; in "Janet's Repentance," 142; in *Shirley,* 197; in *The Heavenly Twins,* 211. *See also* Reform; Reformists

Piano, The (Campion), 1–5

Prince, Mary: *The History of Mary Prince,* 161–62, 165; religious redemption and sexuality, 161–62; censorship of, 161–62, 179; and familial disruption, 164–65*n10*; sold at slave auction, 168*n15*

Promiscuity: upper-class, 48, 49; in *Jane Eyre,* 149, 149*n33*; in *Aurora Leigh,* 51–53; in *The Heavenly Twins,* 203–7, 208–10; working class, 28–29

Prostitution, 8, 61–91; as social issue, 9*n17,* 18–19, 61; and spinsters, 18, 193; "full" and "casual," 30–31; and economics, 31, 66, 90; and nymphomania, 41, 72; child, 49–50; reasons for, 66, 66*n11,* 83*n36*; in "Lizzie Leigh," 78–81; in *Mary Barton,* 84–87; in "Janet's Repentance," 141; in *The Heavenly Twins,* 205–6; and celibacy, 210–11. *See also* Contagious Diseases Acts; Discourse: prostitution; Suicide

Race, 159–88 *passim;* in *Jane Eyre,* 150–54

Rape: in *The Piano,* 2, 4; in *Aurora Leigh,* 8, 48, 53–57; and seduction, 21; in "The Runaway Slave," 182. *See also* Marriage

Redemption. *See* Ideology: maternal; Nursing; Philanthropy

Reform: and women, 15*n24;* and class, 28, 38; Salvation Army, 67; Midnight Missions, 67–68; Female Mission to the Fallen, 68; lock hospitals, penitentiaries, and workhouses, 70; Magdalen homes, 70; Women's Christian Temperance Union, 127*n1. See also* Philanthropy

Reformists: Josephine Butler, 14, 16, 37, 69, 70; women, 15, 15*n24;* Ellice Hopkins, 50; clergy, 67; William Gladstone and William Stead, 67; E. W. Thomas, 67–68; Elizabeth Gaskell and Christina Rossetti, 70; Barbara Leigh Smith Bodichon, 159; Frances Power Cobbe, 192, 211

Retrospect of Western Travel (Martineau), 163–72

Runaway Slave ("The Runaway Slave at Pilgrim's Point"), 180–88

"Runaway Slave at Pilgrim's Point, The" (Barrett Browning), 180–88; as abolitionist discourse, 24; silence, articulation, and appropriation in, 24; infanticide in, 112; lynching in, 182, 186; racism in, 182–83; music in, 184; redemption in, 186. *See also* Race; Rape

Ruth (Gaskell): "once fallen, always fallen," 10; and fallenness and seduction, 38; death and social atonement, 38

Ruth Hilton *(Ruth),* 28, 38–47, 57, 59–60; and seduction, 8; redemption, 17, 32, 44–46; as martyr, 33; appearance of, 36–37, 40–41 44; sexual innocence, 38, 41; maternal ideology, 38, 93; as orphan, 39; as seamstress, 39; dreams, 39, 43; eroticism, 41–42; suicidal, 43; refuses marital legitimation, 42–44; ostracism, 43–44; social impact, 46; as dead angel, 47

Scapegoating: and Ruth, 33; and vanity, 37; of "Crazy Mary," 75; and martyrs, 97*n13*;

35; and working-class morality, 36; and education, 37; absence of, 37; and Nest Gwynn, 74; in *Adam Bede*, 92, 97, 98, 100, 102, 104–5; and Esther, 83–84. *See also* Dress; Hair

Violence: in *The Piano*, 2, 4; in *Aurora Leigh*, 53–54; in *Mary Barton*, 85; in "Janet's Repentance," 138–42; in *Shirley*, 144, 197; in *Jane Eyre*, 145, 150, 153, 154, 155; in "The Runaway Slave," 182, 183, 186

Virginity: as moral standard, 6, 9; as guarantee of legitimacy, 18; exploitation of, 21; and premarital sex, 29–30; as lucrative commodity, 30, 82; in *Aurora Leigh*, 50; in "The Well of Pen-Morfa," 75; and venereal disease, 81; in *Adam Bede*, 98, 103, 108

Voce, Mary, 92–93n2, infanticide, 92; religious conversion, 104, 104n19; execution of, 113; stereotyped, 121. *See also* Hetty Sorrel

Voyeurism: in *Adam Bede*, 99–100, 102, 107, 109–11, 144; foundling hospital "confessions," 118; turning or revolving boxes, 119; in *The Heavenly Twins*, 214

"Well of Pen-Morfa, The" (Gaskell), 17, 21, 71–76; illegitimacy and disfigurement in, 72–74; metaphorical fallenness in, 73; madonnas and harlots in, 74–75; surrogate mothering in, 75

Wet-nursing, 119–20, 136n15

White slavery: needleworking trades as, 20, 30, 33; in *Aurora Leigh*, 49–50, 55;

prostitution rings as, 64; and virginity, 81; and procurers in urban centers, 81–82; drugs, rape, and prostitution, 82; 1885 Criminal Law Amendment Act, 82–83n35; and Stead's "The Maiden Tribute of Modern Babylon," 82–83n35

Women healers: Ruth Hilton, 44–46; Beekeeper, 72–73; Lizzie Leigh, 81; and medical establishment and midwifery, 115–16n31; and maternalism, 127; as occupation, 127; Florence Nightingale, 127, 157, 198; links with promiscuity and fallenness, 127–28; Mrs. Horsfall, 128–29, 197; Janet Dempster, 141–42; Evadne Frayling, 208, 211

Women writers: and class, 10; and gender, 11, 12n21, 13–16; as fallen women, 13–14; narrative ambivalence and redemption, 17–18; on cultural culpability, 18; articulation of fallenness by, 19, 25–26; appropriation by, 24. *See also* Articulation

Workhouse or parish system: and "Crazy Mary," 75; separation of mothers and children, 78; and confinements in "Lizzie Leigh," 78; and prostitution, 78–79; and hair and dress, 79; and Hetty Sorrel, 79, 109n24; illegitimacy in, 113–14n29; in *The Heavenly Twins*, 205

Xenophobia: and slave women's sexuality, 23–24, 183–84; in *Jane Eyre*, 150–51, 153–54, 159–60, 162, 168